The Maska Dramatic Circle

Polish American Theater

in Schenectady, New York

(1933-1942)

By Phyllis Zych Budka

The Maska Dramatic Circle

Polish American Theater
in Schenectady, New York
(1933-1942)

By Phyllis Zych Budka

The Maska Dramatic Circle: Polish American Theater in Schenectady, New York (1933-1942)

By Phyllis Zych Budka

This book is a publication of **Moonrise Press**

P.O. Box 4288, Los Angeles – Sunland, CA 91041-4288 info@moonrisepress.com

www.moonrisepress.com; moonrisepress.blogspot.com

© Copyright 2016 by Moonrise Press and the author, Phyllis Budka

This is a revised edition of a document copyrighted by Phyllis Rita Zych Budka in 2015, *The Maska Dramatic Circle 1933 - 1942: A Window into the Lives of the Schenectady, New York's, First Generation Polish Americans.*

All Rights Reserved

No part of this book may be reproduced or utilized in any form or by any means, electronic or mechanical, including photocopying and recording, or by any information storage and retrieval system, without permission in writing from the publisher.

Book design and layout by Maja Trochimczyk. Cover design by Maja Trochimczyk.

MANUFACTURED IN THE UNITED STATES OF AMERICA

The Library of Congress Publication Data:

The Maska Dramatic Circle: Polish American Theater in Schenectady, New York (1933-1942)

By Phyllis Zych Budka

    264 pages (254 pages + x introductory pages); 21.59 cm X 27.94cm. (8.5 in.X 11 in.)

    Includes illustrations, portraits, facsimiles, and six appendices.

ISBN 978-0-9963981-4-5 (paperback)

ISBN 978-0-9963981-5-2 (eBook – PDF format)

10 9 8 7 6 5 4 3 2 1

The Maska Dramatic Circle

Table of Contents

Chapter 1	The "Maska" Scrapbook – A Family History	1
Chapter 2	Stanley and Sophie – Dad and Mom	7
Chapter 3	Maska is Formed – January 1933 – Summer 1935	15
Chapter 4	The 1935 – 1936 Season; September 1935 – July 1936	33
Chapter 5	The 1936 – 1937 Season; October 1936 – April 1937	59
Chapter 6	The 1937 – 1938 Season; November 28, 1937 – April 3, 1938	67
Chapter 7	The 1938 – 1939 Season; October 9, 1938 – July, 1939	72
Chapter 8	The 1940 Season; December 1939 – August 1940	75
Chapter 9	November 1940 – June 1941	81
Chapter 10	December 1941 – March 1942	85
Chapter 11	1946 – 1980; Reorganization and Reunions	87
Appendix 1	List of Maska Members	91
Appendix 2	List of Maska Patrons	96
Appendix 3	Maska Play List and Time Line	107
Appendix 4	Maska Programs	115
Appendix 5	Maska Buletyns [Newsletters]	172
Appendix 6	Sample Pages from Plays	240
	Pazura (The Claw) – Zygmont Antoni	
	Legionista Na Polu Chwały (Legionnaire on the Field of Glory)	

INTRODUCTION

Capturing the contents of the scrapbook in digital form begun by my Dad, Stanley J. Zych, in 1933, several years before he met my Mom, Sophie Korycinska Zych, has been both a joy and a responsibility. The joy comes from getting to know them as young people, before they became husband and wife, Mom and Dad. The responsibility stems from knowing that no one has told the story of the Maska Dramatic Circle, this unique group of young people, mostly first generation Polish Americans, who contributed so much to the cultural life of their community in Schenectady, New York, between 1933 and 1942. The Maska members were multitalented, hardworking and full of fun. Their world was completely bilingual, with plays in Polish, a newsletter in both English and Polish, and newspaper articles in both the local English newspapers as well as the Polish ones.

The total number of plays given in their 1962 reunion article is "approximately 55." Another reunion article refers to "75 shows." Both may be correct. In the "Play List" (Appendix 3) I can account for 51 plays. Maska publicity refers to some as programs or shows, such as a presentation by the WGY Players. Some plays were announced as part of an upcoming season, but might not have been staged.

Only one study has been identified as dealing in-depth with the regional Polish American community: Robert R. Pascucci Ph.D. dissertation on *Electric City Immigrants: Italians and Poles of Schenectady, N.Y., 1880-1930* (State University of New York, Albany, 1984). According to James Pula's article in the *Polish American Studies* (Spring 2016), "Introducing the Polish American Experience into American History," a serious issue facing Polonia is the disappearance of documentation and memory about the Polish American immigrant experience. While I have approached the Maska book as a family memoir and a local history, I realize that it is very relevant to current concerns in the wider community about the need to document the history of Polish Americans in each area of our country.

I know some Polish and did my best to translate the scrapbook contents, with the help of Google Translate and, occasionally, a bilingual friend. However, the translations are not perfect.

The amazing website fultonhistory.com contributed Maska newspaper articles that helped fill gaps in scrapbook information, for which I am very grateful. Since scans of scrapbook newspaper articles and downloads from fultonhistory.com were not crisp and

clear, I made the decision to retype each one. The digital text will facilitate searching and gathering information on people who were a part of local history and perhaps help others with genealogy searches. While presenting the Maska story through actual newspaper articles is sometimes repetitive, full of names and quite frankly boring, it is done on purpose. Future researchers might find useful information in these texts about the life and culture of a community that shaped the lives of so many people, but exists no more.

Phyllis Zych Budka

ACKNOWLEDGMENTS

My sister and brother-in-law Elizabeth and John Kislinger, passed the yellow box with the Maska scrapbook on to me as they dismantled mom's home after her death in 2001.

Cousins Kelly Norris and Marjorie Norris Brophy "rescued" several Maska play scripts from my grandmother's attic. Treasures!

Seena and Joseph Drapala shared the only two pictures of actual plays found to date. Joanna Socha translated the "Golden Jubilee" article.

Richard Holt, Robert Sullivan and William Buell provided sage advice at a critical stage. I am grateful to editor / publisher Dr. Maja Trochimczyk for her suggestions which have improved the manuscript.

Thank you to everyone!

A special thanks goes to fultonhistory.com and its amazing access to old newspapers.

Phyllis Zych Budka

Maska Dramatic Circle ticket pasted in the scrapbook. Translation: Second Presentation of the Season / Sunday, November 17, 1935 / At the Polish Home, Schenectady / "Hospital for the Insane" and "Catching Fish without Fishing" / The play begins promptly at 7:30 / Special acrobatic presentation / Ticket price 35 cents—Includes dance after the performances

Pulaski Day Essay Contest Winners October 1955: Phyllis Zych (Budka), 8th grade, St. Adalbert's School, and Lawrence Ott, 8th grade, St. Mary's School.

Left to Right: Rev. John Harzynski, Assistant Pastor, St. Adalbert's Church, Lawrence Ott, Schenectady Mayor Archibald Wemple, Phyllis, Unknown man, Rev. Ladislaus Guzielek, Pastor, St. Adalbert's, Unknown man.

The Maska Dramatic Circle

Polish American Theater In Schenectady, New York (1933-1942)

Chapter 1
The "Maska" Scrapbook – A Family History

"Maska," Polish for "mask," was a word I heard many times growing up in the 1940s and 50s on Fifth Avenue in the Mont Pleasant section of Schenectady, New York. The "Maska Dramatic Circle" was where my parents met in 1936. Now, many years later, opening their Maska scrap book full of play programs, newsletters, news clippings and pictures, I am surprised and delighted to learn more about who they were as young people, before they married in July 1940, and before I arrived in 1942.

The scrapbook with the green and gold cover was started by my father and, happily, contains Maska's first program from Sunday, November 1, 1933. The green-cover scrapbook was actually a replacement for the first scrapbook, with smaller pages and flimsy covers. When it started to wear out, its pages were pasted into the larger, more substantial book.

Figure 1a: The MASKA scrapbook. Photo by Phyllis Zych Budka.

Figure 1b: Notes inside the cover of the MASKA scrapbook. Photo by Phyllis Zych Budka.

As I read the contents of the scrap book, both in English and Polish, I realized that this was more than a family history, more than a recounting of the young adult lives of my parents, Stanley Jacob Zych and Sophie Victoria Korycinski Zych. It is the history of a community of first generation Americans, the children of the Polish immigrants who came to Schenectady in the early years of the 20th century, before the Great War, hoping for a better life.

The Maska community was largely centered in Mont Pleasant, the 9th Ward. Few people had cars. Most Maska members lived within walking distance of the Polish National Alliance (P.N.A.) "Home" on Crane Street, their "theater." While I was able to identify the association of most of them with Saint Adalbert's Polish Roman Catholic Church, also on Crane Street, Maska was not affiliated with the Church.

At that time, the General Electric Company and the American Locomotive Company were young and growing enterprises, earning Schenectady the title, "The City That Lights and Hauls the World." The Maska scrapbook pages recount members, including my father, who gained employment at GE in the late 30s. Also evident from the advertising in the play programs is that there were many small businesses owned by the Polish community. Additionally, non-Polish-owned businesses and several local politicians advertised in the Maska programs.

Let me quote from the scrapbook, i.e., the record of Maska's history, Feb. 7, 1939 (this and all subsequent quotes will be indented, in size 10 font):

Maska Dramatic Circle was created on January 20, 1933 at the home of one of the organizers, Daniel Budnick. The latter with Joseph Czyzewski developed the idea of a Polish Group in the City.

In the spring of 1933, the first set of officers was chosen and the name MASKA was formally adopted. By May the membership had grown to about 60.

Maska's first season of plays began in the fall of 1933. The first program, given on Sunday, November 1, 1933, at the Polish Home on Crane Street before a capacity audience, consisted of two one-act plays: ZNAWCA KOBIET (Connoisseur of Women) and SLOWICZEK (Nightingale). This first program proved that Maska possessed not only dramatic talent, but also good voices.

Maska existed from 1933 until 1942, presenting at least 50 plays, all in Polish. In 1946, there was an attempt to revive the group, as documented in a *Gazette* article, but no record was found that this revival occurred. Over its life, Maska had more than 160 members. These young folk were bi-lingual. Many attended St. Adalbert's School, as I did, transitioning to the public schools after the 8th-grade graduation. The Maska members included my father's older brother, Matthew Zych, who served in a technical function, and my mother's younger siblings, Wanda Korycinski Norris and Alexander Korycinski. My future aunt, Jane Wrazen, who would marry my mother's older brother, Peter Korycinski, was also a Maska member. The Maska Members list is found in Appendix 1.

The Maska Dramatic Circle was supported by dues, ticket sales, advertising in the play programs, a newsletter (*Maska Buletyn*), and solid support of the community, with a list of patrons that cumulatively numbered nearly 500. Parents, friends, aunts, uncles and local political figures can be found in the Patrons List in Appendix 2. Anyone who bought a season ticket ($1 for 4 to 5 plays) was listed as a Patron. Prominent local politicians who were Maska Patrons included Oswald D. Heck, Republican, Speaker of the New York State Assembly; Mathias P. Poersch, chair of Schenectady County Democratic Party, 1939; and Judge Morris Marshall Cohn, Democrat.

The scrapbook contains many, but not all, of the play programs. The programs were mostly in Polish, with some advertising in English. Plays were always in Polish and were usually presented on Sunday evenings, often with an afternoon matinee. Sometimes there was a dance after the evening performance. Most performances ranged from one to three acts, with an occasional five act play. Plays included comedies, farces, dramas, and an operetta. Many were written by Polish playwrights; a few were penned by Maska members.

Maska's first presentation on Sunday, November 1, 1933, was *Znawca Kobiet* (Connoisseur of Women), a one- act play by Zygmunt Przybilski, cited as one of the most prolific Polish dramatists of the early years of the 20th century. Subsequently the group also performed Przybilski's *Pierwszy Bal* (The First Ball) and *W Zielonym Gaiku* (In the Dell).

An American favorite, *Charlie's Aunt*, drew rave reviews for its Polish version, *Ciotka Karola*, in February 1936. *Straszna Noc* (Terrible Night) by ZAZ and "*Kobieta Znikła*" (Woman Disappears) by J. Zawistowski, were Polish adaptations of American farces.

Polish culture, American culture, Polish-American culture and even some surprises unfolded before me in the pages of the scrapbook and the associated research. In sharing the joys of this discovery, I wish to pay homage to my parents and the nurturing community of Mont Pleasant in Schenectady, New York, where I grew up.

Maska performed three plays known to be written by Maska members. *Djabel z Monoklem* (Devil with a Monocle), by Zygmunt Brzozowski under the pen name Sigmund Antony, centered around "an ingenious method of smuggling contraband into Poland from Nazi Germany."[1] Fortunately, a manuscript of Brzozowski's three act play, *Pazura* (The Claw), was found recently in the attic of my mother's girlhood home on Forest Road, as the property was prepared for sale. *Pazura* was performed on Sunday, May 14, 1939. The manuscript is typewritten and mimeographed in the familiar blue font. Here, the pen name is Zygmont Antoni. The first page of each scene is found in Appendix 6.

The manuscript page Scene 1 Page 1 illustrates the linguistic world of these mostly first generation Polish-Americans. It is typed on a typewriter which contains the 7 Polish characters not found in the English alphabet. The dialog is in Polish, while the stage directions are in English – well, almost. My translation of the first few lines of *Pazura* (The Claw) is as follows:

> [In Polish]: Scene ------The Library in a Rich Home
> Time: --------11:30 at night
> [In English]: Large old fashioned room, ominous, dark full of shadows and dark corners.
> Door L.--- High backed couch. R. ---Bookcases line the walls at back.
> [In Polish]: When the curtain rises: Kunnegonda comes out, [In English]: followed by Syska.
> Lights. Stage R. Are on!
> Syska: (an old family lawyer. Looks at Polish zegarek [his watch])

This is an amusing linguistic mixture, and probably a reflection of some actual intergenerational conversations.

Maska Director Joseph Czyzewski wrote another play, *Słodkie i Piernie* (The Bitter and the Sweet), about the daily life of a family in the Mont Pleasant area of Schenectady, presented in April 1940. The *Gazette* reported:

> Maska will try an experiment. The play is based on the daily life of a Polish-American family in the Mont Pleasant area. The comedy is full of local color and incidents with which the local Polish-American society comes into contact almost daily. Practical local experience of Polish sales people make the dialogue of the play.[2]

---

[1] Cited from a report in the *Schenectady Gazette,* November 15, 1937.

[2] *Schenectady Gazette,* April 1, 1940 Page 6.

Both my mother and my father were performing in this play. At the time, Mom was a sales woman in a dress shop in downtown Schenectady and Dad had a fruit and vegetable sales business. My guess is that some of their life experiences were captured in this play. I would give anything to have a copy of the manuscript! For additional information on plays and playwrights see Appendix 3 *Maska's Plays*.

As I typed and retyped the many Polish names in this Maska text, my fingers flew to the familiar consonant clusters with ease. My left pinkie finger knows exactly where the z key is, partly from long practice with typing my maiden name, Zych, partly from its over-use in this consonant-filled language. Czyzewski, Cieszynski, Pieszczoch, etc., were no problem to an ear attuned in early childhood to the sounds and spellings.

For ease of reading, I retyped both the *Schenectady Gazette* articles and those from the Polish newspapers. That made me think of the poor *Gazette* typesetters of the 1930s, who, most of the time, spelled these probably unfamiliar names correctly. However, even one of the Maska members had to apologize for mixing up members Joseph Czyzewski and Joseph Cieszynski in print.

As the lists of Maska's many member and patron names grew in my computer, every so often I gave thanks to my many ancestors – AND my husband – that both my maiden name and my married name were short, unaltered from their Polish origins, if also slightly difficult to spell and, as in the case of my maiden name, not quite a pretty sound when pronounced "in English."

The Maska story illustrates how quickly language can change. While all programs and plays were always in Polish, the *Maska Buletyn,* introduced in December 1938, is a delightful language mixture. That first edition is mostly Polish; the December 1940 edition is mostly in English. The *Maska Buletyns* are found in Appendix 5.

The Polish alphabet has 32 letters – 9 vowels and 23 consonants, excluding Q, V and X. Some letters have diacritical marks (slashes, dots or hooks), thereby changing meaning and pronunciation. Information on upcoming plays and reviews of performances appeared not only in Polish language publications such as the *Gazeta Tygodniowa* (The Weekly Gazette)[3] but also in the English-language *Schenectady Gazette*, which lacked the additional fonts.

Thus, Władysława became Gladys; Stanisław – Stanley; Stanisława – Stasia; and Czesław turned into Chester, each losing their <u>Ł</u>s. Other names were also Americanized. Examples are in the table below:

---

[3] Established in 1908, published in Schenectady, New York, in both Polish and English, its masthead proclaims, "The best medium to reach the Americans of Polish extraction in the Capital District of New York State."

Polish Spelling	English Spelling
Aleksander	Alexander
Bronisław	Bernie
Genowefa	Genevieve
Irena	Irene
Jadwiga	Hedwig
Joanna	Joan
Klement	Clement
Liljanna	Lillian
Rozalia	Rose
Ryszard	Richard
Stefania	Stephanie
Waleria	Valerie

In Polish, the feminine version of a surname ending in "ski" is "ska." In the February 1939 *Maska Buletyn*, mom's name in the Polish editorial credits is listed as Zofja Korycinska. Later in the issue, in the English *Social Gossip*, she is Sophie Korycinska. Her cover art on the May 1940 issue is signed "Sophie Korycinski." In some places, the correct Polish spelling, with a diacritical mark on "n" is given: Koryciński.

Another example of a language change – perhaps even language confusion – is the various spellings for Maska Program and Buletyn cover artist and scenery designer, Zygmond or Zygmunt Kilian or Kiljan. The same goes for another Zyg. The 1939 May Buletyn "Gossip About the Semi-Formal" has two spellings within one English section for the same person: Zygmunt Brzozowski and Zygmund Brzozowski; the 1939 December Buletyn has yet another variation, Zygmont Brzozowski, in a Polish section.

Chapter 2
Stanley and Sophie – Dad and Mom

Stanley Jacob Zych

The first documented occurrence of my father's involvement with Maska is in the program for May 27th, 1934: "The Maska Circle orchestra during the entr'acte and dance is under the direction of Mr. Zych." A note in the program states that the orchestra, under the direction of Stanley Zych, will play during the presentation and for the dance [following the play]. My mother played the piano all her life, but I did not usually associate my father with music. My only clue is a memory of a silver clarinet on which I took my first lessons; it had been his.

His first stage appearance was on September 16, 1934, as Kwasnicki [Mr. Sour], the vinegar maker, in *The Live Ghost* (*Żywy Nieboszczyk*). That phrase, "żywy nieboszczyk" is a part of my limited childhood Polish vocabulary because my parents would chuckle in describing someone with little personality as a "żywy nieboszczyk."

My father was always an entrepreneur. I knew that he sold fruit and vegetables at some point. A scrapbook article from the December 27, 1934, *Gazeta Tygodniowa*, (Weekly Gazette) in the column, "With Our Folks Around Town," by Luczek, refreshes my memory; he was 21 years old at the time:

> Personality Stan. Z., our vegetarian, who can sell anything from apples to zebras, has taken a new interest in plugs – not spark plugs, but Sparky! We know he'll have no difficulty convincing his hoss that he's pulling a good load of delicacies – Aw-Ow!

Figure 2: Stanley Zych and Sparky July 1934 – From the Scrapbook

The March 24, 1935 Maska program features the following advertisement:

> Sending Congratulations
> The Brothers Zych
> Purveyors of fruits and vegetables - Scrapbook

Stanley Zych's older brother, Matthew, was his partner in this Depression Era enterprise. Another clipping from the January 24, 1935 "With Our Folks Around Town" by Luczek, sounds like delicious gossip:

> Stan Zych received a letter from "Frances." We don't know if it's an Avenue or a ……? Take it easy on the sales talk, Stan.[4]

The columnist "Luczek," a Polish diminutive of "Lucjan" (Lucyan) was Lucian Sekowski, a very active Maska member.

> At the last meeting we decided to accept the *Weekly Gazette* (Polish *Gazeta Tygodniowa*) as our local authority. We have to admit that this writing has contributed to our development, and to the success of our presentations.[5]

As I organized the scrapbook items into a time sequence, I realized that there was a gap in the early months of 1936 and immediately knew why. On January 6, 1936, my grandfather Joseph Zych, a General Electric Co. retiree, was struck by a hit and run driver. The next day, it was my father who identified him at Ellis Hospital. Joseph died a few days later.

Later that year, my father, who was a Polish Boy Scout Leader (Harcestwo) was one of two Maska members selected to represent the local Polish National Alliance on a month long trip to Poland. He and Maska friend Agnes Pieszczoch sailed in early July on the SS Batory along with more than 100 Polish American young adults to become acquainted with their parents' homeland.

How convenient that the February 14, 1939 *Maska Buletyn* with Mom and Dad among the several editors, featured a picture of Dad on the cover and included the following biography, which I translated from Polish:

> Stanley Jacob Zych is a happy, well dressed young man whose picture is found on the "Maska Bulletin" cover.
> [Stanley Zych was born on May 2, 1913 in Schenectady. He is 5 foot 7 and weighs 154 pounds.]
> He attended Saint Adalbert School and later McKinley Junior High School. He finished Nott Terrace High School in 1930.
> Stanley had his own business for a few years selling fruits and vegetables and then worked in the

---

[4] Francis Avenue is a street in the Mont Pleasant district of Schenectady.

[5] *Gazeta Tygodniowa,* January, 1935. – Scrapbook.

General Electric Company. These days we can see Stas [diminutive of Stanley] near the register of the A&P Company [super market] on Crane Street.

In 1933, Stanley joined the Maska Dramatic Circle. From that time he was president twice and is currently the stage manager. His first performance was as Krasnicki, a businessman, in the play "The Living Corpse." Stanley had parts in the following plays: (1) as Zdzislaw, the philanderer in "Councilor of Mr. Councilman," (2) as the father Grubinski in "Adventures on a Honeymoon," (3) Jozef Bandl, a fire sergeant in "Marriage on Trial," (4) Policeman and Jew Fulgedesang in "The Terrible Aunt," (5) Professor Inicki in "Galoshes," (6) Ocetkiewicz, a stuttering man, in "Dress Rehearsal," (7) Wojtek the lover in "Catching Fish without Fishing," (9) Hydrogen, the crazy doctor in "Hospital for the Insane," (10) Professor Safandurski in "The Professor's Wig," (11) Jacob Kwiecinski, the father, in "A Basket of Flowers," (12) Marcin Grabicki in "Terrible Night," (13) Inspector Piernik in "Woman Disappears," and (14) Stanko the hunchback in "Devil with a Monocle."

When General Electric had its Gold Jubilee [May 21, 1936], Stanley Zych had the honor of playing the inventor Charles Steinmetz on the float under the title "Their Last Meeting," which represented Polonia, and won first prize. See Chapter 4.

In addition to acting, Stanley likes to skate, go for walks, and fish. Wallace Beery and Myrna Loy are his favorite actors.

For his participation in (PNA) Council 53's Scouts [Harcestwo], Stanley was awarded a trip to Poland where he spent the summer of 1936.

Stanley Zych was the artistic director of the play, "Legionnaire on the Field of Glory." That play was the first Maska K. D. [Dramatic Circle] triumph of 1938. He will also be the director of the next play which will be given on April 23rd at the Polish Home.[6]

We sincerely wish him further accomplishment, luck and prosperity. - Scrapbook

Figure 3: Stanley J. Zych – Maska Buletyn, February 1939 – Scrapbook

---

[6] There is no record of a play on that date. He is listed as co-director for the May 14, 1939 play, *Pazura*.

As I read, re-read and translated the newspaper articles, the following item from the April 2, 1936, *Gazeta Tygodniowa*, made my heart sing:

> Unlike previous productions "Koszyk Kwiatow" was a drama abounding with scenes of poignant human emotion unfolding the experiences of Marynia, an innocent girl, accused of a larceny. Miss Agnes Pieszczoch, portraying the part of Marynia, interpreted with much realism the demands of a difficult role and **Stanley Zych, as her father, rendered a convincing type of parent much concerned over his child's fate**.

Maska members were patriotic young Americans, whose parents had become naturalized US citizens, like my grandparents. Yet, the scrapbook is filled with evidence of love for their Polish heritage and concern for Poland, whose 123-year-old struggle for independence became a reality in October 1918.

The scrapbook article, "Polish Dramatics Vital" dated March 12, is probably from either 1935, when Dad became Maska president for the first time, or the following year.[7]

Polish Dramatics Vital

> "As in every other thing dramatics have their purpose. Greater interest and support of Polish dramatic productions by the young element of this city would preserve and bring about a better understanding of the language and culture of our forefathers.
> "Many a dramatic production recalls to the minds of the audience memories of the past and the joys and privations of others.
> "Dramatics are vital to the preservation and wide-spread use of the Polish language and provide a cultural asset to all participants.
> "Support Polish dramatic activities by all means!"
>
> Stanley J. Zych, distributor, Fifth Avenue

Preludjum Chopina (Chopin's Prelude), a one-act drama, was presented in December 1934. An historical drama (title unknown) was performed in March 1934, listed in the *Gazette* with the headline, "Poles to Honor Joseph Pilsudski." *Koszyk Kwiatów or Los Sieroty* (Basket of Flowers or Fate of the Orphan), from March 1936, is listed as a melodrama of Polish village life, a tense drama of human faith and suffering occurring in Poland in 1858.

Their American pride and patriotism were exhibited in the theme of the prize-winning float in the 1936 General Electric Gold Jubilee parade titled, "Their Last Meeting," between Steinmetz and Edison, in which dad portrayed Steinmetz. See Chapter 4.

There is little information on the tableau, *Żywy Obraz* (Living Picture) from October 1937, commemorating the 29th anniversary of the founding of the Polish Army of America. The following year, my father directed a five act patriotic tragedy, *Legjonista na Polu Chwały* (Legionnaire on the Field of Honor), by Antoni Jax, a play based on the experience of Polish Legions on the Eastern Front in 1916. The play was chosen by

---

[7] Letter to the editor, newspaper not identified; date March 12, 1935 or 6 – Scrapbook.

Maska as commemoration of the 29th anniversary of the Declaration of Polish Independence by the Warsaw Committee.

As I write this, the 4.5 inch by 6 inch, 72-page *Legionista* manuscript sits on my desk, another recent attic find. I am reminded of the comment in one of the *Maska Buletyns* that Stanley Zych's "recent trip to Poland" influenced several of Maska's program selections. *Legionista* was undoubtedly one them.

Sophie Victoria Korycinski Zych

My mother Sophie probably joined Maska after she graduated from Mont Pleasant High School in June 1936. At that point, Maska was well-established and receiving enthusiastic support from the community. Mom is in the picture of members and guests at the Maska installation banquet on February 4, 1937. The headlines read:

> From Schenectady N.Y.
> Walter Sekowski Takes an Oath from the New Administration of the Maska Dramatic Circle
> A varied installation program was presented at the Polish Home
> Fine speeches during the banquet
> Many guests
> The ranks of the Circle is increased with some new members
> The following were received into the Circle:
> Sophie Korycinska, Zygmunt Wisniewski, Matthew Ozarowski and Stanley Plocharczyk.[8]

Stanley Zych, the current Maska President, was not in the picture. A small article pasted in the scrapbook alongside the large banquet article, explains his absence:[9]

> **Remaining Under Doctor's Care**
> The President of the Maska Dramatic Circle Mr. Stanley Zych, as well as Mr. John Laniewski, a member of the group, were both ill with colds and remained in bed, under the care of the doctor. Everyone wishes that they quickly return to health.

Sophie Korycinski and Stanley Zych appeared together for the first time in the play, *Kobieta Znikła* (Woman Disappeared) on Sunday, February 21, 1937. What fun to learn the following:[10]

> **Entertained Presentation Amateurs**
> Miss Sophie Korycinska, daughter of Mr. and Mrs. Peter Korycinski, was hostess at a warm welcome at her home on Forest Road for all amateurs from the "Maska" Dramatic Circle who took part in Sunday's presentation. The following were present:
> Sophie Chojnicka, Agnes Dmochowska, Mary Dziuba, Helen Kilian, Wanda Korycinska, Agnes Pieszczoch, Genevieve Stelmach, Mary Zborowska, Zygmunt Brzozowski, Joseph Czyzewski, Bernard Deptula, Tad Kilian, Bronislaw Kalinowski, Leo Marcinek, Matthew Ozarowski, Lucian

---

[8] *Dziennik dla Wszystkich* (Everybody's Daily), February 9, 1937.

[9] Clipping from *Dziennik dla Wszystkich* [Everybody's Daily] February 9, 1937, Scrapbook translated by PZB.

[10] Clipping from *Dziennik Dla Wszystkich* [Everybody's Daily] February 26, 1937. Scrapbook, translated by PZB.

Sekowski, Stanley Zych as well as Mr. and Mrs. Peter Korycinski, Mr. and Mrs. Rudolph Woltner.

This brought a smile to my face! How typical of Miss Sophie, who loved people and parties, to celebrate her new Maska "career" with a party! And kudos to her parents for obviously supporting this activity!

Sophie Korycinski became an editor of the *Maska Buletyn* which appeared in December 1938. Her artwork is on the May 1939 cover. While *Buletyn* articles, art work and newsy notes usually have no author names, I can hear her voice, intelligence and sense of humor come through the pages and the years.

The May 1939 *Maska Buletyn* features Mom's picture on the cover with a brief biography:

> Sophie Korycinska was born in Schenectady in the area of Avenue B, on October 2, 1918. She started her education at Yates Elementary School. When Sophie was seven years old, her parents moved to Forest Road, where they live now. From this location, Sophie went to the parish school (Saint Adalbert's), where she received an award for good scholarship. Then she went to Pleasant Valley School, McKinley Junior High School, and Mont Pleasant High, where she graduated in 1936.
>
> Sophie joined the Maska Dramatic Circle in 1936 and had parts in several plays, including (1) the servant, Crazy Dorothy, in "Woman Disappears," (2) Basia Niedoszyta, a 12 year old girl, in "Cares and Worries," (3) Arora Misenki, a countess, in "Legionnaire on the Field of Honor," (4) Izabela Zielonka, a farmer, in "Speedy Work," and also (5) Klara Makowaka, in "Trapped" [also known as "The Claw"]. She was the secretary of the Circle during the 1938 - 1939 season and is also the Circle's press agent.
>
> Sophie likes to ice skate, fish, and loves handwork, music and writing articles. Sophie currently works at the Berkeley-Smith Dress Shop.

Figure 4: Sophie Korycinski - *Maska Buletyn* May 1939 (Scrapbook).

Stanley and Sophie - February 1937

To assist in untangling the mass of scrapbook items found in early 1937, I decided to list the information in a time sequence. *Kobieta Znikła* [A Woman Disappeared], presented on Sunday, February 21, 1937, is one of the best documented plays in the scrapbook. It is notable for several reasons:

- This play drew the largest audience in Maska history – nearly 500 people, "including several from out of town" as reported by *Dziennik Dla Wszystkich*
- Stanley Zych was the newly elected Maska president. Sophie Korycinski had joined the group a few months earlier and this was their first performance together.
- From a *Dziennik Dla Wszystkich* article: "Stan Zych, in the role of Konstanty S. Piernik, as the police inspector, played like a professional actor." It listed the women in the cast, including Sophie Korycinska, "who performed their roles famously."
- And, last but not least, the cast includes a real cat named Toby.

February 1937 – the time period rang a bell in my brain, already littered with a mass of items from my genealogy research. I dove into my files, searching for my paternal grandmother Rozalia Zych's application for Naturalization. The application listed my mother and her mother, Victoria Korycinska, as Rozalia's sponsors. The application form asked how long the candidate had known the sponsors. Typed in was the date "Feb. 14, 1937." When I received the papers from the Schenectady County Clerk's Office a few years ago, it struck me that that was probably the first time the two families met.

Now, I THINK I know something else! Again, diving into my files, I checked the date on the scrapbook clipping below. It not only reflects the bilingual "flavor" of 1930s Mont Pleasant, but also, suddenly, I have the realization that it is "the gleam in Dad's eye." Oh my gosh! My father is in love with my mother!

> One of our Polish young people received the following card on St. Valentine's Day, on which was written the following verse:
>
> My Love,
> What can I do,
> I can not sleep
> The whole night thru.
> Everywhere I turn
> I think of you.
> I seems to me
> That I love you.

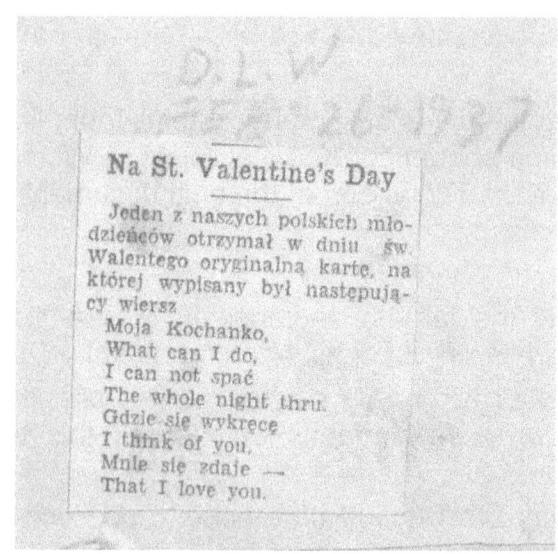

Figure 5: Valentine's Day entry from 1937.

My parents were married on July 27, 1940, in Saint Adalbert's Church.

Their personal history is interwoven with Maska's history, extending even into the 1980 Maska reunion.

Figure 6: Left to Right: Walter Sekowski (Maska), Jessie Nisiobencka, Zygmunt Brzozowski (Maska), Helen Kudrewicz, Matthew Zych (Maska), Wanda Korycinska (Maska), Sophie Korycinska Zych (Bride), Stanley J. Zych (Groom), Statia Zych Jendzejczyk, Anthony Pajak, Jessie Krasnowska Rozen and Peter Korycinski – July 27, 1940.

Chapter 3
The Early Years (January 1933 – Summer 1935)

January 20, 1933 – Maska Is Formed

The scrapbook contained a "gift" that was a great help in getting this project underway: Dated February 7, 1939, and titled "Maska Dramatic Circle," seven typed and yellowed pages documented Maska's birth in 1933 until the end of 1938. The history, thankfully in English, was compiled by "Researcher George W. Briskie, Jr." from "Information received from Joseph Czyzewski, Secretary." It concludes with a statement that "MASKA has become a Polish institution here in Schenectady and in the Capital District."

An institution indeed! In this first subscription season, the group of 38 Maska members presented 11 plays; the majority were "comedies of a farcical nature."

Maska's story unfolds below, compiled from scrapbook programs, newspaper clippings in English and Polish, the *Maska Buletyn* newsletter, and a modern wonder, the "Fultonhistory.com" website's newspaper scans.

1933 – January 20

As reported in the history of the group in the Scrapbook:

> Maska Dramatic Circle was created on January 20, 1933 at the home of one of the organizers, Daniel Budnick. The latter with Joseph Czyzewski developed the idea of a Polish Group in the City. Those present at the first meeting were: Nellie Petera, Mary Dziuba, Irene Brzostowski, Wanda Golembiowski, Sadie Zablocki, Mrs. Budnick, Mrs. Szymanowski, Mrs. Toniszewski, Chester Rudowski, Raymond Golembiowski, Stanley Golembiowski and the two organizers. These were the charter members. It was decided to present the plays in the new Polish Community Home that was as then being rushed to completion. The first task was to raise money for the construction of scenery and property effects. In April, 1933, MASKA sponsored a Card Party and Entertainment. Two sketches marked the beginning of Maska's Dramatic efforts. Those taking parts in the sketches were: Nellie Petera, Sadie Zablocki, Raymond Golembiowski and Joseph Czyzewski. The evening was a huge success.

In the spring of 1933, the first set of officers was chosen and the name MASKA was formally adopted. By May the membership had grown to about 60. The first set of officers consisted of the following:

President and Coach	Daniel V. Budnick
Vice President	Mrs. R. Zielanis
Secretary	Joseph Czyzewski
Treasurer	Nellie Petera

Business Manager	Michael Tytko
Stage Manager	Zygmunt Kilian
Art Manager	Wanda Hennel
Electrician	T. Noskowiak
Property Manager	Chester Rudowski

1933 – Sunday, November 1

How fortunate that the very first program was in the scrapbook! While my father apparently did not join Maska at its first organizing meeting, he must have joined shortly after and attended that first performance, one of the "capacity audience."

> Maska's first season of plays began in the fall of 1933. The first program, given on Sunday, November 1, 1933 before a capacity audience, consisted of two one-act plays: ZNAWCA KOBIET (Connoisseur of Women) and SŁOWICZEK (Nightingale). This first program proved that Maska possessed not only dramatic talent, but also good voices. Sadie Zablocki proved to be an able soprano; Klement Olszewski an excellent tenor and Michael Tytko, a pleasing basso. Maska was on the way to a permanent Polish Dramatic organization in Schenectady.

Znawca Kobiet (Connoisseur of Women) was written by Zygmunt Przybylski; 1856-1909), a prolific Polish author of popular comedies and theater criticism, active in Kraków and Warsaw. Przybylski's plays include romantic intrigues (*Antkowe Wesele, Debiutantka, Sposób na żony*), comedies of manners (*Wicek i Wacek, Wojna domowa, Wdowa z musu*), and humorous portrayals of life of Polish gentry in the countryside (*Dwór we Włodkowicach, Dzierżawca z Olesiowa*).

Słowiczek (A Little Nightingale) was an operetta. The program cover art, which decorated subsequent programs as the Maska logo, contains the initials, "Z.K.", for Zigmunt Kilian, listed as Scenery Director, who became an artistic mainstay of the group. The program introduces several local individuals and institutions that were supportive of Maska's budding theatrical efforts.

The action took place in the Nightingale's florist workshop. Maska founding member, Aniela Pitera, donated the flowers for the play. Aniela, variously listed over time as "Nellie Petera," was the owner of a "Polish Greenhouse" florist shop. Nellie's firm provided artistic designs for funerals, wedding bouquets and flowers for all occasions. My sister, Betty [Elizabeth Zych Kislinger], recalls getting corsages for her Notre Dame High School event from Nellie's florist shop in the early 1960s.

Michael Tytko, the "pleasing basso," later attended Union College, and continued his involvement as prompter in later performances. As I grew up, I knew him as Dr. Michael Tytko, a local general practitioner.

The entr'act and accompaniment to *Słowiczek* were played by C. Zeltman's Orchestra. The program notes that after the presentations there would be a dance by Mr. C. Zeltman's Orchestra. These post performance dances at the P.N.A. Home became a staple of many of Maska's Sunday evening plays.

The Polish-Artistic Society "Polart" built and installed the scenery. Polart was an art organization composed of young Polish-American students of art under the leadership of Joseph Czechowicz and Zygmond Kilian.

Furniture was donated by Mr. Stanislaw Bartosiewicz of The Mt. Pleasant Furniture House, on Crane Street, across from the P.N.A. Home. I recall several visits to that establishment to select pieces of furniture as I grew up.

Backdrops and scenery were a gift to the Polish (P.N.A.) Home from the firm, "Community Garage," Railroad St., Brothers Korkosz and Wrazen, Proprietors. More correctly, they were brothers-in-law. The Garage could provide towing as well as used car parts. Mr. Wrazen's only child, Jane, married my mother's older brother, Peter Korycinski. Aunt Jane Wrazen Korycinska had parts in a few plays.

Waclaw Daniel Przybylek, pharmacist and chemist serving Polish clientele for 15 years, Please come see us at MYERS' PHARMACY, on the corner of Crane St. & Francis Ave. This program ad brought a smile of memory to me. My husband, Alfred John Budka, who also grew up in the Mont Pleasant community, worked at Myers' Pharmacy as a "soda jerk" when he was young. I can still remember Myers' delicious vanilla ice cream sodas.

> The last program page is still firmly affixed to the scrapbook, so the heads of two local politicians are partially missing from the ads. Joseph P. Coffey, Democratic Candidate for Mayor, and Mathias P. Poersch, Democratic Candidate for Municipal Court, both send greetings.

1933 – December 9

The English-language *Schenectady Gazette* reports:[1]

> The Polish Dramatic Club "Maska" will present its second production of the season tomorrow afternoon and night at the Polish home on Crane street. This program will consist of three one-act plays – a comedy, a drama and an operetta.
> First on the program will be the operetta, "Plaything." This is a short playlet concerning a Polish-American business man who leaves his business in the care of his nephew when he goes away to New York City to buy supplies. Upon leaving for the big city, he instructs his nephew to pay strict attention to business and above all leave the ladies alone. The nephew disregards such instruction, and marries a young lady. When the uncle returns, the nephew finds himself in a pickle. The dénouement of the play is quite interesting.
> The second play is a serious drama dealing with the up-to-date marriage problems. This

---

[1] *The Schenectady Gazette,* December 9, 1933, Page 6.

> play, "Chopin's Prelude in C Minor," centers around three people – one a young man, though madly in love with his ideal, gives up his place to his best friend, because he thinks himself physically incapable of undertaking marriage. Chopin's famous "Prelude" is the theme of the play. The marriage of his best friend, Ludwig, and the maiden, Laura, proves to be a path of thorns.
>
> The third play will be a comedy, "Uncle Arrives." The scene of the play is modern Krakow. The story deals with a nephew who has been playing "hookie" and his wealthy uncle who lived on a manor in northern Poland. Finally, the uncle decides to pay his nephew a visit which places the nephew in a most precarious position. When the uncle arrives, things happen rapidly. The uncle discovers that his nephew had been receiving money under false pretense. Enraged the uncle plans his revenge.
>
> This program has been under rehearsal for the past three weeks and every effort is being made to produce a smooth production. The scenery and effects are being constructed by the Polart Club.
>
> The musical scores are being arranged by Stanley Petera and Charles Zeman. There will be a matinee at 2:30 o'clock at the Polish home on Crane street. The evening performance will begin at 7:30 o'clock. This production has been under the direction of Daniel Budnick with Miss Agnes Pieszczoch and Joseph Czyzewski as assistants.

The first play, or rather an operetta, with the Polish title Cacusia (Plaything), was written by Stanislaw (Stanley) Zenon Wachtel (1887-1959) a prominent Polish-American actor and playwright. It was publlished in 1915 with music by M.A. Rozycki. The third play, *Stryj przyjechał (Uncle Arrived),* was written by Count Władysław Koziebrodzki (1839-1893), Polish writer, politician, and community activist from Galicia (the partition of Poland ruled by Austria). The play was published in 1900.[2]

The newspaper article presents a capsule of information about the course that Maska was setting at least for the near future: a) a three-week rehearsal period, b) the role of Polart Club, c) the performance as a Sunday matinee plus an evening performance, and d) the mentorship of Daniel Budnick.

The role of Stanley Petera, Nellie's father, in the formation of Maska and his own musical background is unclear, but his influence remains intriguing, and is discussed below.

1933 – December 26

The local newspaper reports:[3]

To Conduct Party at Polish Center

> The Polish Community Center will hold a Christmas tree party tonight for the children of the community. A large tree has been set up and decorated in the auditorium of the hall. Distribution of gifts to each child present at the meeting will begin the program.
>
> Following this there will be recitals and songs. Speakers will be the president of the Polish Welfare League and the president of the Community 53 [Polish National Alliance number]. Organizations which are co-operating in the program are the Kalina Glee Club, the Young Men's Polish Association and the *Maska Dramatic Club*.

Thus, Maska takes its place in the Polish-American community along with two

---
[2] Information from Dr. Karen Majewski, email of February 19, 2016.
[3] *The Schenectady Gazette,* December 26, 1933, Page 3.

established groups.

1934 January – March

The English-language history of Maska in the scrapbook continues:

> The Last program of the season was given in March, 1934, consisting of a three-act play GRUBY SZKANDAL (Great Scandal). Maska finished a very successful season. That Spring it was decided to have season tickets and to have a list of patrons and patronesses on each program of the season.
>
> Daniel Budnick did a splendid job of directing during 1933 and could not devote the time he wished to the Presidency. He also gave coaching advice to J. Czyzewski and Agnes Pieszczoch. When the election of January, 1934 came around Dan Budnick declined the presidency. The set of officers elected for 1934, were:
> - President: Joseph Czyzewski
> - Vice-President: Agnes Pieszczoch
> - Secretary: Wanda Hennel
> - Treasurer: Nellie Petera
> - Historian: Mary Dziuba
> - Marshall: Karol Szymanski
> - Director: Daniel Budnik
> - Assistants: J. Czyzewski and Agnes Pieszczoch
> - Art Manager: Mary Zborowski
> - Stage Manager: Chester Rudowski
> - Property Manager: John Zielanis
> - Business Manager: Joseph Czechowicz and Zygmunt Brzozowski
>
> Daniel Budnick continued his coaching until 1935, when other duties forced him to retire from active work in Maska. Joseph Czyzewski and Agnes Pieszczoch took over the coaching and continued to work together until the end of the 1937-38 season.
>
> The last official program of the 1934-35 season included three one-act plays, WET ZE WET (Eye for Eye), KALOSZE (Galoshes) and STRASZNA CIOTUNIA (The Terrible Aunt). KALOSZE is one of Alexander Fredro's popular comedies. Fredro was the greatest comedy writer of the 19th century in Poland
>
> In May 1934, Maska participated in a one-act play contest with the Polish Dramatic Club of Amsterdam and the Polish Literary Club of Albany. Each club presented a one act play and the program was repeated in each city. In Schenectady the contest ended on May 27, 1934. Maska presented PIERWSZY BAL (The First Ball), a light comedy by Zygmunt Przybylski, one of the most prolific Polish dramatists of the early years of the 20th century. Maska's presentation made a deep impression. The judges were split in their decision and there were no prizes awarded. The whole affair was a huge financial success.

1934 March Press Reports

The *Schenectady Gazette* reports:

> The Polish Dramatic Circle "Maska" will present its Lenten production Sunday night at 7:30 o'clock at the auditorium of the Polish Community Home. The program consists of a 3-act comedy and a skit.
>
> The main attraction is the comedy entitled, "Big Scandal" written by a Polish-American writer, J. Michalski. This play portrays a bit of life in a mining town where everyone struggles for his very existence. The theme of the play is the duping of a large home-owner into marrying an

old maid whom he detests. The most comic element is the way in which the old maid tried to ingratiate herself with this man. The old maid is the eldest of a large family of girls all old enough to be married, but the father sticks to an old custom which forbids the marriage of younger sisters before the eldest daughter of the family is safely married. Thus all the sisters of the old maid do their bit in making sure that their sister "lands" her perspective groom. This creates an amusing situation which finally brings about the much sought solution – the marriage of the old maid. This play presents the amusing side of the life of Polish-American miners.

An additional feature of the program is a skit portraying the domestic differences in a family where the husband is inclined to be a partaker of strong beverages.

Another *Schenectady Gazette* report is entitled "Poles to Honor Jos. Pilsudski – Will Join in Celebration of St. Joseph's Day as Mark of Respect"

Poles of this city will join in a two-day celebration of St. Joseph's day, tomorrow and Monday as a manifestation in honor of the name day of Marshal Joseph Pilsudski, founder of the Republic of Poland. The observance will inaugurate an annual nation-wide affair.

Arrangements for the celebration are in the hands of the Polish National Alliance "Gmina" with Stanley Sadowski as general chairman.

Attorney Thaddeus S. Ogonowski and Ludwig Blinkowski, publisher of the Polish Weekly of Utica, will be the principal speakers at a meeting tomorrow afternoon at the Polish Community Home. Sigmund Illnicki, president of the executive committee of "Gmina," will open the session at 3 o'clock. The program will include, besides the addresses, violin and piano solos, recitations, choral selections by the Chopin male chorus under the direction of Edmund Kulakowski, and a one-act historical drama given by the Maska Dramatic Club.

Monday night a dance will conclude the manifestation. The observance is free to the public.

Other members of the committee on arrangements are the executive committee of "Gmina," president, Sigmund Illnicki; vice-president, S. Skrzynski; vice-president, Mrs. Mary Lisinska, M. A. Rekucki, Benjamin Garuski, W. Zalewski, Frank Rosiak, B. Kaszubski, and the social committee, Bernard Luniewski, Adam Adach, J. Sarnowski, T. Marcinkiewicz, T. Jaroszewski, Adam Nosal, Casper Wojcicki, John Galkiewicz and Mrs. K. Styczynski.

1934 April Press Reports

On April 14, 1934, The *Schenectady Gazette* published the following announcement:

The Maska Dramatic Club will hold its spring novelty ball tonight at the P. N. A. Home on Crane street. All arrangements have been completed for this unusual event.

The club has been fortunate in obtaining the services of Bill Mayotta and his well-known orchestra. He brings with him an entirely new collection of dance music and innovations. The dance committee has prepared added attractions for the evening. There will be a great assortment of novelties, funmakers and souvenirs for everyone. The committee consists of Agnes Pieszczoch, Florence Bylewicz, Walter and Lucian Sękowski and Joseph Czyzewski.

The proceeds of this event will make it possible for the Maska Dramatic Club to participate in the One-act play contest between Amsterdam and Albany dramatic clubs and that of the Schenectady club. This will be the first contest of this nature held by Polish dramatic clubs in this section of the state.
The soiree begins at 9 o'clock.

1934 – May 27

In May 1934, Maska joined the Literary Circle of Albany and the Amateur Circle of

Amsterdam in a play contest. The groups performed the following together in all 3 communities:

- The Literary Circle of Albany, NY: *O.S.S.* or *The Marriage Portion.*
- Amateur Circle of Amsterdam, NY: *Fledgling Kokusia* by Pobratym
- Maska Dramatic Circle of Schenectady, NY: *The First Ball* by Zygmunt Przybylski

The Maska Circle orchestra during the entr'acte and dance is "under the direction of Mr. Zych." The program pages from the Schenectady event are the only record.

1934 – November 18

On Sunday, November 18, 1934, Maska presented the three act play, *Radcy Pana Radcy* (Councilors of Mr. Councilor), written in 1867 by Michał Bałucki (1837-1901), a well-known Polish playwright, novelist, and poet, author of 12 novels and over 10 comedies and satirical plays.

The following entry in the Scrapbook commemorated this premiere:

> The second program of the season consisted of a three-act play RADCY PANA RADCY (Councilor of Mr. Councilman) an outstanding Polish play written by that Great Polish artist Michael Balucki of the 1890s.

Listed in the program as External Advisors to the Maska Circle were:
- The Honorable Mr. Roman Kwiecien, Consul
- Mr. Jerzy Orzarzewski, New York
- The Honorable Professor Stefan P. Mierzwa
- Mr. Wladyslaw Lesiakowski

The same names were again found in the February 7, 1939 "Maska History:"

> During the 1934-35 season Maska gained a great deal of prominence. Dr. Roman Kwiecien, Polish Consul at New York; George Orzarzewski, New York City producer of Polish plays, and Dr. Stefan P. Mierzwa became advisors to Maska. Maska also became a member of the Institute Teatrow Ludowych of Warsaw, Poland (Institute of Polish National Theaters) and also of Polish-American Cultural Union at Chicago, Illinois. Maska on March 19, 1925 [error 1934] presented a historical drama in honor of the late Marshal Pilsudski.

Stefan Mierzwa (1892-1971) was the founder of The Kościuszko Foundation (KF) based in New York City, still a force in today's US-Poland relations. Founded in 1925, the Kościuszko Foundation promotes closer ties between Poland and the United States through educational, scientific and cultural exchanges. Also known as Stephan Mizwa, the long-time president of the Foundation is described as a talented and energetic Polish immigrant who has made a difference in the lives of many. Reading through to

the end of this history revealed an additional surprise:[4]

> In 1950, Stanislaw Petera, a retired worker from General Electric, met with Mizwa to explain that his last will and testament would leave $25,000 in government bonds to the Foundation. To honor the Foundation's 25th anniversary, he wanted to donate the money sooner. Petera's attorney created a living trust, which gave his assets to the foundation. The money was invested in stocks and Petera received a 2.5% yield to cover his living expenses, while the Kosciuszko Foundation paid off its mortgage. It was a brilliant act of charity that benefitted Petera and Polonia.

Stanislaw Petera?! GE retiree! THAT name rang a bell! Mr. and Mrs. Stanley Petera are in the list of Maska Patrons. Aniela (Nellie) Petera (a.k.a. Pitera), one of Maska's founding members, is probably their daughter. While a definite connection between Stanislaw Petera, the Kosciuszko Foundation benefactor, and Stanley Petera of Schenectady is yet to be confirmed, both individuals are very likely to be the same person. The listing in the November 1934 Maska program of Mierzwa as an advisor to Maska indicates there might have been a personal connection between the two men as early as 1934.

1934 – December 16

The Scrapbook continues the Maska narrative:

> The third program was patterned after the first and its three one-act plays were: W PUŁAPCE (Trapped), PRZYGODY MAŁŻENSKIE W PODRÓŻY POSLUBNEJ) (Adventures on a Honeymoon) and one of the greatest Polish one-act plays ever written BŁAZEN (The Jester). BŁAZEN is a play based on the life of a jester in the 18th century in Poland. It was written by that great Polish novelist and playwright, Alexander Swiętochowski. Zygmunt Kilian as the Jester turned in a magnificent performance.

Przygody Małżeńskie w Podróży Poślubnej (Adventures on a Honeymoon), a one-act play premiered on December 16, 1934 featured Stanley Zych as Grubinski, father of Laura and Rozalja (Rosemary) Gontarska was Laura's mother.

The play was written by Antoni Jax (1850-1926), popular Polish-American playwright, based in Chicago since 1889. Jax wrote sixteen plays on American subjects, including political satires, and nineteen plays set in Poland. The "American" plays included political satires (*Alderman's Daughters, The Mayor's Son*), portrayals of current social issues (*Freedom and Slavery, From Pennsylvania to California, The Chicago Street Urchin*), and relations of emigrants to their Polish families (*The Aunt from America, His Young Lordship in America, The Cousin from America* and *The Uncle from America*). The Polish plays explored folk tales (*Pan Twardowski*), patriotic themes linked to national uprisings and wars (*The Legionnaire On the Field of Honor; As Long as Poles Live, Poland Will Not Perish*), and comedies of manners (*A Professor's Wig, The Honeymoon*).[5]

---

[4] http://www.thekf.org/about/mission_history/
[5] See Rev. Joseph Krzyszkowski, S.J. (transl. Sr. M. Charitina, C.S.S.F). "Anthony Jax - A Forgotten Playwright" *Polish American Studies* 9, no. 1-2, (1952).

Błazen (*The Jester*) by Aleksander Świętochowski (1849-1938), a famous Polish novelist, political writer, philosopher, and dramatist, the leader of the Positivism movement, was a portrayal of a court jester that hid his wisdom and presented warnings to the king in jokes. Swietochowski wrote numerous novels and plays, edited an influential newspaper, published political-social essays in regular columns, and supported universal education and work "at the foundations" as a way of transforming society.[6]

Figure 7: Rosemary Gontarska and Stanley Zych, in
Przygody Małżeńskie w Podróży Poślubnej. Sunday, December 16, 1934.

The program of *Przygody Małżeńskie w Podróży Poślubnej.* preserved in the Scrapbook features Stanley Zych's signature on the first page and is decorated with several autographs (Appendix 4), including a flourish marking "Lord Thaddeus Kilian" on page 3. The most intriguing note of all is faintly visible on the cover:

> Because other people have feathers on their hats—My friends call me "Jennie" - Please be my friend and call me that also
> Genevieve Skizinski 180 Second St. Albany, NY—Age 18 Nov. 9, 1934 Senior at Albany High School

---

[6] See his biography on: http://literat.ug.edu.pl/autors/swietoch.htm.

No, I don't know who she was! The second page of the program has another name and address from an Albany woman.

1935 – Officers

The record for 1935 notes a change in officers of the Maska organization:

> The set of officers elected for the year 1935 were as follows:
> - President: Stanley Giniecki
> - Vice President: Walter Sekowski
> - Secretary: Wanda Hennel
> - Treasurer: Nellie Petera
> - Marshal: Karol Szymanski
> - Parliamentarian: Roberta Tytko
> - Business Managers: V.W.Plath & Joseph Czechowicz
> - Coaches: Agnes Pieszczoch & Joseph Czyzewski
> - Stage Manager: Zygmunt Kilian
> - Art Manager: Zygmunt Brzozowski
> - Property Manager: Lucian Sekowski
> - Wardrobe Managers: Lillian Wanik & Thaddeus Kilian
>
> In 1935, Stanley Giniecki resigned as president of Maska and Walter Sekowski took his place. Zygmunt Kilian went away to school in September 1935 and Matthew Zych became stage manager. Roberta Tytko resigned and Joan Penichter became parliamentarian. Carl Szymanski went away to the CCC [Civilian Conservation Corps] and Anthony Kopec became Marshal.

1935 – February 3

The premiere of the three-act comedy *Marriage on Trial* (*Małżenstwo na próbę*) took place on February 3, 1935 and was documented in the Scrapbook in two press clippings in Polish (translated below), and an English language article, describing the author, Francis Wysocki as a "master of comedy." Two translations from the Polish papers and an English article about the upcoming play are presented together to highlight the difference in writing styles: The Polish versions exude a sense of enthusiastic support, while the English version, probably from the *Gazette*, is matter of fact.

Article 1, translated from the "Maska" Dramatic Circle Scrapbook, reads as follows:

> On Sunday, February 3rd, at the Polish Home on Crane Street the "Maska" Dramatic Circle will present a three act play, "Marriage on Trial," by the slapstick humorist Francis Wysocki. Play directors are Miss Agnes Pieszczoch and Mr. Joseph Czyzewski.
> Those taking part in the play are as follows: Miss Ida Moros, Miss Genevieve Stelmach, Miss Mary Dziuba, Miss Joan Lisowicz, Miss Leokadia Wanik, Miss Sophie Chojnicka, Miss Valeria Szymanska, Mr. John Laniewski, Mr. Stanley Zych, Mr. Joseph Czyzewski, Mr. Alexander Dzierwa, Mr. Lucian Sekowski, Mr. Frank Borkowski, Mr. Joseph Czechowicz and Mr. Anthony Kopec.
> After the presentation there will be a dance. A popular orchestra will play American and Polish songs. Tickets can be obtained from members or at the door.
> At the last meeting the board of directors laid plans for a special musical program for our next monthly meeting. In addition there is another surprise. Mr. Walter Sekowski, chairman of the

board of directors, finished an outline of the program, which Agnes Pieszczoch will direct. All members of our group are expected at that meeting.

Last week there was a mistake in relation to the director of the play that we will present next week. The name printed was Mr. Joseph Czechowicz instead of Mr. Joseph Czyzewski. It is not very surprising, for the names both begin with "Cz." For the second time we will have to distinguish between these two members by adding "blonde or brunette."

For consideration: "Who gives love?" – The Maska Dramatic Circle – K.D.M. [Maska]. We congratulate our member Mr. Richard Olkowski who was called to be the president of the "Chopin" choir.

At the last meeting we decided to accept the "Weekly Gazette" (Polish "Gazeta Tygodniowa") as our local authority. We have to admit that this writing has contributed to our development, and to the success of our presentations.

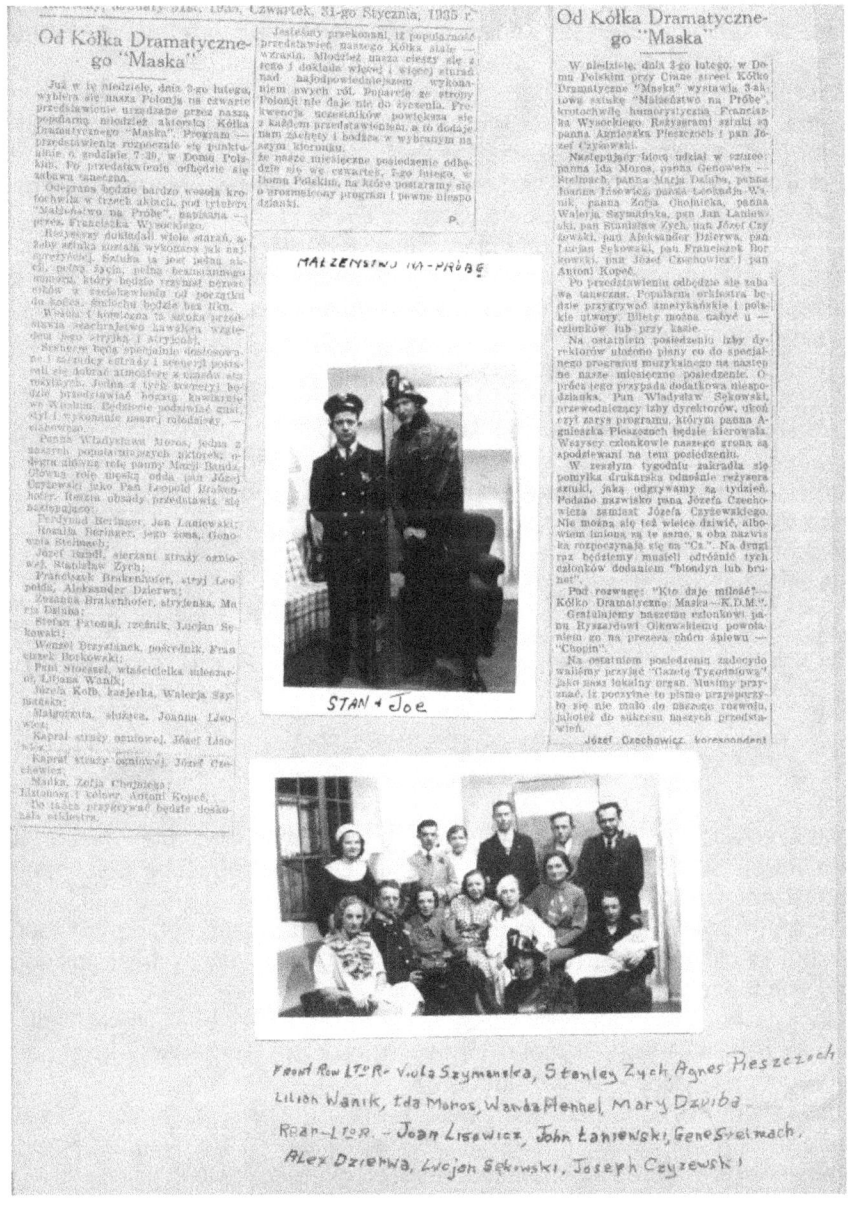

Figure 8: *Marriage on Trial* – Top photo: S. Zych played Fire Sergeant Jozef Bandl; Joe Czechowicz was a Fire Corporal; The cast is shown in bottom photo. Scrapbook.

The second article included in the Scrapbook contained the following:

From the "Maska" Dramatic Circle

This coming Sunday, February 3rd, our Polonia will gather for the fourth presentation given by our popular young actors the "Maska" Dramatic Circle – the performance will begin promptly at 7:30 in the Polish Home. There will be a dance after the performance.

The play will be a very happy pastime in three acts, entitled "Marriage on Trial," written by Francis Wysocki.

The directors have made a great effort so that the play will be very energetic. The play is full of action, full of life, full of continuous humor, which will hold the audience's attention from beginning to end, with countless laughs. It shows the misdeeds of his bachelor uncle and aunt.

The scenery will be specially tailored and the stage manager tried to choose the atmosphere of old times. One of the scenes takes place in a fancy café in Vienna. You will marvel at the taste, style and performance of our young people, - emphatically.

Miss Wladyslawa Moros, one of our most popular actors, will play the main role of Miss Marja Banda. The Lead male role will be played by Mr. Joseph Czyzewski as Mr. Leopold Brakenhofer. The rest of the cast are as follows:

Ferdinand Beringer, Jan Laniewski; Rozalja Beringer, his wife, Genevieve Stelmach; Jozef Bandl, sergeant of the firefighters, Stanley Zych; Franciszek Brakenhofer, Leopold's uncle, Alexander Dzierwa; Zuzanna Brakenhofer, niece, Mary Dziuba; Stefan Patonaj, butcher, Lucjan Senkowski; Wenzel Brystanek, intermediary, Francis Borkowski; Mrs. Stoessel, owner of ?, Lilian Wanik; Josephine Kolb, cashier, Valerie Szymanski; Malgorzata, maid, Joanna Lisowicz; corporal of the firefighters, Joseph Lisowicz; corporal of the firefighters, Joseph Czechowicz; Manka, Sophie Chojnicka; postman and waiter, Anthony Kopec.

An excellent orchestra will play for the dance.

We are confident that the popularity of our Circle is increasing. Our young people take pride in that and put more and more effort into their roles. Support from Polonia leaves nothing to be desired. The turnout of the participants increases with every performance, and this gives us the stimulus incentives in our selected direction.

Our monthly meeting will be on Thursday, February 7, at the Polish Home, at which we will have a varied program and some surprises.

The third article appeared in English in the *Schenectady Gazette* on February 2, 1935, a day before the premiere:[7]

Maska Club To Stage Comedy

The Maska Dramatic Club will present the fourth production of its play season tomorrow night in the auditorium of the P. N. A. Community Home, Crane street. The presentation is a three-act comedy, "Malzenstwo na Probe" by Franciszek Wysocki.

A cast of 15 will take part in the production. The stage setting will represent a dwelling and tap room in old Vienna. The main roles will be portrayed by Miss Ida Moros and Joseph Czyzewski with the following supporting cast:

Genevieve Stelmach, Valeria Szymanska, Mary Dziuba, Lillian Wanik, Joan Lisowicz, Sophie Hojnicka, Stanley Zych, John Laniewski, Lucien Sekowski, Alexander Dzierwa, Frank Borkowski, Joseph Czechowicz and Anthony Kopec.

During intermissions between acts Edward Gurzinski, accordion soloist, will play a few selections. Dancing will be featured during the remainder of the evening. Final preparations are being supervised by the production staff comprised of the following:

Agnes Pieszczoch and Joseph Czyzewski, directors; Zygmond Kilian, stage manager; Zygmond Brzozowski, art director; Wanda Hennel, assistant art director; Joseph Czechowicz and

---

[7] Clipping from the *Schenectady Gazette*, February 2, 1935, p.10

Victor W. Platt, financial managers; Lucien Sekowski, property manager, Helen Kilian and Regina Giniecka, makeup artists; Lillian Wanik and Thaddeus Kilian, wardrobe managers, and Matthew Zych, electrician.

The sub-committee: Jessie Penichter, Mary Zborowska, Hedwig Godlewska and Julia Belniak, Victor W. Platt, Joseph Czechowicz, Leon Marcinek, Daniel Budnik, Thaddeus Kilian, Bronislaw Deptola, Walter Sekowski and Richard Olkowski.

This play program, full of autographs, contains my all-time favorite autograph and I can still picture the mustachioed writer in my mind's eye. The son of A.B. Brzozowski Funeral Home owner, Zigmunt Brzozowski, writes across the family firm's program ad shown below:

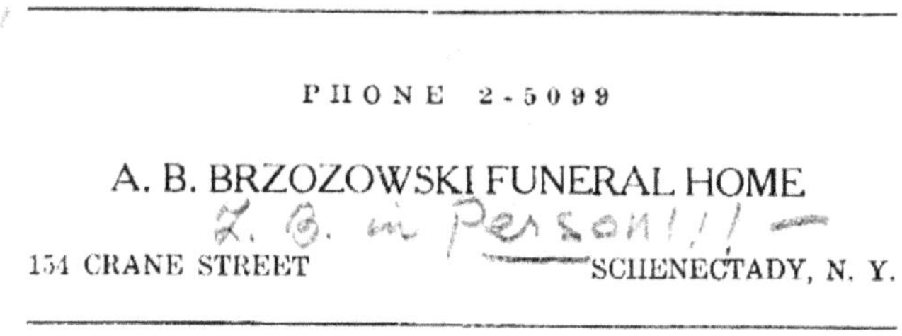

PHONE 2-5099

A. B. BRZOZOWSKI FUNERAL HOME

Z. B. in Person!!!

154 CRANE STREET — SCHENECTADY, N. Y.

Figure 9: Zygmunt Brzozowski's note found in a program, February 3, 1935.

1935 – February 23

The *Schenectady Gazette* published the following announcement on p. 4:

Polish Clubs Council Will Meet on Monday
The Central Council comprised of young people of Polish extraction belonging to various clubs will meet Monday night at 8 o'clock at the P. N. A. hall. This will be the second meeting of this body. The initial meeting was held February 10. Officers will be elected and plans will be made for a field day and other activities during the summer months at Monday's meeting. Peter Lewandowski, chairman, has requested the following organizations to send delegates to Monday's meeting:
Kalina Glee Club, St. Adalbert Athletic Club, Chopin Male Chorus, St. Adalbert Choir, Maska Dramatic Club, Young Men's Polish Association, and the St. Joseph's Athletic Club.

1935 – March

A note in the Scrapbook stated:

The last official program of the 1934-35 season included three one-act plays, WET ZA WET (Eye for Eye), KALOSZE (Galoshes) and STRASZNA CIOTUNIA (The Terrible Aunt). KALOSZE is one of Alexander Fredro's popular comedies. Fredro was the greatest comedy writer of the 19th century in Poland.

1935 – March 23

The *Schenectady Gazette* announced the upcoming performances of Maska as follows (p. 9):

Maskas Give 3 One-Act Plays

Three one-act comedies having unusually fine casts are to be presented by the Maska Dramatic Club players tomorrow night in the auditorium of the P. N. A. community home, Crane street. The production marks the close of the current subscription season during which five play productions have been staged.

The comedy triad includes "Wet za Wet" by Marja Finklowna; "Kalosze" by Alexander Fredro, and, "Straszna Ciotunia" by Ary Jawicz. Twenty-three characters constitute the complete casts of the three presentations.

"Wet za Wet" (Tit for Tat) is a ludicrous illustration of what happens when a husband, completely preoccupied with his professional interests as a chemist, neglects his romantic wife, who craves affectionate attention. The locale of the story is set in the suburb of Fontannelles, a district near Paris. The roles are Gaston Baudoin, Lucyan Sekowski, Madame Baudoin, Miss Genevieve Stelmach; Ludwig Colombin, Richard Olkowski; Mlle. Colombin, Miss Wanda Gerut; Claude Barrois, Frank Borkowski; M. Le Capitaine Gabriar, John Laniewski, and Marietta, Miss Joan Lisowicz. The play is directed by Joseph Czyzewski.

"Kalosze," a farcical comedy, by the "Moliere of Polish Comedy," Alexander Fredro, is a portrayal of the eccentricities of a crotchety old professor, whose main concern is the selection of a suitable husband for his only daughter. A pair of common and seemingly unobtrusive galoshes are an important factor throughout the play, providing a great deal of amusing situations. The cast for this comedy, which is directed by Joseph Czyzewski, is as follows: Pan Inicki, Stanley Zych; Emilia, Miss Irene Witkowska; Balbina, Miss Velma Domkowska; Karol Butowski, Alexander Dzierwa; Fillowicz, Joseph Czyzewski; Zyzla, Miss Joan Lisowicz, and Chlopiec (Boy), Anthony Kopec.

The final presentation, directed by Miss Agnes Pieszczoch, entitled "Straszna Ciotunia", is an intimate sketch of family life occurring in a picturesque quarter of a health resort. The action is replete with buffoonery and without a moment of tedium. The title role of Hermina is portrayed by Miss Jessie Penichter. Other members of the cast are Pafnucy Mekalski, Leon Marcinek; Konegunda, Miss Rosemary Gontarska; Aniela, Miss Helen Kilian; Boleslaw, Bronislaw Deptula; and Stanley Zych, John Laniewski, Thaddeus Kilian and Anthony Kopec.

The stage settings were designed by Zygmond Brzozowski, art director, and a system of effective lighting has been produced by Zygmond Kilian, stage manager. The following also compose the production staff; Misses Regina Giniecka and Helen Kilian, Makeup artists; Lucyan Sekowski, property manager; Miss Lillian Wanik and Thaddeus Kilian, wardrobe managers; and Joseph Czechowicz and V. W. Platt, financial managers.

The general committee and program board include: Joseph Czechowicz and V. W. Platt, chairmen; Misses Sophie Hojnicka, Stella Wojtulewicz and Wanda Hennel; and Stanley Giniecki, Walter Sekowski and Theodore Czyszczon.

During the brief interim between plays, there will be a musical interlude featuring Edward Gurzinski, accordion soloist.

A large attendance is anticipated with many guests from Albany, Amsterdam and Cohoes.

The program for these performances (Appendix 4) contains vivid evidence of my father's entrepreneurial spirit, an ad for The Brothers Zych, Purveyors of fruits and vegetables. It also testifies to Maska's success: the addition of 16 new advertisers: Pleasant Valley Dairy; Advanced Bakery; Carlson's, a paint store with 2 locations; District Attorney's Office; Snyder's Tavern; F.L. Leszczynski Funeral Director; Market

Filling Station with "Smiling Service;" Dr. M.E. Finkel Dentist; Dr. B.C. Mazurowski; Mt. Pleasant Theater; and Z.B. Kilian Signs and Show Cards, the Maska Art Director; Dr. A.F. Korniejewski; Clement Olszewski, Jeweler; Mt. Pleasant Laundry; and Dr. M.J. Dybich, our family doctor who delivered me at the Bellevue Maternity Home.

The impressive list of Patrons on the program's back page includes Pani J. Zych (Mrs. Joseph Zych) my father's mother and Pani J. Wrazen, my Aunt Jane's mother, whose husband is included in the ad at the top of that page. There is a catch in my throat as I recall so many of these people from my childhood community.

1935 – April 12

The report in the *Schenectady Gazette* (p. 26) pointed out the successful season with eleven plays and as many as 38 performers:

**Maska Enjoys Good Season –
Eleven Plays are Staged by Polish Dramatic Club;
38 Players in Parts**

The Maska Dramatic Club recently completed its first successful subscription play season presented on schedule since last fall in the auditorium of the P. N. A. Community Home, Crane street. The close of the season of dramatic productions, numbering 11 in all, marks the attainment of a goal and stands out as a splendid record of achievement and co-operative effort in the history of the comparatively young organization of Polish-American drama devotees. The season comprised five presentations and the various casts engaged 38 different players.
    The play productions during the season were under the direction of Miss Agnes Pieszczoch, Joseph Czyzewski, Daniel V. Budnik, Miss Wanda Hennel and Chester Rudowski. Joseph Czyzewski ably directed four plays; Miss Agnes Pieszczoch was in charge of three; Daniel V. Budnik directed a comedy in three acts; Miss Wanda Hennel and Chester Rudowski jointly directed one play; and one three-act production was under the collaborated direction of Miss Agnes Pieszczoch and Joseph Czyzewski.
    "The Plays Presented"
The plays presented were as follows: "W Zielonym Gaiku," Przybylski; "Tatus Pozwolil," Mozer; "Zywy Nieboszczyk," Belly; "Radcy Pana Radcy," Balucki; "W Pulapce," Alf; "Przygody Malzenski w Podrozy Poslubnej," Jax; "Blazen," Swietochowski; "Malzenstwo na Probe," Wysocki; "Wet za Wet," Finklowa; "Kalosze," Fredro; and "Straszna Ciotunia," Jawicz. The majority of the stage offerings were comedies of a farcical nature.
    The following formed the casts of the productions staged: The Misses Florence Beleus, Velma Dombkowska, Agnes Dmochowska, Mary Dziuba, Wanda Gerut, Regina Giniecka, Hedwig Godlewski, Rosemary Gontarska, Sophie Hojnicka, Helen Kilian, Joan Lisowicz, Ida Moros, Jessie Penichter, Eleanor Piorowska, Genevieve Stelmach, Valeria Szymanska, Lillian Wanik, Irene Witkowska, Stella Wojtulewicz, and Frank Borkowski, Joseph Czechowicz, Thaddeus Czyszczon, Joseph Czyzewski, Bronislaw Deptula, Alexander Dzierwa, Thaddeus Kilian, Zygmond Kilian, Anthony Kopec, John Laniewski, Henry Lewkowicz, Leon Marcinek, Richard Olkowski, V. W. Platt, Lucyan Sekowski, Walter Sekowski, Carl Szymanski, Michael Tytko, Stanley Zych.
    "Those Outstanding"
The list of those who were outstanding in the portrayal and excellent characterization of roles include Genevieve Stelmach, Ida Moros, Regina Giniecka, Florence Beleus, Mary Dziuba, Helen Kilian, Rosemary Gontarska, Jessie Penichter, Eleanor Piorowska, and Stanley Zych, Joseph Czyzewski, Bronislaw Deptula, Lucyan [Sekowski], Richard Olkowski, Frank Borkowski, Leon Marcinek, Alexander Dzierwa, Michael Tytko and John Laniewski.

The members of the production staff in charge of scenic requirements, properties, make-up wardobe and general business management were Misses Wanda Hennel, Regina Giniecka, Helen Kilian, Jessie Penichter, Aniela Pitera, Roberta Tytko. Lillian Wanik, Mary Zborowska, Gertrude Zielanic, and John Belniak, Zygmond Brzozowski, Joseph Czechowicz, Stanley Giniecki, Zygmond Kilian, Thaddeus Kilian, Henry Lewkowicz, V. W. Platt, Lucyan Sekowski, Walter Sekowski and Matthew Zych.

Summer Fun – 1934 - 1936

Individual pictures on the two scrapbook picture pages are labeled "Garkowski's Farm" (1934) or "Galway Lake." In addition, two large, independently mounted photo duplicates were found with the scrapbook:

- S. Zych with the horse (Sparky, I am sure) is labeled: "HERE'S A GOOD PLUG FOR 'STAS'" 1st Picnic of M.A.S.K.A. July 15, 1934. Garkowski's Farm. Photo by- Joseph W. Carroll, 1331 Keyes Avenue, Schenectady, N.Y. 12309."

- S. Zych playing horseshoes with Frank Borkowski, horse in the background, is labeled: "'FRAN' & 'STAS' READY FOR A RINGER" M.A.S.K.A. 1st Picnic July 15, 1934 at Garkowski's Farm."

The group picture in Figure 10 shows 31 happy picnickers at the event. A news article from June 30, 1936, probably refers to the pictured event:

"The Maska Dramatic Club opened its summer recreation program with a sports outing Sunday at "Kamp Korkosz", Galway lake."

The significance of the pinned ribbon (Fig. 11) is unknown. What is obvious in these pictures is the fun and fellowship that characterized Maska during its life.

Figure 10: Maska outings – Garkowski's Farm – 1934; Galway Lake – June 1936. Scrapbook.

Figure 11: Maska outings – Garkowski's Farm – 1934; Galway Lake – June 1936. Scrapbook.

Chapter 4
The 1935 – 1936 Season
September 1935 – July 1936

Maska's status in the cultural life of Schenectady's Polish American community, often referred to as "Polonia," grew significantly during the 1935 – 1936 season. A total of eight plays were presented on five Sundays (counted as five productions) to audiences of up to 400 people. Production planning, a season ticket sales campaign, a season-long stage personality contest, a card party, the first newsletter (Maska Buletyn) and the inclusion of the wider community in several programs mark the increase in Maska activity. Each Sunday Maska event included a matinee for children and a dance after the evening performance at the P.N.A. home on Crane Street.

Maska programs included information about and ads from the Chopin Male Chorus, the Union College fencing team, the Polish University Club, Our Lady of Czestochowa [aka St. Mary's] Dramatic Circle, the Albany Dramatic Club, the Union College Mountebanks, the WGY Players and radio stations WGY and W2XAF.

In September 1935, a party was held for several members departing for college.

A second group of Polish American thespians was formed in the fall of 1935. In contrast with Maska, the Our Lady of Czestochowa Dramatic Circle was affiliated with one of the two local Polish Roman Catholic Churches, also known as St. Mary's; St. Adalbert was the other. Maska members attending the performance probably included my father, since the program was pasted in the scrapbook. The play, *Miracle on Clear Mountain*, was presented in the auditorium of St. Mary's School. Program pages list characters and scenes and their many ads for local small businesses testify to strong community support.

The Stage Personality Contest

From the Maska History: "…all those who participated in the plays of that season (1935 – 1936) were eligible to win the award as the best male actor and the best female actress of the season. The judges were present at each play and gave a rating to each player in each play. Judges Dr. M. J. Dybich and Dr. Bruno C. Mazurowski, were local physicians; Stanley Kosinski was a local musician who gave Sophie Korycinski (my mother) piano lessons; Stanley Belniak of unknown background, and Dr. Bradley H. Kirschberg.

In December 1935, Stanley Zych was elected Maska president. His older brother, Matt, was elected stage manager. The Maska year 1936 began with the January 10th, 1936 inauguration banquet. Sophie Korycinski was among the 14 new members welcomed into Maska.

Soon after, a tragedy struck. The father of Stanley and Matt Zych, Joseph Zych, died on January 12th from injuries sustained in a hit and run accident on January 6th, 1936.

In the process of reading and translating the scrapbook contents, some mysteries appeared. One of these mysteries was the identity of Dr. B. H. Kirschberg, a personality contest judge, and his connection to the Maska Dramatic Circle. Untangling his relationship with Maska was an interesting challenge.

Who was Dr. B. H. Kirschberg?

The inclusion of Dr. Bradley H. Kirschberg as a judge in the Maska stage personality contest in the fall of 1935 puzzled me, since I had never heard of him. A web search turned up the information below.[1]

> Dr. Bradley H. Kirschberg (1883?-1941), chemist and head of the New York State Police Laboratory. Born in Poland, he immigrated to the United States and took a doctorate in chemistry from New York University. From 1912-1935 he served as city chemist for Schenectady. In 1936 he was appointed director of the New York State Police Laboratory, in which position he served until his death. (According to his obituary in the *New York Times* (29 May 1941), he died of a heart attack on the job.)

This is when I realized the possible connection: My father's older brother, my Uncle Matt and Maska's technical director, was a deputy sheriff and Dr. Kirschberg worked for the New York State Police! What is also very interesting is that Dr. Kirschberg was a translator of Polish poetry. Several news articles in the scrapbook included his translations of Polish poetry by Kornel Ujejski (1823-1897), a well-known poet, patriot and political writer, including such verse as "Marsz Pogrzebowy" ("Funeral March") and "Wniebowzięcie" ("Assumption"), providing poetic interpretations of Chopin's work.[2] It may be interesting to know that Ujejski's poem Hagar in the Wilderness was a favorite of actress Helena Modjeska, who knew it by heart and often selected this poem when asked to recite a verse.

The following pages include newspaper articles found in either the family scrapbook or on-line at fultonhistory.com. that I retyped for readability. Articles from the Polish newspapers are translated. Although several articles repeat accounts of the same event, they are included to illustrate the publicity effort that Maska made as well as some differences in depth and tone of coverage.

<u>1935 - August 22, *Schenectady Gazette*</u>

Five Plays for Polish Drama Group Season

> Preliminaries for the forthcoming fall and winter subscription season of the Polish drama productions by the Maska Dramatic Club on the stage of the P. N. A. Community home auditorium are progressing rapidly and give promise of great gains in every respect. The

---

[1] From Flickr on-line source, accessed on December 1, 2015:
https://www.flickr.com/photos/58558794@N07/6703795259/
[2] *Gazeta Tygodniowa*, December 26, 1935.

schedule for the season includes five productions to be presented on dates listed on the season tickets already on sale.

1935 - November 14, 1935, *Gazeta Tygodniowa*

This report, published in Polish, includes the only mention that matinees were designated for children. There is no indication whether they were in any way different from the evening performances.

> The presentations of these young people are already an important component of the life of Polonia here, without which it would be hard to dispense. Support is high and avid followers are steadily increasing. Sunday's show promises further popularity and rightly deserves the heart of local Polonia.
>
> The initial production, slated for October 6, consists of a set of comedies entitled: *Krewniak z Ameryki* [Relative from America] by Marja Dabrowska and *Generalna Próba* [General Rehearsal] by W. Roart. Both presentations have been especially selected for the spontaneity of real humor that pervades them. The directors for the plays are Miss Agnes Pieszczoch and Joseph Czyzewski.
>
> The dates set for the remaining four productions are November 17, December 15, February 2 and March 20. Social dancing will supplement every evening performance. Matinees for children will take place in the afternoon. The plays chosen for enactment on the above dates are as follows: *Ciotka Karola*, [Charlie's Aunt] by T. Brandon; *Zmartwychwstanie* [Resurrection] from Teatr Ludowy [Folk Theater]; *Cyganki* [Gypsies] by Pauline Witkońska; *Fatalna Szata*, [Fatal Garment] by Apolinary Twaciński; *Marcowy Kawaler* [The March Bachelor] by Joseph Gliziński; *Świat bez Męszczyzn* [A World Without Men] by Alexander Engel; *Na bezrybiu i rak ryba* [Catching Fish Without Fishing] by Karl Wachtel; *20 Dni Kozy* [20 Days of Jail] by Maurice Hennequin; *Kto się Spodziewal* [Who Would Have Thought] by Władysław Renz; *Szpital Waryjatów* [Hospital for the Insane] by Eugene Augustin and Augustin; and *Peruka Profesora* [The Professor's Wig] by Anthony Jax.
>
> The production staff that confers during rehearsals includes Miss Agnes Pieszczoch and Joseph Czyzewski, drama directors; Zygmond Kilian, stage manager; Zygmond Brzozowski, art manager; Joseph Czechowicz and V. W. Platt, financial managers; Miss Genevieve Stelmach, Miss Sophie Hojnicka and Miss Helen Kilian, makeup artists; Lucyan Sekowski, property manager; Miss Lillian Wanik and Thaddeus Kilian, wardrobe managers.
>
> A special meeting will be held tonight to make plans for the final outdoor event of the summer.

The list of plays included in the report above contains several that were probably under consideration at the time, but apparently were not performed. There is no additional mention of the following plays in subsequent Maska information: *Zmartwychwstanie; Cyganki; Fatalna Szata; Marcowy Kawaler; Świat bez Męszczyzn; 20 Dni Kozy* and *Kto się Spodziewal.*

1935 – Fall, Unidentified Press Clipping in the Scrapbook

Maska Dramatic Club Has Party for Sales Victors

A group of 42 joined in merry-making at the fall roundup party of the Maska Dramatic Club, arranged by the male members of the organization for the young women winners of the club's recent season tickets sales campaign. Various dances and singing were the most popular divertissements. The musical portion of the program was executed by Anthony Laniewski, accordionist, and his band, which included Anthony Kopec, drums; John Laniewski, clarinet; Matthew Zych, violin and harmonica, and Victor Harasimowicz, musical pipe and saw.

Those attending the party were the Misses Mary Dziuba, Aniela Pitera, Alice Nowicka, Stephania Lewkowicz, Valeria Szymanska, Wanda Gerut, Regina Gensen, Wanda Hennel, John Penichter, Genevieve Stelmach, Jo[an] Lisowicz, Sophie Hojnicka, Frances Harasimowicz, Irene Witkowska, Victoria Tupacz, Jane Zaleska, Helen Kilian, Mary Zborowska, Hedwig Godlewska, Agnes Dmochowska.

Leon Marcinek, chairman; John Laniewski, Thaddeus Kilian, Matthew Zych, Joseph Czyzewski, Walter Sekowski, Henry Lewkowicz, Rudolph Woltner, Anthony Harasimowicz, Joseph Czechowicz, Zygmond Kilian, Stanley Zych, Anthony Laniewski, John Belniak, Victor Harasimowicz, William Bonczyk, Charles Taylor, Anthony Kopec, Joseph Drapala, Joseph Bonczyk and Edward Mack.

1935 – September 20, *Schenectady Gazette* (Page 30)

Maska Dramatic Club Rehearsing for 2 Comedies

The production of two hilarious comedies for the fall opening of the Maska Dramatic Club subscription play season is well under way, according to reports of Directors Agnes Pieszczoch and Joseph Czyzewski. Many new members will make their stage debut in this initial presentation to be staged on October 6 in the auditorium of the P. N. A. community home, Crane street.

At a recent meeting of the board of directors, leaves of absence were granted to the following members entering institutions of higher education: Raymond Budny, a graduate of Union College, left for Western Reserve University in Cleveland, O., to complete his studies for a career in the medical profession; Zygmond Kilian, stage manager for the past two years, enters Cooper Union in New York to follow a calling in art; Andrew Podbielski, enlisted with the United States Army for Military service in the Hawaiian Islands; Miss Rosemary Gontarska, pursuing art studies in Salem, Mass; Miss Gertrude Zielanis, a student of Barnard College of Columbia University, resumes her studies as a sophomore; Carl Szymanski, on a tour of the states, visited Zane Grey, famous western story writer, while en route in Oregon; Zygmunt Brzozowski, art director, leaves for Syracuse early in October to enter the Simmons School of Embalming.

Members appointed to official capacities vacated by absentees include Miss Wanda Hennel, art director; Miss Jessie Penichter, parliamentarian; Matthew Zych, stage manager, and Anthony Kopec, sergeant-at-arms.

Those newly joined and participating in the coming production are Miss Alice Nowicka, Miss Frances Harasimowicz, John Potocki, Joseph Grapala (error: Drapala) and Henry Wienclawski.

1935 – September 23, *Schenectady Gazette* (Page 10)

Hold Farewell Party for 2 Dramatic Club Men

A farewell party in honor of Zygmond Kilian and Zygmont Brzozowski, both prominent in activities of the Maska Dramatic Club, who are leaving for study at educational institutions, was held Saturday evening by members of the dramatic group. Kilian, who was stage manager of the club's production staff, is leaving for New York for art studies at Cooper Union College. Brzozowski, art direct of the production staff, will study at the Simmons School of Embalming in Syracuse, N. Y. Matthew J. Zych was chairman of the affair.

The following attended: Mr. and Mrs. Daniel V. Budnik, Mr. and Mrs. John Zielanis, Mr. and Mrs. Boleslas Kilian, Mr. and Mrs. John Kilian, Miss Irene Jablonska, Miss Agnes Dmochowska, Miss Velma Dombkowska, Miss Sophie Honicka, Miss Frances Harasimowicz, Miss Wanda Gerut, Miss Irene Lanier, Miss Lillian Wanik, Miss Joan Lisowicz, Miss Helen Kilian, Miss Alice Nowicka, Miss Irene Witkowska, Miss Helen Kowalska, Miss Jessie Penichter, John Belniak, William Bonczyk, Michael Bryniarski, Joseph Czechowicz, Stanley Decker, John Laniewski, Leon Marcinek, Thaddeus Kilian, V. W. Platt, John Mack, Henry Wienclawski, Matthew Zych, Stanley Zych and Edward Godlewski.

The clipping was accompanied by the attached advertisement of the upcoming performance:

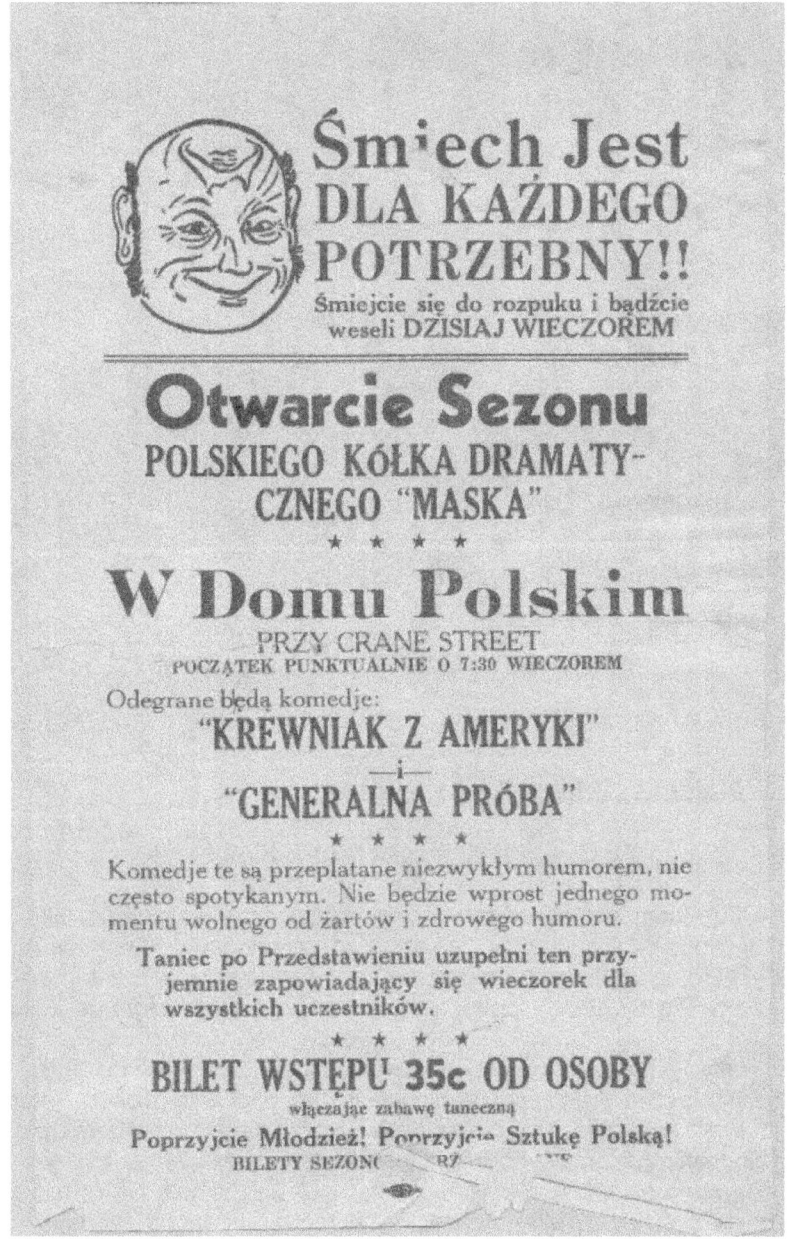

Figure 12: Poster for two plays by Maska. From the Scrapbook.
Translation of Text by PZB: "Laughter is Necessary for Everyone!! Laugh your head off and be merry this evening The season opener of the Maska Dramatic Circle At the Polish Home on Crane Street, starting punctually at 7:30 Two comedies will be presented, *Relative from America* and *Dress Rehearsal*. These comedies are interspersed with extraordinary humor, not often encountered. There will not be a single moment free of jokes and healthy humor. A dance after the presentations will complete this pleasant evening for participants. Admission is 35c per person including the dance. Support the Young Folk! Come to the Polish Play!"

Figure 13: "*Krewniak z Ameryki*," October 1935. Photo courtesy of Seena and Joseph Drapala.

1935 – October 8, *Schenectady Gazette* (Page 8)

Over 400 at Maska Club's First Plays

Upwards of 400 persons witnessed the opening of the Maska Dramatic Club play season at the presentation of two farcical comedies, Sunday in the auditorium of the P. N. A. Community Home, Crane street. The cast in the performance earned many points of merit in the first competition of the "Stage Personality Contest," sponsored by the board of directors as a special feature of the season.

The comedy program proved a great success. The action of the one-act comedies sustained the interest of the record audience to the end and evoked frequent applause. The colorful settings and costumes also made the productions the most attractive ever staged.

The first offering of the performance entitled, *Krewniak z Ameryki*, by Marja Garson-Dabrowski, portrayed an unusual episode in the gay and simple life of a neighborhood in rural Poland, and was directed by Miss Agnes Pieszczoch. *Generalna Próba*, under the direction of Joseph Czyzewski, depicted the manner in which a group of village mountebanks of the year 1902 carried on at a final rehearsal.

A committee of three judges rated the individual merits of the players mainly in regard to diction, gesticulation and mimicry. The following participated in the competition: Miss Ida Moros, Miss Valeria Szymanska, Miss Sophie Hojnicka, Miss Helen Kilian, Miss Mary Dziuba, Miss Alice Nowicka, Miss Hedwig Godlewska, Miss Agnes Dmochowska, Miss Irene Witkowska, Miss Joan Penichter, Leon Marcinek, Joseph Drapala, Walter Sekowski, Stanley Zych, Zenon Sekowski, John Laniewski, Lucyan Sekowski, Joseph Czechowicz, Victor Harasimowicz, Anthony Kopec and Edward Gurzynski.

The production staff included: Miss Agnes Pieszczoch and Joseph Czyzewski, drama directors; Miss Wanda Hennel, art director; Matthew Zych, stage manager; Joseph Czechowicz and Victor W. Platt, finances; Lucyan Sekowski, properties; Miss Lillian Wanik and Thaddeus Kilian, wardrobe and the Misses Genevieve Stelmach, Helen Kilian and Sophie Hojnicka,

makeup. Others on the general committee were: Miss Joan Lisowicz, Miss Wanda Gerut, Miss Joan Penichter, John Belniak, Edward Godlewski, Henry Wienclawski and Daniel V. Budnik.

1935 – November 9, Report in the Scrapbook

Maska Players Rehearsing for November 17 Event

Rehearsals are in full swing by the Maska Dramatics Club players for the presentation of two hilarious comedies on Sunday, November 17, in the second scheduled presentation of the current subscription play season to be staged in the auditorium of the P. N. A. Community home, Crane street. It will be the second opportunity for the participating casts to compete for merits in the "Stage Personality Contest", sponsored by the directors for the entire season's activity.

To comply with the many requests for a comedy program similar to the season's first success, Directors Agnes Pieszczoch and Joseph Czyzewski selected the comedies, *Szpital Waryjatów* [Hospital for the Insane] by Eugene Augustin, popular Romanticist dramatist of the early 19th century, and *Na Bezrybiu i Rak Ryba* [Catching Fish Without Fishing] by Karol N. Wachtel, a noted Polish playwright. Both of the one-act comedies abound in humorous situations and witty dialog.

The cast of *Szpital Waryjatów*, directed by Miss Agnes Pieszczoch, includes Miss Agnes Dmochowska, Miss Frances Harasimowicz, Miss Sophie Chojnicka, Miss Joan Penichter, John Laniewski, Joseph Drapala, Stanley Bonczyk, Stanley Zych, Anthony Kopec, Edward Godlewski, Thaddeus Kilian, Lucyan Sekowski, Willian Bonczyk and Victor Harasimowicz.

In *Na Bezrybiu i Rak Ryba*, under the direction of Joseph Czyzewski, are cast Miss Wanda Gierut, Miss Aniela Pitera, Miss Sophie Chojnicka, Henry Lewkowicz, Leon Marcinek, Joseph Czyzewski and Stanley Zych.

Stage requirements are being made ready by the production staff including Matthew Zych, stage manager; Miss Wanda Hennel, art director; Joseph Czechowicz, and W. W. Platt, business manager; Lucyan Sekowski, property manager; Miss Lillian Wanik and Thaddeus Kilian, wardrobe managers, and the Misses Genevieve Stelmach, Helen Kilian and Sophie Chojnicka, make-up artists.

A special acrobatic exhibition will be featured as an added attraction to the program of dramatics and social dancing.

1935 – November 14, *Gazeta Tygodniowa*

Maska Dramatic Circle's Second Presentation on Sunday

The second presentation of the season of the popular "Maska" Dramatic Circle will take place this coming Sunday, November 17th, at the Polish Home. Besides there is another piece of the contest for the prize of all people taking part in various roles.

Two comedies will be presented: *Catching Fish without Fishing* by Wachtel and *Hospital for the Insane* by Eugene Scribe and Auguste Augustin, popular 19th-century playwrights. Twenty people will take part in these two plays. Rehearsals have been taking place the past 3 weeks under the direction of Miss Agnes Pieszczoch and Mr. Joseph Czyzewski, who unanimously predict that Sunday's program will exceed all presentations to date from the view of good humor and sequence.

In *Catching Fish without Fishing*, directed by Mr. Czyzewski, scenes revolve around a group of Polish-Americans, settling in a small town in the western states, where they started to build a railroad.

The second play, *Hospital for the Insane,* is also interspersed with humor from beginning to end. The play director is Miss Agnes Pieszczoch. – The cast includes doctors, nurses, madmen, patients and so forth.

Miss Helen Grzyms [Grzywna] and Mr. Chester Napiorski, well known acrobats, will occur in their familiar roles, as an additional part of the program. This pair has won many prizes for various performances, and on Sunday the opportunity promises a "handkerchief episode" which will delight the viewers.

The program will begin punctually at 7:30, and the dance begins at 9:30.

The presentations of these young people are already an important component of the life of Polonia here, without which it would be hard to dispense. Support is high and avid followers are steadily increasing. Sunday's show promises further popularity and rightly deserves the heart of local Polonia.

1935 – November 16, Report in the Scrapbook

Second Maska Plays Sunday – Polish Group To Present Comic Stage Vehicles at P.N.A. Crane St. Home

Presenting the second play of the subscription season, the Maska Dramatic Club players will enact the comedies, *Na Bezrybiu i Rak Ryba*, by Karol. N. Wachtel, and *Szpital Warjatow*, by Eugene A. Scribe and Augustin, tomorrow at 7:30 p. m. in the auditorium of the P. N. A. Community home, Crane street. The casts of the two comic plays have entered in the "stage personality contest" inaugurated at the season's initial performance. An acrobatic and balancing exhibition will be an added feature of the evening's entertainment.

On the program will be *Na Bezrybiu i Rak Ryba*, under the direction of Joseph Czyzewski. This one-act comedy is a portrayal of amusing courtship proceedings in the home of Polish inhabitants in western United States at the beginning of the 20th century. The cast includes the following characters:

Pan Dobrzycki, Joseph Czyzewski; Irene, his daughter, Miss Wanda Gierut; Leokadya, his sister, Miss Aniela Pitera; Wladyslaw Zawilowski, railroad employee, Henry Lewkowicz; Edward Granski, his friend, Leon Marcinek; Hipolit Majdalewicz, suitor of Irene, Stanley Zych, and Kasia, chamber maid, Miss Sophie Chojnicka.

An asylum for the demented is the scene for the comic play, *Szpital Warjatów*, directed by Miss Agnes Pieszczoch. It is adapted from the French and reveals the unusual experiences of a sane person mistaken for an idiot while visiting an institution. In the cast are:

Doktor Jancym, John Laniewski; Jadzia, his daughter, Miss Agnes Dmochowska; Hydrogen, mad physician, Stanley Zych; Edward, captain of cavalry, Joseph Drapala; Jakob, interne at the asylum, Lucyan Sekowski; nurses Miss Sophie Chojnicka and Miss Frances Harasimowicz; lunatics, Leon Marcinek and Victor Harasimowicz; attendants, Miss Genevieve Stelmach and Miss Wanda Hennel; patients in cells, Thaddeus Kilian, Anthony Kopec, Edward Godlewski, Willian Bonczyk and Henry Wienclawski.

Judges in the "stage personality contest," who will rate the acting of the casts in regard to diction, gesticulation and mimicry, are Dr. B. H. Kirschberg, Professor Stanley Kosinski and Dr. B. C. Mazurowski.

The added attraction of the evening, the acrobatic and balancing exhibition, will be presented by Miss Helen Grzywna and Chester Napiorski, who will give a varied repertoire of stunts and balancing acts. The team has made many appearances in this vicinity.

The production staff is as follows: Miss Agnes Pieszczoch and Joseph Czyzewski, drama directors; Matthew Zych, stage manager; Miss Wanda Hennel, art manager; Joseph Czechowicz and V. W. Platt, finances and publicity; Lucyan Sekowski, properties; Misses Genevieve Stelmach, Sophie Chojnicka and Helen Kilian, make-up, and Miss Lillian Wanik and Thaddeus Kilian, wardrobe. Auxiliary committee is composed of Miss Alice Nowicka, Miss Irene Witkowska, Walter C. Sekowski, Henry Wienclawski, John Belniak and Leon Marcinek. Dancing will follow the program.

Matthew Zych, stage manager of the Maska Dramatic Club, has built very realistic stage settings for "Szpital Warjatow" one of the comedies to be presented Sunday at the Maska event. The set is representative of barred cells of the "lunatics" in the play.

1935 – November, Report in the Scrapbook

350 Witness Polish Plays –
Maska Dramatic Club's Players Effective as Is Acrobatic Dancing Team

Approximately 350 attended the second production of the cycle of five play presentations scheduled for this fall and winter season by the Maska Dramatic Club players, Sunday night, in the auditorium of the P. N. A. community home, Crane street. The program staged included two comic plays, "Na Bezrybiu i Rak Ryba" by Wachtel and "Szpital Warjatow" by Scribe and Augustin, and a specially featured acrobatic and balancing exhibition. The casts of both plays were rated by a staff of three Judges in the "Stage Personality Contest," a competition for stage honors conducted regularly during this season.

The comic presentations were enthusiastically received by the large audience. The bits of repartee and droll situations confronting the characters in the productions brought forth frequent peals of laughter. Splendid effects and atmosphere were supplied by realistic stage settings.

First was "Na Bezrybiu i Rak Ryba," a humorous portrayal of a courtship in which rival suitors with diverse love-making technique, finally attain desired ends. In "Szpital Warjatow" the action depicted a confusion of affairs at an insane asylum because of a mistaken identity of a visitor to the sanitarium. The plays were under the direction of Miss Agnes Pieszczoch and Joseph Czyzewski.

The acrobatic and balancing exhibition by Miss Helen Grzywna and Chester Napiorski was a fine showing of athletic prowess.

Those on the judging staff of the stage personality contest were Dr. B. H. Kirschberg, W. Elwood McAllaster, Stanislaus Kosinski and Dr. B. C. Mazurowski. The following received ratings:

Misses Wanda Gierut, Aniela Pitera, Sophie Chojnicka, Agnes Dmochowska, Frances Harasimowicz, Genevieve Stelmach, Wanda Hennel and Joseph Czyzewski, Henry Lewkowicz, Leon Marcinek, Stanley Zych, John Laniewski, Joseph Drapala, Lucyan Sekowski, Victor Harasimowicz, Thaddeus Kilian, Anthony Kopec, Henry Wienclawski, Boleslas Bonczyk and Edward Godlewski.

The management of the production was as follows: Matthew Zych, stage; Miss Wanda Hennel, art; Joseph Czechowicz, and V. W. Platt, finances and publicity; Lucyan Sekowski, properties; Miss Lillian Wanik and Thaddeus Kilian, wardrobe; Misses Helen Kilian, Genevieve Stelmach and Sophie Chojnicka, make-up; and Miss Alice Nowicka, Miss Irene Witkowski, Miss Hedwig Godlewska, John Belniak Walter C. Sekowski, Henry Wienclawski and Edward Godlewski,

DNIER 21ST, 1935, CZWARTEK, 21GO LISTOPADA, 1935

MASKA PLAYERS GAIN APPLAUSE IN THEIR COMEDY PRESENTATION

The presentation of the second play performance of the scheduled subscription play season of the Maska Dramatic Club on Sunday, November 17, in the auditorium of the P. N. A. Community Home on Crane street, was attended by upwards of the 300 people, who expressed approval of the program with frequent outbursts of laughter and applause. The casts of the two comedies given received merit ratings in the stage personality competition in effect this season. The acrobatic and balancing exhibition featured was accorded enthusiastic appreciation.

A humorous episode of courtship procedure was depicted in the first offering entitled "Na Bezrybiu i Rak Ryba", a one-act comedy by Karol Wachtel, presented under the direction of Joseph Czyzewski. In Scribe & Augustin's "Szpital Warjatow", directed by Miss Agnes Pieszczoch, mirthful events occurring in a sanitarium for the demented were portrayed by a large cast. The stage settings added a touch of realism to both presentations. The acrobatic and balancing feature by Miss Helen Grzywna and Chester Napiorski was a great success. The stunt team executed a variety of acts and several encores with experienced skill.

On the judges staff in the stage personality competition were: Dr. B. H. Kitzenberg, W. Elwood McAllister, Professor Stanislaus Kosinski and Dr. B. C. Mazurowski.

Three participating in the production and stage contest are as follows; the Misses Wanda Gierut, Anielia Pitera, Sophie Chojnicka, Agnes Dmochowska, Frances Harasimowicz, Genevieve Steimach, Wanda Hennel, and Joseph Czyzewski, Henry Lewkowicz, Leon Marcinek, Stanley Zych, John Janiewski, Joseph Drupala, Lucyan Sekowski, Victor Harasimowicz, Thaddeus Killam, Anthony Kopec, Henry Wienchwski, Boleslaw Bonczyk and Edward Godlewski,

MASKA TO PRESENT BIG PROGRAM SUNDAY

The Maska Dramatic Club is presenting a varied program including a set of one-act comedies, an acrobatic exhibition and a dance, Sunday evening, November 17, in the auditorium of the P. N. A. Community Home, Crane street. The event is the second scheduled presentation of the subscription play season, which features a "Stage Personality Contest" for all the members participating in productions during the entire season of dramatic presentations.

The comedies to be enacted are "Na Bezrybiu i Rak Ryba" by Karol W. Wachtel, and "Szpital Warjatow," by Eugene Augustin Scribe and Augustin, popular playwrights of the Romanticist era in the early nineteenth century. The casts of the two plays number twenty persons. Rehearsals have been carried on for the past three weeks under the direction of Miss Agnes Pieszczoch and Joseph Czyzewski, who unanimously declare that the program prepared "surpasses all previous productions in respect to abundance of humor and repartee."

"Na Bezrybiu i Rak Ryba," directed by Joseph Czyzewski, represents an amusing incident in the lives of a group of Polish-Americans settling in a small town in western United States where a railroad is under construction. The cast and their respective roles are as follows: Joseph Czyzewski, Pan Dobrzycki; Miss Wanda Gierut, his daughter; Irene; Miss Anelia Pitera, aunt of Irene; Henry Lekowicz, Wladyslaw Zawilowski; and Leon Marcinek, Edward Granski, both railroad employees; Stanley Zych, Hipolit Majdalewicz, suitor of Irene; and Miss Sophie Chojnicka, chamber-maid of the Dobrzyckis.

There will be laughs galore in the "Szpital Warjatow", under the direction of Miss Agnes Pieszczoch. This comic play, adapted from the French, is set in a sanitunry for the

Dalszy triumf młodzieży Kółka Dramatycznego "Maska".

Ubiegłej niedzieli wieczorem młodzież kochana zgrupowana w Kółku Dramatycznem "Maska" święciła dalszy triumf swych zabiegów z wieniem dwóch pełnych humoru i ciekawej sekwencji jednoaktowych komedjęk pod tyt. "Na Bezrybiu i Rak Ryba", i "Szpital Warjatów".

Pomimo czterech konkurencyjnych zabaw tego wieczoru publiczność dopisała nadspodziewanie dobrze, uczestników bowiem do 400 osób.

Pierwsza sztuka, "Na Bezrybiu i Rak Ryba", była wyreżyserowana przez p. Józefa Czyżewskiego, które były obsadzone znakomicie, scenerja była kompletowana należycie. Panna Wanda Gierut w roli Ireny, i panna Anelia Pitera w roli Leokadji, wywiązały się ze swego zadania wyśmienicie. Panowie Henryk Lewkowicz i Leon Marcinek, urzędnicy kolei, doprali wszystkim wymaganiom; p. Józef Czyżewski w roli pana Dobrzyckiego, jak również dopisał siedmioletni, panna Zofja Chojnicka w roli Kasi, również nie zawiodła.

Główną rolę męską, Hipolita Majdalewicza odegrał p. Stanisław Zych. Jeszcze w uszach naszych dźwięczy nieżyjącej a częścią zachwalone "od samego dziecka". Pan Zych grał jak zawodowy aktor, umiał dostosować się do każdej okoliczności. Całość sztuki zdawała się dostosowane.

Zaledwo doszliśmy do "normalnego" stanu rzeczy", a kurtyna podnosi się na znak otwarcia drugiej sztuki "Szpital Warjatów", reżyserowanej przez panne Agnieszkę Pieszczoch. Widzimy wspaniałą scenę urządzeń szpitalnych, krzaty przechodzące pielęgniarki, doktorów, internistów, warjatów i cała usłaną szpitała. Przez kilka minut pod czas występnego epizodu uwolnienia się warjatów, padały kaskady śmiechu, nie możliwe do powstrzymania. Epizod ten wywiał wprost formalną furorę, tak też i całość sztuki do samego końca.

Rolę doktora Janczyna grał p. Jan Laniewski; Jadzi, Agnieszka Dmochowska; Hydrogena, łużka porbawionego zmysłów, p. Stanisław Zych; Edwarda, p Józef Drupała, Jakóba, p Lucjan Sekowski: pielęgniarek, panny F Harasimowicz i Z Hojnicka, głównych warjatów, pp. Leon Marcinek i Wiktor Harasimowicz; służących w szpitalu, panny Genowefa Steinach w

pala. Lucyan Sekowski, Victor Harasimowicz, Thaddeus Kilian, Anthony Kopec, Henry Wienclawski, Boleslas Bonczyk and Edward Godlewski.

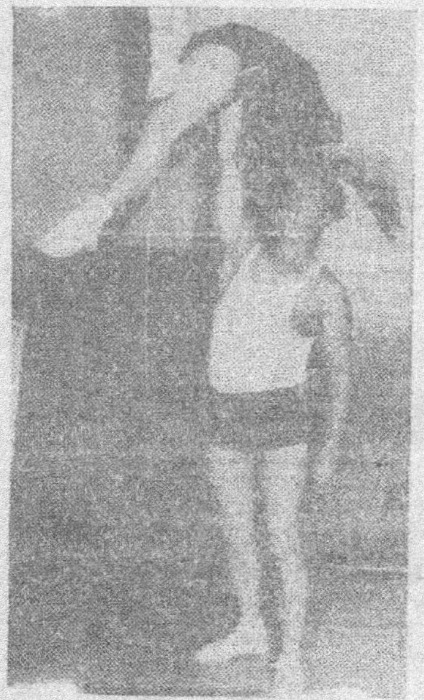

CHESTER NAPIORSKI AND HELEN GRZYWNA IN ACROBATIC EXHIBITION

The production was managed by Matthew Zych, stage; Miss Wanda Hennel, art; Joseph Czechowicz and V. W. Platt, finances and publicity; Lucyan Sekowski, properties; Miss Helen Kilian, Miss Genevieve Stelmach and Miss Sophie Chojnicka, make-up; Miss Lillian Wanik and Thaddeus Kilian, wardrobe; and the auxiliary committee composed of Miss Alice Nowicka, Miss Irene Witkowska, Miss Hedwig Godlewska, John Belniak, Walter Sekowski, Henry Wienclawski, and Edward Godlewski.

There will be laughs galore in "Szpital Warjatow," under the direction of Miss Agnes Pieszczoch. This comic play, adapted from the French, is set in a sanctuary for the insane, where a series of monstrously droll events occur. The following have parts in the production; John Laniewski, Doktor Jancym; Miss Agnes Dmochowski, Jadzia, his daughter; Stanley Zych Hydrogen, demented physician; Joseph Drapala, captain of cavalry; Lucyan Sekowski, interne at asylum; Miss Sophie Chojnicka and Frances Harasimowicz, nurses; Leon Marcinek and Victor Harasimowicz, two lunatics; Misses Genevieve Stelmach and Wanda Hennel, maid-servants; and Thaddeus Kilian, Anthony Kopec, Henry Wienclawski, Edward Godlewski and William Bonczyk, patients at asylum.

An acrobatic and balancing exhibition by the popular team, Miss Helen Grzywna and Chester Napiorski, will be a special added feature of the program. The team has won many prizes in past competitive exhibitions and has prepared a new handkerchief stunt, which will be very thrilling to see.

The production staff in charge of affairs includes: Miss Agnes Pieszczoch and Joseph Czyzewski, play directors; Matthew Zych, stage manager; Miss Wanda Hennel, art director; Joseph Czechowicz and V. W. Platt, business managers; Lucyan Sekowski, property manager; Miss Lillian Wanik and Thaddeus Kilian, wardrobe managers; and the Misses Genevieve Stelmach, Sophie Chojnicka and Helen Kilian, make-up artists.

The play presentation begins at 7:30 p. m. Dancing from 9:30 p. m.

Lucjan Sękowski; pielęgniarek, panny F. Harasimowicz i Z. Hojnicka; głównych warjatów, pp. Leon Marcinek i Wiktor Harasimowicz; służących w szpitalu, panny Genowefa Stelmach i Wanda Hennel; pacjentów w szpitalu, panowie Tadeusz Kilian, Antoni Kopeć, Henryk Wienclawski, Bolesław Bonczyk i Edward Godlewski.

Wszyscy amatorzy spisali się ze swego zadania bez najmniejszego zarzutu. I tu również w głównej roli Hydrogena wywiązał się znakomicie, jak i w pierwszej sztuce, pan Stanisław Zych. Rzeczywiście i bez przesady oddał tę rolę tak naturalnie, z taką swadą i pewnością, iż w zachwyt wprowadził zebraną publiczność.

Po przedstawieniu nastąpił występ panny Heleny Grzywnej i p. Czesława Napiorskiego w akcie akrobatycznym, poczem uczestnicy udali się w tany.

Po niedzielnem przedstawieniu pozostają miłe tylko wspomnienia. Uczestnicy sztuki polskiej tak już polubili naszą młodzież Kółka, iż nie mają wprost słów uznania za te biesiady, jakie nam programowo urządza.

Stoją przed oczyma jeszcze wspaniałe dekoracje sceny, widok wnętrza domu warjatów, czego mistrzami są — członkowie tego kochanego naszego zespołu.

Cały wieczór przeszedł pod znakiem dużych rzeczy. Wysiłki kwiatu tej — młodzieży naszej, tu zrodzonej, są należycie oceniane, chociaż nie wszyscy zdają sobie sprawy z trudów, borykań, nawet i przeszkód, z jakiemi przygotowania i uzupełniania każdego wystawianego programu są połączone.

Postęp na każdym kroku jest widoczny. Nasza młodzież nie tylko że nie ustępuje lecz i przewyższa zespoły większych osiedli polskich w Ameryce. Jesteśmy z niej słusznie dumni, rokując dla niej bardzo różową przyszłość na desce scenicznej, w czem tylko podzielamy zdanie rzeczoznawców, których szczególnie ubiegłej niedzieli nie było brak.

Będąc jeszcze pod miłem wrażeniem zeszłoniedzielnej biesiady, już nieco niecierpliwie oczekujemy następnego programu tej kochanej naszej młozieży.

Figure 14b: Bottom half of newspaper article.

1935 – November 21, Report in the Scrapbook

Kirschberg To Address Club
Polish University Group Hear Lecture Nov. 29
by Chemical Consultant

Pursuing its educational activity, the Polish University Club of this city has completed arrangements for a program of cultural interest, featuring Dr. Bradley H. Kirschberg, chemical consultant of the New York State Association of Police Chiefs, who will deliver a lecture on "The Esthetics of the Spoken Word," on November 29 at 8 p. m. in the P. N. A. Community Home, Crane street. Included on the program will be a eulogy in observance of the 75th birthday anniversary this month of Ignace Jan Paderewski, celebrated concert pianist, statesman and patriot of Poland.

The lecture to be given by Dr. Bradley H. Kirschberg, who is well known as an accomplished speaker and linguist, will be based on the work of Professor Julius Tanner and will deal with the biological chemic-mechanical and esthetic evolution of human sound. Dr. Kirschberg has made a thorough study of the sounds of the Romanic, Slavonic and Germanic languages and is the translator of many literary works in both the Polish and English languages.

In illustrating the co-relationship between music and the spoken word Dr. Kirschberg will make recitations of several poems from the cycle called "Chopiniana," a collection of verse inspired by the composer, Frederic Chopin, and written by his contemporary, Kornell Ujejski, a Polish Poet. The rhythmic distinction of sound will also be demonstrated by means of a rendition of both Polish and English of a number of these poems which Dr. Kirschberg has translated into English.

Musical selections on the program will be rendered by Miss Florence Lewienski, secretary of the Polish University Club, and by Robert Stone, director of the WGY Players.

1935 – November, Report in the Scrapbook

Speech and Music Linked
Dr. B.H. Kirschberg Demonstrates for Polish Group Relationship of the Two

Dr. Bradley H. Kirschberg, chemical consultant of the New York State Association of Police Chiefs, in a lecture on "The Esthetics of the Spoken Word," sponsored by the local Polish University Club, Friday night, in the P. N. A. Community Home, Crane street, gave an impressive demonstration of the co-relationship between music and the human sound. To show that languages of human speech and music are synonymous in expressing the emotions recitations in Polish and English of a famous poem by the Polish poet, Kornell Ujejski, were given in unison with the somber strains of Chopin's "Funeral March."

In introducing his subject, Dr. Kirschberg described the evolution of sound in respect to the animal kingdom and explained the production of transmission of human sound by means of the physical instruments of speech. He spoke of the mouth as the "typical concert hall of human speech," pointing out the various influences that determine the richness of language, and how colors are compared with sounds indicative of human emotion.

Speaking on the beauty of sound he said that "the esthetics of the spoken word occupies an important position in general esthetic education. Besides the individual pleasure, the nursing of a spoken word has a significant social and national importance. One can almost say nation and that the soul of the nation is its speech.

"Early in the 19th century the idea that all emotions are centered in the heart passed out of existence. Speech then commenced to travel in three directions – logical, depending upon the sense of the matter; psychological, reflecting a proper attunement, and finally, esthetic, expressing beauty.

"The interpretation 'what touches us in a spoken word' is not the subject of which we are being told, but rather the emotion of the one who speaks to us. The triumph of an actor is the ability to be forgotten, which means that he is forgotten but the character which he reproduces stands apparent before you."

Several translations in English from Ujejski's cycle of verse, "Chopiniana," inspired by the musical compositions of Frederic Chopin, served to illustrate the theme of the lecture. Recitations were given by Stanley J. Zych, of the Maska Dramatic Club players; S. Ralph Cohen, a member of the Union College Mountebanks, and Dr. Kirschberg. Assisting on the piano were Robert Stone, drama director at the WGY broadcasting studios, and Miss Florence Lewienska, secretary of the university body.

Thaddeus Ogonowski, president of the University Club, expressed the appreciation of the group at the conclusion of the program.

1935 –December 5, *Schenectady Gazette* (Page 28)

Ask St. Mary's Circle Repeat Polish Vehicle

The St. Mary's Dramatic Circle made a successful debut into the dramatic world Sunday by the presentation of a Polish melodrama *Cud na Jasnej Gorze* ["Miracle at Jasna Gora," a place in southern Poland] by J. S. Zielinski. The enthusiastic audience of over 500 persons has requested a repetition of the drama for the benefit of those who have missed the first performance.

Excellent work on the part of the cast is being complimented by critics but special mention is due Frank Halturewicz who not only played the part of a count impressively but also directed the drama. Miss Helen Roginski also impressed as the heroine. Others in the cast were Victor Rucinski, John Millewski, Mary Mozgawa, Brennen Warlik, Stanely Karpinski, Edward Stuczko, Anna Mae Kluczynski, Walter Duszynski, Eleanor Przekop, Jean Idzikowski, Florence Kiszka, Helen Nicos, Philamena Gwiazdowski, Statia Stempkowski, Irene Krasucki, Clara Krasucki, Cecelia Szuba, Lillian Kalabus, Stella Puszcz, Helen Duszynski, Helen Przekop, Stella Pawlaczyk, Bernice Mozgawa and Helen Kosielski.

Singing was under the direction of Brennen Warlik and Miss Sophie Witkowski was at the piano and organ.

Joseph Dmochowski, assistant stage manager of the Plaza Theater and honorary member of the circle, supervised the stage setting and scenery. Assisting him were Harry Razewski, Albert Kaczmarek, Frank Retajczyk, and Joseph Bojczuk.

Among those in the audience were the Maska Dramatic Club of Schenectady and the Albany Dramatic Club who were entertained after the performance by the St. Mary's Dramatic Circle. Miss Bernice Rogowicz, vice president, was master of ceremonies, and the following spoke extending their congratulations and best wishes for future success: Edward S. Wojtal, director of the Albany Dramatic Club; Walter Senkowski, president of Maska Dramatic Club; Waclaw Grodkiewicz, scout director and member of Maska; John Bonczyk, Albany Dramatic Club; Frank Leszczynski, Arthur Sarnowski, Mrs. John Zielanis, honorary member of Maska; Agnes Pieszczoch and Joseph Czyzewski, directors of Maska; Benjamin Kazyaka, assistant direct of St. Mary's Dramatic Circle; Joseph Dmochowski and Frank Halturewicz, president of St. Mary's Dramatic Circle.

1935 – December 6, *Schenectady Gazette* (Page 10)

Kirschberg Will Address Polish Group Tonight

A program of cultural interest, sponsored by the local Polish University Club, featuring a lecture by Dr. Bradley H. Kirschberg, chemical consultant of the New York State Association of Police Chiefs, will be presented tonight at 8 o'clock in the P. N. A. Community Home on Crane street.

"The Esthetics of the Spoken Word" will be the subject of the talk by Dr. Kirschberg, who has made a special study of this phase of linguistics. His address will trace the evolution of human sound and show the co-relationship between music and human sound. It will be based on the works of Professor Julius Tenner and will include several original translations in English from Polish literature.

Participating in the program will be Robert Stone, drama director of the WGY broadcasting studio; Stanley J. Zych, vice-president of the Maska Dramatic Club; S. Rolfe Cohan,

member of the Mountebanks at Union College; and Miss Florence Lewienska, secretary of the University Club, who will be piano accompanist in the musical portion of the program.

Educational groups throughout this vicinity including the local Conrad Literary Fellowship and Maska Dramatic Club have been invited to attend.

Much favorable comment has been received by the University body in regard to the special radio broadcast commemorating the 75th birthday anniversary of the eminent virtuoso and the statesman, Ignace Jan Paderewski, presented last week in co-operation with stations WGY and W2XAF of Schenectady.

1935 – December 6, From *Union–Star*[3]

Maska Names Zych President – Polish Dramatic Group Holds Annual Meeting; Plans Plays

Figure 15: Scrapbook page with two clippings about Zych's election to Maska president.

---

[3] Reproduced in the Scrapbook. The reference to "Honeymoon Special" is unknown.

1935 December 11, *Schenectady Gazette*

Election of Leaders of Maska Dramatic Club

At a recent election of officers of the Maska Dramatic Club, Stanley J. Zych was chosen president and Leo P. Marcinek, vice-president and chairman of the board of directors.

Mr. Zych has been active in the organization continuously for the past two years. He has portrayed many leading roles and is a former vice-president.

Mr. Marcinek has gained popularity acting in the club's presentations and has been active in promoting social and production affairs of the group. Recently he was chairman of the ticket sale campaign for subscribers to the season, which includes five plays for this fall and winter.

Other officers are Miss Wanda Hennel, secretary; Miss Amelia [Aniela] Pitera, treasurer; Walter C. Sekowski, business manager; Willian Bonczyk, sergeant-at-arms; Miss Alice Nowicka, parliamentarian; Matthew Zych, stage manager; Miss Wanda Hennel, art manager; John Laniewski, property manager; Miss Helen Kilian, Miss Genevieve Stelmach, Miss Hedwig Godlewska and John Belniak, wardrobe managers; Joseph Czyzewski and Miss Agnes Pieszczoch, drama directors.

The board of directors is comprised of Leon P. Marcinek, chairman; Walter Sekowski, Joseph Czechowicz, Stanley Zych, Miss Amelia [Aniela] Pitera, Miss Wanda Hennel, Joseph Czyzewski, Miss Agnes Pieszczoch and Matthew Zych.

Installation of officers will be held at the January meeting.

1936 – January (after the 10th), Report in the Scrapbook

Maska Dramatic Club Holds Installation Fete

Members of the Maska Dramatic Club gathered at the P. N. A. Community Home on Crane street on January 10 at 8 p. m. to witness the annual installation ceremonies of the newly-elected officers and the initiation of new members. A program of entertainment and refreshments preceded the main event of the evening. Joseph Drapala was master-of-ceremonies.

The officers installed include: Stanley J. Zych, president; Leo P. Marcinek, vice-president; Miss Wanda Hennel, secretary; Miss Nellie Pitera, treasurer; William Bonczyk, sergeant-at-arms; Walter C. Sekowski, business manager; Matthew J. Zych, stage manager; John Laniewski, property manager; John Belniak, wardrobe manager; Joseph Czechowicz, publicity manager; the Misses Helen Kilian, Genevieve Stelmach, Hedwig Godlewska and Jane Dlugosinska, make-up artists; and Miss Agnes Pieszczoch and Joseph Czyzewski, drama directors.

The members initiated are as follows: Miss Jane Dlugosinska, Miss Frances Harasimowicz, Miss Alice Nowicka, Miss Sophie Korycińska; Miss Hilda Saniewska, Miss Jessie Niesobienska, Miss Jane Kozlowska, Miss Stephanie Lewkowicz, Miss Irene Nowicka, Joseph Drapala, Willian Bonczyk, Stanley Godlewski, Henry Wienclawski, and Henry Klejsmyt.

The committee in charge consisted of Miss Agnes Pieszczoch and Joseph Drapala, co-chairmen; and the Misses Wanda Hennel, Stephanie Lewkowicz, Frances Harasimowicz, and Joan Penichter.

1936 – January 25, *Schenectady Gazette* (Page 9A)

Maska Club to Stage Comedy – Success of 10 Years Ago to be Given February 2; All Actors in Stage Contest

The Maska Dramatic Club will present the popular American stage and screen success of a decade ago, "Ciotka Karola," a three-act farcical comedy by Brandon, at the fourth scheduled performance of its current subscription season, Sunday, February 2, in the auditorium of the P. N. A. community home on Crane street. Rehearsals by the cast of 11 eligible to compete for stage laurels in this season's specially featured "stage personality contest" are progressing under

direction of Joseph Czyzewski. Supplementing the program of dramatics there will be a dueling exhibition by varsity members of the Union College fencing team.

The farcical drama, "Ciotka Karola," has all the prerequisites of ideal humorous entertainment. Its main action centers about the ludicrous impersonation of an old aunt by an English nobleman, who masqueraded as a lady, is induced to chaperone a house party for young people. Situations of unusual dramatic appeal abound in every act and contain a lively wit infallible in producing laughs.

Heading the cast is Leo P. Marcinek, who plays the part of Lord Fancourt Babberly. The other portrayals are Jacob Chesney, John Laniewski; Brassett, Thaddeus Kilian; Karol Wycham, Henry Klejsmyt; Sir Francis Chesney, Joseph Czyzewski; Anna Spettigue, Miss Irene Wikowska; Kasia Verdun, Miss Alice Nowicka; Stephen Spettigue, Joseph Drapala; Donna Lucia D'Alvadorez, Miss Lillian Wanik; Ella Dellahay, Miss Irene Brzostowska and Marynia, Miss Aniela Pitera.

Stage settings and business arrangements are being supervised by the production staff of the following:

Matthew Zych, stage manager; Walter Sekowski, business manager; Zygmont Brzozowski, art director; John Laniewski, property manager; John Belniak and Miss Stephanie Lewkowicz, wardrobe; Misses Helen Kilian, Genevieve Stelmach, Hedwig Godlewska and Jane Dlugosinska, make-up; Joseph Czechowicz, publicity; Miss Helen Dziuba and Miss Wanda Hennel, prompting.

The auxiliary committee includes Miss Aniela Pitera and Miss Stephanie Lewkowicz, checking; Miss Frances Harasimowicz and Miss Sophie Chojnicka, program distribution; Victor Harasimowicz, door tickets. Walter Sekowski, Lucyan J. Sekowski and Leon Marcinek, program advertisements.

1936 – January 31, *Schenectady Gazette* (Page 25)

College Fencers Will Be Seen on Maska Program

Featuring the fourth scheduled presentation of the current subscription season by the Maska Dramatic Club on Sunday, in the auditorium of the P. N. A. community home, Crane street, will be an exhibition of fencing by Captain James Righter, '37, of Altamont, and Elmer Sheldon, '37, of Scotia, veteran swordsmen of the Union College varsity fencing team, with Kurt von Forstmeyer as coach. The exhibition will include matches with the foils, sabers and epees.

Experience of three years continued practice, including two years with the college varsity, indicates the Garnet duelers will stage a spectacular demonstration of thrusts and parries. With the enlivened interest in the sport locally it is expected that many fencing enthusiasts will attend the bouts.

In the first Union fencing engagement this season with Colgate University last week Captain Righter won five matches including three foil bouts and two saber matches to make a perfect score. His conquests were the main factor in the Garnet victory over the Maroon swordsmen in the nine encounters. Elmer Sheldon, participating in the saber and foil events, was winner in the foil contest with the score of 5 to 2.

Announcement of phases of the exhibition will be made by Michael J. Tytko, 36 [Class of 1936], of Schenectady. Arrangements have been completed by W. C. Sekowski, business manager of the group.

1936 – February 1, *Schenectady Gazette* (Page 7)

Leo Marcinek To Play Lead Role in Farce

Leo P. Marcinek, 1530 Third avenue, will portray the leading role of Lord Fancourt ("Babbs") in the three-act farcical comedy, *Ciotka Karola*, by Brandon, which will be presented by the Maska Dramatic Club players tomorrow night at the P. N. A. Community Home, Crane street.

The characterization of this part includes an impersonation of a woman named Donna Lucia D'Alvadorez, played by Miss Lillian Wanik. The complete cast, consisting of 11 persons, is concluding rehearsals under the direction of Joseph Czyzewski.

Mr. Marcinek has been active in the group's stage productions during the past year and has participated in every presentation of the current subscription season. During the season ticket drive he was captain of the sales team and at the yearly election of officers he was chosen vice president and chairman of the board of directors.

Other members of the cast are Miss Irene Witkowska, Miss Alice Nowicka, Miss Aniela Pitera, Miss Irene Drzostowska, John Laniewski, Thadeus Kilian, Henry Klejsmyt and Joseph Drapala. Judges in the stage personality contest will be Stanislaus Kosinski, Stanislaus Belniak and Dr. Myron J. Dybich.

The program will be concluded by a fencing exhibition by the members of the Union College varsity team.

1936 – February 2, Unknown Newspaper Report [4]

Ciotka Karola, a three-act farcical comedy by Brandon, is the fourth scheduled performance of its current subscription season, Sunday, February 2, in the auditorium of the P. N. A. community home on Crane street. Rehearsals by the cast of 11 eligible to compete for stage laurels in this season's specially featured "stage personality contest" are progressing under direction of Joseph Czyzewski. Supplementing the program of dramatics there will be a dueling exhibition by varsity members of the Union College fencing team.

Figure 16: *Ciotka Karola* [Charlie's Aunt]. February 1936 - Leo P. Marcinek, "bride," is Lord Babberly ' Charlie's "Aunt". Photo Courtesy of Seena and Joseph Drapala.

---

[4] Fultonhistory.com , accessed on November 15, 2015. Newspaper Source unknown

1936 – Report in the Scrapbook

Maska Farce Drama Pleases
Actors Excellent in Roles
Fencing Exhibition Features Program

Portrayal of the entertaining stage and screen comedy hit of former years, Brandon's *Ciotka Karola* in three acts, by the Maska Dramatic Club players, Sunday night, on the stage of the P. N. A community home, Crane street, registered frequent applause from an enthusiastic audience. The excellent work of the cast received high rating in the season's "stage personality" competition. All attending acclaimed the featured exhibition of swordsmanship by the members of the Union College varsity fencing team.

    In a story of a comic impersonation of an aunt by a titled Englishman, Ciotka Karola presented the manner in which the deception involved others in a series of amusing complications. Playing the role of Lord Fancourt ("Babbs") Babberly, who posed as the aunt of an Oxford student at a house party, Leo P. Marcinek enlivened the main action with an effective rendition of a dual personality. Miss Lillian Wanik, as Donna Lucia D'Alvadorez, the real aunt delayed in arriving from Brazil on a visit to her nephew, interpreted her role with realistic grace and dignity. Depicting the part of Brassett, the butler, was Thaddeus Kilian, who enhanced the humorous developments with an expression of constant serenity. Anna Spettigue and Kasia Verhun enacted by Miss Irene Witkowska and Miss Alice Nowicka respectively, supplied the love interest in fine style. John Laniewski and Henry Klejsmyt, who made his stage debut in the play, ranked well as the two student lovers, Jacob Chesney and Karol Wycham. True characterization was given to the parts of Sir Francis Chesney and Stephen Spettigue by Joseph Czyzewski and Joseph Drapala. Miss Irene Brzostowska as Ella Dellahay and Miss Aniela Pitera as Marynia, the maid, did a fine piece of acting. The production was under the direction of Joseph Czyzewski.

    The exhibition of fencing tactic was given by Captain James Righter and Elmer Sheldon, veteran swordsmen of the Union College varsity team coached by Kurt von Forstmeyer. Matches with the foils and sabres with explanation of the various types of thrusts and parries by Michael J. Tytko '36, of Schenectady, combined to make the feature an excellent bit of instructive entertainment.

    Those active in the arrangement of the program were as follows: Zygmont Brzozowski, art; Walter Sekowski, business; John Laniewski, properties; Miss Stephanie Lewkowicz and John Belniak, wardrobe; Matthew Zych, stage; Miss Helen Kilian, Genevieve Stelmach, Hedwig Godlewska and Jane Dlugosinska, make-up; Misses Mary Dziuba, Wanda Hennel and Agnes Dmochowska, prompting; Joseph Czechowicz, publicity; William Bonczyk and Lucyan Sekowski, entrance; and Miss Frances Harasimowicz and Miss Sophie Chojnicka, programs.

    The fifth and final presentation of the current season will be staged on March 29.

1936 – February 4, *Schenectady Gazette* (Page 8)

Maska Comedy Well Received – Fourth Subscription Play
to Be Presented; Union Fencers Give Exhibition

An excellent performance of the gay and diverting three-act farcical comedy, *Ciotka Karola*, by Brandon, given by the Maska Dramatic Club players at the fourth scheduled presentation of the current subscription season Sunday night, on the stage of the P. N. A. community home, Crane street, drew forth enthusiastic applause from approximately 300 people. The cast in the production rated highly in "stage personality" competition for acting honors. The fencing exhibition by varsity swordsmen of Union College proved instructive.

    The story of *Ciotka Karola* concerned an amusing deception of an elderly aunt by a man of English peerage, Lord Fancourt Babberly, who perpetrated the impersonation for two fellow classmates in need of a chaperone for a house party. In the portrayal of the false aunt, which was the motivating factor in the play, Leo P. Marcinek demonstrated a true type of capricious femininity. Prior to the arrival of the real aunt, Donna Lucia D'Alvadorez, played by Miss Lillian

Wanik, the action was enlivened by ludicrous love-making. Revelation of real identities climaxed the final denouement of the play.

Completing the cast were Jacob Chesney, John Laniewski; Brassett, Thaddeus Kilian; Karol Wycham, Henry Klejsmyt; Sir Francis Chesney, Joseph Czyzewski; Anna Spettigue, Miss Irene Witkowska; Kasia Verdun, Miss Alice Nowicka; Stephen Spettigue, Joseph Drapala; Elia Dellahay, Miss Irene Brzostowski, and Marynia, Miss Aniela Pitera.

An exhibition of fencing, including matches with the foils and sabres, was given by Captain James Righter and Elmer Sheldon, varsity member of the Union College team coached by Kurt von Forstmeyer, Michael J. Tytko '36 of Schenectady explained the various thrusts and parries with combinations as demonstrated by the fencers.

The presentation was supervised by the production staff comprised of the following:

Joseph Czyzewski, drama director; Zygmont Brzozowski, art director; Walter C. Sekowski, business manager; John Laniewski, properties; John Belniak and Miss Stephanie Lewkowicz, wardrobe; Matthew Zych, stage; Misses Helen Kilian, Genevieve Stelmach, Hedwig Godlewska and Jane Dlugosinska, make-up; Joseph Czechowicz, publicity; Miss Helen Dziuba and Miss Wanda Hennel, prompting.

The auxiliary committee included Miss Stephanie Lewkowicz, Miss Aniela Pitera, Miss Frances Harasimowicz, Miss Sophie Chojnicka, William Bonczyk and Lucyan Sekowski.

The final presentation of the season will be staged March 29.

1936 – February, Report in the Scrapbook

Maska Card Party Entertainment to Be Held
Next Week Committee Plans Unusual Program

Who craves amusement? All normal persons living in this workaday enjoy being entertained – and rightly so! The opportunity is at hand to experience that necessary pleasure of social activity without the aid of a divining rod or even a genuine reproduction of Aladdin's mystical lamp. Read on!

A card party with special entertainment and door prizes will feature next week's social program at the P. N. A. community home on Crane street. The Maska Dramatic Club is sponsoring the event arranged by a special committee of seventeen for Thursday evening, February 27, at 7:30 p. m. The affair will be the group's first social activity this year. The program will include variety entertainment and refreshments will be served. Tickets are on sale by all members of the group.

The committee in charge of arrangements is comprised of Walter C. Sekowski, chairman; Miss Genevieve Stelmach, mistress of ceremonies; Miss Sophie Chojnicka, Miss Frances Harasimowicz, Miss Lillian Wanik, Miss Alice Nowicka, Miss Irene Witkowska, Miss Jane Dlugosinska, Miss Wanda Hennel, Miss Stephanie Lewkowicz, Miss Joan Penichter, Miss Agnes Pieszczoch, Lucyan Sekowski, Henry Klejsmyt, Stanley Zych, Henry Lewkowicz, and Edward Hennel.

1936 – March, Report in the Scrapbook

After Card Party

The Maska Dramatic Club held a successful card party last week at the Polish community home. Featuring the evening's entertainment was a variety program with the following participating: Peter Lewandowski, Jr., accompanied by Miss Sophie Witkowska, song; Joseph Czechowicz accompanied by Matthew Tyborowski, violin solos; Edward Gurzynski, accordion selections; Miss Aniela Pitera, accompanied by Miss Witkowska, buck tap dance; and last but not least, Joseph Czyzewski and Miss Pitera, dramatic skit, "Kasia Przy Telefonie." Miss Genevieve Stelmach was mistress of ceremonies.

The committee was comprised of Walter C. Sekowski, chairman; Miss Genevieve Stelmach, program; Miss Stephanie Lewkowicz, refreshments; Lucyan Sekowski, finances; and

Miss Sophie Chojnicka, Miss Frances Harasimowicz, Miss Lillian Wanik, Miss Wanda Hennel, Miss Alice Nowicka, Miss Irene Witkowska, Miss Jane Dlugosinska, Miss Agnes Pieszczoch, Henry Klejsmyt, Edward Hennel, Henry Lewkowicz, and Stanley Zych.

1936 –March, Unidentified Press Clipping in the Scrapbook

Maska Players Prepare Melodrama
Season's Final Production to Be Staged March 29

Rehearsals are nearing completion by members of the Maska Dramatic Club preparing the final production of the current subscription season to be presented on Sunday, March 29, in the auditorium of the P. N. A. community home on Crane street. The performance will feature a three-act melodrama entitled *Koszyk Kwiatów* [A Basket of Flowers] adapted by Józef Chociszewski from a stirring tale of profound emotional appeal written by X. Schmider, and will conclude the "stage personality contest" in effect throughout this season's activity.

Koszyk Kwiatów, or Los Sieroty [A Basket of Flowers, or the Orphan's Fate] is a tense drama of human faith and suffering occurring in Poland in the year 1858. The locale of the story is the estate of a wealthy noble who employs a retinue of peasant workers to farm his fields. A series of unusually pathetic events gives the production a touch of realism and illustrate a well-known truth of civilization. The play is in three acts and includes five changes of scenes.

The principal role of Marynia will be portrayed by Miss Agnes Pieszczoch, who will make her first appearance as an actress in the group's productions, having previously been in charge of directing the play presentations. Others comprising the cast are Jakub Kwiecinski, Stanley Zych; hrabia (Count), Henry Lewkowicz; hrabina (Countess), Miss Wanda Hennel; Zofja, Miss Wanda Gierut; sedzia (judge), Leo P. Marcinek; Stanislaw, Bernard Deptula; Antoni, Lucyan J. Sekowski; Szymon, Henry Klejsmyt; Joanka, Miss Frances Harasimowicz; Katarzyna, Miss Aniela Pitera; Jedrzej, Frank Borkowski; Brygida, Miss Hedwig Godlewska; ksiadz (priest), V. W. Platt; and two court guards, Thaddeus Kilian and William Bonczyk.

Special stage settings are being painted by an art crew headed by Miss Wanda Hennel. The stage production staff includes Joseph Czyzewski and Miss Agnes Pieszczoch, drama directors; Walter C. Sekowski, business manager; John Laniewski, property manager; Miss Stephanie Lewkowicz, wardrobe; Misses Helen Kilian, Genevieve Stelmach, and Jane Dlugosinska, make-up artists; Joseph Czechowicz, pubicity; and a general committee consisting of Misses Sophie Chojnicka, Agnes Dmochowska, Irene Nowicka, Alice Nowicka, Velma Dombkowska, Stephanie Lewkowicz, and William Bonczyk. A musical interlude will be heard during the presentation.

1936 – March, Report in the Scrapbook

Maska Present Final Drama Sunday Evening
To Stage *Koszyk Kwiatów* Melodrama
Stage Competition Will Close

Presenting the fifth and final play production of the current subscription season the Maska Dramatic Club will stage *Koszyk Kwiatów*, a three-act melodrama based on a popular story, Sunday, at 7:30 p. m. in the auditorium of the P. N. A. community home on Crane street. The regular featured "stage personality" contest in which the participating casts receive ratings on acting ability, will be brought to a close at the presentations.

Adapted from a remarkable story of X. Schmider by Jozef Chociszewski the drama depicts the unfortunate destiny of an orphaned peasant maiden, who becomes charged with a criminal offense in spite of her alleged innocence. The action occurs on the country estate of a rich Polish count in the early nineteenth century. Events of strikingly excellent emotional appeal abound in nearly every scene and are certain to pull the heartstrings of many in the audience. The principal role of Marynia represents one of the most serious and realistic characterizations ever attempted by the group. The play is in three acts and five scenic transitions and will be produced under the co-direction of Miss Agnes Pieszczoch and Joseph Czyzewski.

Appropriate stage scenery and lighting arrangements have been completed by Miss Wanda Hennel and a selected art staff. Among the settings to be represented is the exterior and interior of the nobleman's country home and the prison where the blameless victim is incarcerated. Costumes in colorful pattern have been supplied for the production.

The main role will be played by Miss Agnes Pieszczoch, who has directed many of the past season's successes. The remaining cast includes Misses Wanda Hennel, Wanda Gierut, Frances Harasimowicz, Aniela Pitera, Hedwig Godlewska, and Stanley Zych, Bernard Deptula, Leo P. Marcinek, Henry Klejsmyt, Henry Lewkowicz, Lucyan Sekowski, Frank Borkowski, V. W. Platt, Thaddeus Kilian and William Bonczyk.

Those serving on the production staff are Walter Sekowski, business and program; Miss Wanda Hennell, art and stage; John Laniewski, properties; Miss Stephanie Lewkowicz, wardrobe; Misses Helen Kilian, Genevieve Stelmach and Jane Dlugosinska, make-up; J. W. Czechowicz, press; Misses Sophie Chojnicka, Agnes Dmochowska, Alice Nowicka, Irene Nowicka, Velma Dombkowska, Stephanie Lewkowicz, and William Bonczyk, auxiliaries.

Judges in the stage contest will include Prof. Stanislaus Kosinski, Prof. Stanislaus Belniak, and Dr. Myron J. Dybich.

The Chopin Male Chorus under the direction of Felix Woznicki will render several choral selections on the program.

1936 – March 26, *Schenectady Gazette* (Page 14)

Maska Dramatic Club Holds Final Play Rehearsal

Final rehearsals are in progress by the Maska Dramatic Club players on the fifth and last production of the current subscription season, *Koszyk Kwiatów*, a three-act melodrama adapted by Josef Chociszewski from a popular story by X. Schmider, to be presented Sunday in the auditorium of the P. N. A. Community Home, Crane street. The performance will mark the close of the "stage personality" contest effective throughout the entire season.

In the production of *Koszyk Kwiatów*, there is a deviation from the accustomed policy of the group to stage only dramas of light and comic nature. The present drama is a serious portrayal of an orphaned peasant maiden's plight upon becoming innocently involved in a robbery offense. The locale of the story is the country estate of a wealthy nobleman living in Poland about the year 1858. Fifteen participate in the cast under direction of Miss Agnes Pieszczoch and Joseph Czyzewski. Elaborate stage settings have been completed by an art staff headed by Miss Wanda Hennel.

Several choral selections by the Chopin Male Chorus under the direction of Felix Woznicki will be a supplementary feature of the program.

1936 – March 28 *Schenectady Gazette* (Page 8)

**Polish Cast to Give Last Play; Maska Dramatic Club
Will Present Play Tomorrow at P.N.A. House**

Completing a season of five play performances the Maska Dramatic Club will present its final stage production, *Koszyk Kwiatów*, a three-act melodrama by Joseph Chociszewski, tomorrow at 7:30 p. m. in the auditorium of the P. N. A. community home on Crane street. The performance will mark the close of the "stage personality" contest.

The role of Marynia is portrayed by Miss Agnes Pieszczoch, who has directed many of the productions of the past two seasons. Other characterizations are enacted by Jakub Kwiecinski, Stanley Zych; hrabia (Count), Henry Lewkowicz; hrabina (Countess), Miss Wanda Hennel; Zofja, Miss Wanda Gierut; sedzia (judge), Leo P. Marcinek; Stanislaw, Bernard Deptula; Antoni, Lucyan J. Sekowski; Szymon, Henry Klejsmyt; Joanka, Miss Frances Harasimowicz; Katarzyna, Miss Aniela Pitera; Jedrzej, Frank Borkowski; Brygida, Miss Hedwig Godlewska; ksiadz (priest), V. W. Platt; and two court guards, Thaddeus Kilian and William Bonczyk.

Stage settings have been completed by a special art staff under supervision of Miss Wanda Hennel, art director. The sets constructed include an interior and exterior of a country house, a prison chamber and a court room.

The production will be presented under direction of Miss Agnes Pieszczoch and Joseph Czyzewski. Others in charge of arrangements include Walter C. Sekowski, business and program; John Laniewski, properties; Miss Stephanie Lewkowicz, wardrobe; Misses Helen Kilian, Genevieve Stelmach, and Jane Dlugosinska, make-up; J. W. Czechowicz, press; auxiliary committee Sophie Chojnicka, Agnes Dmochowska, Alice Nowicka, Irene Nowicka, Velma Dombkowska, Stephanie Lewkowicz, and William Bonczyk.

Judges in the rating of the acting ability of the cast in the "stage personality" competition are Stanislaus Kosinski, Stanislaus Belniak, and Dr. Myron J. Dybich.

Supplementing the program will be choral selections by the Chopin Male Chorus under the direction of Felix S. Woznicki.

1936 – March 29, Report in the Scrapbook

Final production of the current subscription season to be presented on Sunday, March 29, in the auditorium of the P. N. A. community home on Crane street. The performance will feature a three-act melodrama entitled *Koszyk Kwiatów* adapted by Jozef Chociszewski from a stirring tale of profound emotional appeal written by X. Schmider, and will conclude the "stage personality contest" in effect throughout this season's activity.

1936 – March 31, *Schenectady Gazette* (Page 11)

Final Play by Maska Actors Well Received

Koszyk Kwiatów, in three acts by Chociszewski, was presented by the Maska Dramatic Club before approximately 360 people Sunday night in the season's final performance at the P. N. A. community home, Crane street. Players received merits in the concluding run of the "stage personality" competition and choral selections by the Chopin Male Chorus were well received.

Opening in a garden scene of rural Poland, *Koszyk Kwiatów*, adapted from a novel of X. Schmidt, enfolded in striking detail the hardships of a young peasant maiden accused of stealing a ring from her nobleman employer's chateau. Miss Agnes Pieszczoch, as Marysia, the unfortunate victim in the plot, turned in a masterful portrayal requiring much emotional interpretation, as did Stanley Zych, her father, who played a difficult role with accustomed ease. Lesser roles were represented with excellent characterization by Misses Frances Harasimowicz, Wanda Gierut, Hedwig Godlewska, Aniela Pitera, Leon P. Marcinek and Lucyan J. Sekowski. The remaining cast included Miss Wanda Hennel, Bernard Deptula, Henry Klejsmyt, Frank Borkowski, Henry Lewkowicz, V. W. Platt, Thaddeus Kilian and William Bonczyk.

The production was under direction of Miss Agnes Pieszczoch and Joseph Czyzewski. Judges in the "stage personality" contest were Stanislaus Kosinski, Stanislaus Belniak and Dr. M. J. Dybich. Stage settings were designed by Miss Wanda Hennel. Selections by the Chopin Male Chorus, directed by Felix S. Woznicki, included "Wisla" of F. Wiedeman, "The Bubble" by Rudolf Friml and "Dunika" by St. Niedzielski.

Those serving on the production staff comprised Zygmont Brzozowski and Lucyan Sekowski, stage; Walter Sekowski, business and program; John Laniewski, properties; Miss Stephanie Lewkowicz, wardrobe; Misses Helen Kilian, Genevieve Stelmach and Jane Dlugozinska, make-up; Joseph Czyzewski, press; Miss Sophie Witkowska, music; Misses Sophie Chojnicka, Agnes Dmochowska, Alice Nowicka, Irene Nowicka, Velma Dombkowska and Edwsard Hennel, Victor Harasimowicz and William Bonczyk, auxiliaries.

1936 – April 2, *Gazeta Tygodniowa*

Maska Drama Season Ends; Final Play Given Sunday; Concludes Stage Contest

The Maska Dramatic Club brought to a close its season of five scheduled play productions with an excellent presentation of a three-act melodrama depicting a Polish orphaned maiden's destiny, *Koszyk Kwiatów*, by Josef Chociszewski, Sunday, on the stage of the P. N. A. community home, Crane street. An attendance of about 300 witnessed the performance which concluded the "stage personality" contest conducted regularly during the season. Several choral selections by the Chopin Male Chorus directed by F. S. Woznicki featured ?? The program.

Unlike previous productions *Koszyk Kwiatów*, was a drama abounding with scenes of poignant human emotion unfolding the experiences of Marynia, an innocent girl, accused of a larceny. Miss Agnes Pieszczoch, portraying the part of Marynia, interpreted with much realism the demands of a difficult role and Stanley Zych, as her father, rendered a convincing type of parent much concerned over his child's fate. The remaining characters in the cast included Misses Frances Harasimowicz, Wanda Gierut, Hedwig Godlewska, Aniela Pitera, Wanda Hennel, and Leo P. Marcinek, Lucyan Sekowski, Bernard Deptula, Henry Klejsmyt, Frank Borkowski, Henry Lewkowicz, V. W. Platt, Thaddeus Kilian and William Bonczyk.

Final ratings on the stage deportment of the cast entered in the regularly conducted "stage personality" competition averaged into one of the highest scores received during the season. Announcement of the complete scores will be made at a later date.

Those active in the production were Zygmont Brzozowski, Lucyan Sekowski, Walter Sekowski, Edward Hennel, Victor Harasimowicz, Joseph Czechowicz, and Misses Stephanie Lewkowicz, Genevieve Stelmach, Helen Kilian, Jane Dlugosinska, Sophie Chojnicka, Alice Nowicka, Velma Dombkowska, Irene Nowicka, Agnes Dmochowska, and Sophie Witkowska.

An attendance of about 300 witnessed the performance which concluded the "stage personality" contest conducted regularly during the season. Several choral selections by the Chopin Male Chorus were featured.

Final ratings on the stage deportment of the cast entered in the regularly conducted "stage personality" competition averaged into one of the highest scores received during the season. Announcement of the complete scores will be made at a later date.

The "Maska" Dramatic Circle Prepares Itself for the Coming Season's Performances

Everything is ready for the stage programs for the coming 1936-1937 season, and they predict excellent progress on all aspects. The program for this season includes four productions at the Polish Home.

Figure 17: Press Clipping from *Gazeta Tygodniowa*, June 18, 1936.

1936 – May 21, General Electric Jubilee Parade

There are moments, there are occasions, which raise the spirits of us Poles; which give us pride; which our Polish name, so often encountering obstacles in daily life, places above (respect); which build and give us a much needed boost, - and of these moments, an undeniable opportunity was last Saturday's parade, the finale of a two day excellent manifestation combined with the ceremony of the golden jubilee in the city of our enterprises – the General Electric Company.

This was the largest and most impressive parade in the history of this city – everyone agrees. Up to 30 organizations and groups took part, more than 10,000 people. There were up to 25 bands. The entire event was great and colorful, not missing a step. And the most important fact, it was calculated that more than 125 thousand people saw the parade, lured by good publicity, excitement and extraordinary weather.

Through that manifestation, and in that parade the Polish division, gathered under the flag of the Polish Supervisory Board, won first prize for the best float, the first prize for exposing the best chariot and the second prize for the largest performance and another prize for the best in?debut?, in fact we were the largest division, but some circumstance wanted and cut off us a few points.

The competition for the first prize among the floats was fierce. There were 20 floats. Some organizations spent from 350 to 500 dollars on building their floats. The budget for the Polish division was relatively modest because it allowed only 100 dollars. But the difference was the passion, desire, ability and talent of our youth, who constructed the float. Once thought of as a difficult idea, it was constructed in just two weeks from when we received the invitation to be in the parade.

Our float was excellent, beautiful and in good taste, full of color, and most important and depicted as necessarily required – the progress of the General Electric. The meeting of Mr. F. G. Halturewicz in the role of Edison, and Mr. Stanley Zych in the role of Steinmetz, surpassed all expectations. Thanks to the excellent and professional characterization, they were such original approximations to the real geniuses, that those, who knew them could hardly believe their eyes. The excellent float showed the laboratory at the General Electric and the last meeting there between Edison and Steinmetz.

The applause did not stop along the entire parade route. Photographers, amateur and professional, took pictures of the float every few steps, being convinced that here would fall victory. Admiration was universal. And that our float had the right to win the first place, say facts such as: first, the decision of the six judges was unanimous; second, there is no one in town who would deny us that honor, admitted that, considering the competition, this is exceptional.

Our young people deserve deep appreciation. They acted disinterestedly. They proved that when it comes to ideas, talent, finishing tasks, they do not give way to any other group. Here we must underline the names of Miss Agnes Pieszczoch, Mr. Joseph Dmochowski, Mr. S. Ratajczyk, Mr. F. G. Halturewicz, Mr. Thaddeus Kiljan, Mr. Zygmunt Kiljan, Mr. Zygmunt Brzozowski, Casimir Kupinski, Mr. Heronimus Razewski, Mr. F. Leszczynski, and lawyer A. G. Sarnowski, who… [text truncated – PZB]

Even today our ears are resonating with the loud applause with which the viewers of our division showed their admiration. There were about 1250 compatriots in the division. The banner of the Polish Welfare Council, division 1, was carried by two Polish scouts (harcerzy). Next came the priests. Fathers F. Ren and E. Tanski, next marshals Mr. J. Cieplinski and A. B. Brzozowski and the president of the Polish division, Mr. K. S. Ogonowski. Next came Mrs. Kozlowska, members of the St. Teresa Society, of Polish Union, as a champion body; the band of the Polish Welfare Council, the St. Teresa Society in beautiful and colorful native costumes with capes; Polish and American flags; the float; a band of drummers from the "Wyszomirski Post" from Amsterdam; flags of other sections; Society of Veterans of the Polish Army; Society of Unification and Unity, and at the end of our division, the auxiliary body in their uniforms gave a pleasant impression.

Pleasant comments were heard along the entire line of march. Father Pastor F. Ren and his assistant Father T. Tanski contributed to the gravity of our division. With the performance,

Father Ren captured the hearts of all the compatriots and earned the great respect, because he proved that when it comes to showing our strength and unity we can always count on him.[5]

1936 – June 4, *Gazeta Tygodniowa*

The best play production of the 1935 – 1936 season of dramatic presentation by the Maska Dramatic Club, according to averaged cast ratings in the regularly featured "stage personality" contest was the three-act melodrama, *Koszyk Kwiatów*, of Chociszewski, directed by Miss Agnes Pieszczoch and Joseph Czyzewski. Others in order of merit were "Ciotka Karola," Brandon; "Peruka Profesora," Jax; "Na Bezrybiu i Rak Ryba," Wachtel; "Generalna Proba," Roart; "Szpytal Warjatow," Scribe and Augustin; "Krewniak z Ameryki," Gerson-Dabrowska; and "Pokoj do Wynajecia," Poplawski and Golanski. Winners of the main awards in the stage competition judged by a committee of five were Miss Aniela Pitera and Leo P. Marcinek. Donors of the prizes, a silver loving cup and silver medal, were Walter C. Sekowski and Stanley J. Zych. Merit certificates were received by all the participants in the casts. And that's that – a la Healey!

1936 – June 30, *Schenectady Gazette* (Page 8)

The Maska Dramatic Club opened its summer recreation program with a sports outing Sunday at "Kamp Korkosz", Galway lake. Thirty-six members and friends attended.
Entertainment included baseball, volley-ball, softball, swimming, boating and choral singing. During the refreshment recess, Stanley Zych, who will soon leave for a two months' tour of Poland, spoke.

Members of the arrangements committee were Joseph Drapala, chairman; Miss Frances Harasimowicz, Miss Genevieve Stelmach, Miss Irene Witkowski, Miss Sophie Chojnicka, Miss Hedwig Godlewska, Miss Alice Nowicka, Leon Marcinek, Henry Klejsmyt and Stanley Zych. Mr. and Mrs. Stanley Korkosz were hosts.

Those present were Miss Katherine Borejka, Miss Irene Brzostowska, Miss Sophie Chojnicka, Miss Helen Czyszczon, Miss Agnes Dmochowska, Miss Velma Dombkowska, Miss Frances Harasimowicz, Miss Hedwig Godlewska, Miss Mary Flis, Miss Agnes Pieszczoch, Miss Genevieve Stelmach, Miss Nellie Bonczyk, Miss Philomena Gwiazdowska, Miss Alice Nowicka, Miss Irene Nowicka, Miss Cecelia Wisniewska, Miss Florence Kiszka, Miss Gertrude Sliner, Miss Irene Witkowska, Miss Jane Zalewska, Miss Julia Malinowska.

Zygmont Brzozowski, Stanley Zych, Joseph Drapala, Leo Marcinek, Rudolph Waltner, Victor Harasimowicz, Chester Garkowski, Zygmond Kilian, Zygmond Ozarowski, Stanley Bonczyk, Henry Klejsmyt, Bernard Deptula, Lucyan Sekowski, Victor Platt, Water Sekowski, Thaddeus Kilian and Willian Bonczyk.

Pictures of this event are found at the end of Chapter 3.

1936 – July 2, *Gazeta Tygodniowa*

The Year's Activities of the "Maska" Dramatic Circle

The first prizes in the stage contest were won by Mr. Leon P. Marcinek and Miss Aniela Pitera. Prize Donors and Production Managers Did Not Take Part in the Contest. Certificates of honorary remembrance were received by: Stanley Zych, Miss Agnes Pieszczoch, Lucian Sekowski, Joseph Czyzewski and Miss Lucy Wanik.

Certificates of special merit were obtained by: Miss Wanda Hennel, Miss Wanda Moros, Joseph Drapala, Miss Helen Kilian, Miss Francis Harasimowicz, and Miss Irene Witkowski.

Certificates of appreciation were received by: Miss Alice Nowicki, Miss Genevieve Chojnicka, Miss Agnes Dmochowska, Miss Stefanie Lewkowicz, Miss Irene Brzostowska, Miss

---

[5] Translation by Joanna Socha.

Sophie Stelmach, Miss Joan Penichter, Miss Valerie Szymanska, Francis Borkowski, Walter Bonczyk, Victor Harasimowicz, Joseph Czechowicz, John Laniewski, Bernard Deptula, Henry Klejsmyt, Anthony Kopec, Henry Lewkowicz, Victor Platt, Walter Sekowski and Henry Wienclawski.

1936 – July 2, *Gazeta Tygodniowa*

This past season 1935-1936 was extremely abundant in the treatments and the work done among our young people in the popular "Maska" Dramatic Circle. The young people during that time presented a number of Polish dramatic plays for the entertainment of our Polonia, showing great thrift and work in completion – all plans and productions were connected.

The Circle did not expend a lot of money and did not always experience deserved support, however with perfect direction they went forward without complaint. To date the following plays have been presented:

Koszyk Kwiatów, ("A Basket of Flowers") by Chociszewski under the direction of Miss Agnes Pieszczoch and Mr. Joseph Czyzewski; "Ciotka Karola" ("Charlie's Aunt"); "Peruka Profesora"("Professor's Wig"); "Na Bezrybiu I Rak Ryba" (Catching Fish Without Fishing"); "Generalna Proba" ("Dress Rehearsal"); "Szpital Wariatow" ("Hospital for the Insane"); "Krewniak z Ameryki" ("Relative from America") and "Pokoj do Wynajecia" ("Room To Rent"), -- The theatrical "stage personality" contest was conducted during all the productions, which was formally ended with giving out prizes on May 24th by Father Professor Stanislaw Sobieniowski.

Those donating the prizes were Water C. Sekowski and Stanley J. Zych, and the production managers Miss Agnes Pieszczoch and Joseph Czyzewski, were not eligible for the contest.

The first prize, a silver goblet [puchar] was won by Leon P. Marcinek, vice-president and director of the "Maska" Circle. He was also captain of the ticket sellers and took part in five plays. Second prize, a silver medal, was given to Miss Aniela Pitera, treasurer since the group's inception. She took part in three plays and was active in various committees.

Chapter 5
The 1936 – 1937 Season
October 1936 – April 1937

Maska, born in the depths of the Great Depression, continues to grow and thrive. Maska members and Polish Scout leaders (Harcerstwo) Agnes Pieszczoch and Stanley Zych return from their month-long trip to Poland. The news article of September 24 (below) states that Mr. Zych returned with several plays that were hits in Poland. While four plays were announced for the upcoming season, there is information for only three. A record audience of 500 attends the farce presented in February that includes a live cat.

1936 – September, *Gazeta Tygodniowa*

Our young people, centered in the "Maska" Circle will receive more recognition in their work, when they perform this season.

Tickets for the season are ready and have been distributed to the members. We are pleased to report that ticket sales are going well. We ask the honored public not to forget that the season ticket entitles one to admission to four presentations, and costs only one dollar. Everyone who holds a season ticket is considered a Circle Patron and their names will be printed in every program. Tickets can be purchased from members of our group, from Mrs. Władysława Sekowski, at 1116 Fourth Avenue or from the editors of the "Weekly Gazette."

We ask the honorable public for cooperation. Season tickets will be available only until October 25th. The time is short, thus we ask that all lovers of Polish presentations and our supporters to purchase their tickets as early as possible.

Production dates are as follows: Sunday, October 25th, December 13th, February 21 and April 18th. We ask and have excellent support from our patrons as we had last year. We are striving to add new names to that list.

1936 – September 24, *Schenectady Gazette* (Page 14; see Figure 18 below)

The list of season ticket customers which we had the pleasure to count last year is as follows:

The Maska Dramatic Club has begun its third subscription drive for the 1936-37 season. No change will be made in the price of the season ticket. Tickets have been allotted to the members of the organization for sale. Additional acting material has been acquired. The season ticket campaign will end October 25.

This season the club will give four productions. The dates set for the season are October 25, December 13, February 21 and April 18. Again the auditorium of the P. N. A. home on Crane street will serve as the playhouse.

Stanley J. Zych, president, will continue his role as actor. He has been an active member for the past two years.

The names of patrons and patronesses will appear on the program of the season productions.

The directors chosen for the season are Miss Agnes Pieszczoch and Joseph Czyzewski. Mr. Czyzewski will direct the season's first play, *Niewinność Zwycięża*, or *Innocence Triumphs*, a melodrama in three acts. Rehearsals have been under way for the past week. The cast consists

of Miss Genevieve Stelmach, Miss Alice Nowicka, Miss Nellie Pitera, Lucyan Sekowski, Stanley Zych, Henry Klejsmyt, Bernard Deptula.

The club's audience will see several plays which were brought from Poland by Mr. Zych. These plays were "hits" abroad.

The Maska Dramatic Club will participate in the Polish University Club program in October. Joseph Czyzewski, director, has selected two skits, one in Polish and the other in English, *Nazajutrz Po Ślubie* and *The Man Upstairs*.

1936 – October 24, *Schenectady Gazette* (Page 10)

Maska Players Begin Season

Innocence Conquers, (*Niewinność Zwycięża*) will open the third consecutive season of the Maska Dramatic Club when the first presentation is given at P. N. A. hall, Crane street, tomorrow night. The production, which is being directed by Joseph Czyzewski, has been in preparation for several weeks.

Members of the cast are Matthew, Lucyan Sekowski; Kathryn, Miss Genevieve Stelmach; Agnes, Miss Alice Nowicka; Jadwiga, Miss Eugenia Kilian; Stanley, Bernard Deptula; Adelbert, father of Stanley, Henry Klejsmyt; Agatha, Agnes' aunt, Miss Nellie Pitera; Icek, Stanley Zych.

Zygmunt Kilian, stage manager, and Zygmunt Brzozowski, art manager, have supervised renovation of the stage and the building of new scenery. The production staff includes Miss Agnes Pieszczoch and Joseph Czyzewski, directors; Walter C. Sekowski, business manager; Lucyan Sekowski, publicity; Agnes Pieszczoch, Sophie (C)Hojnicki and Irene Nowicki, make-up artists; Miss Sophie (C)Hojnicki Irene Nowicki and Agnes Pieszczoch, costumes; Mrs. Wanda Lewkowicz, Agnes Dmochowska, Stephanie Lewkowicz, Wilma Dombkowski, Leo Marcinek, Thaddeus Kilian, Victor Platt, William Bonczyk, Anthony Kopec and Carl Szymanski, general committee.

1936 – October 29, *Schenectady Gazette* (Page 8)

Maska Players Present Initial Play of Season

Maska Dramatic Club opened its current season Sunday with the presentation of *Innocence Conquers*, (*Niewinność Zwycięża*) at P. N. A. Home, Crane street.

Members of the cast were Lucyan Sekowski, Miss Genevieve Stelmach, Miss Alice Nowicka, Miss Eugenia Kilian, Bernard Deptula, Henry Klejsmyt and Stanley Zych.

Members of the production staff were Zygmont Kilian and Zygmont Brzozowski, stage and art; Walter C. Sekowski, business; Miss Agnes Pieszczoch, make-up and wardrobe; Sophie Chojnicki, Irene Nowicka, Lucyan Sekowski, publicity; John Laniewski, properties; Victor Platt, program, and Michael J. Tytko, prompter.

Those serving on the auxiliary committee included Mrs. Wanda Lewkowicz, Agnes Dmochowski, Miss Irene Witkowski, Miss Stephanie Lewkowicz, Henry Lewkowicz, William Bonczyk, Carl Szymanski, Anthony Kopec, Teddy Kilian and Leon Marcinek.

The second production of the season will be presented December 13 at P. N. A. hall.

1936 – November 24, *Schenectady Gazette* (Page 8)

Maska Drama Club to Present Farce Dec. 4th

The Maska Dramatic Club will present *Prędka Robota* as the second offering of the season on Sunday, December 4. This play is a farce in three acts. *Prędka Robota* is the life-picture of the second generation of Polish-Americans, a portrayal of the problems of youth. Adolf Smietanka, main character of the play, is a business executive of a food products company in Brooklyn, but a business executive in name only. His father, after a long struggle, had built up this business and then left it all to his only son, who has no head for business and who placed all responsibility on

the shoulders of his attorney, David Kohn, a shrewd attorney who has developed a fondness for the reckless youth and acts as his guardian.

The rehearsals are under the direction of Joseph Czyzewski. The play will be staged in the auditorium of the Polish community house.

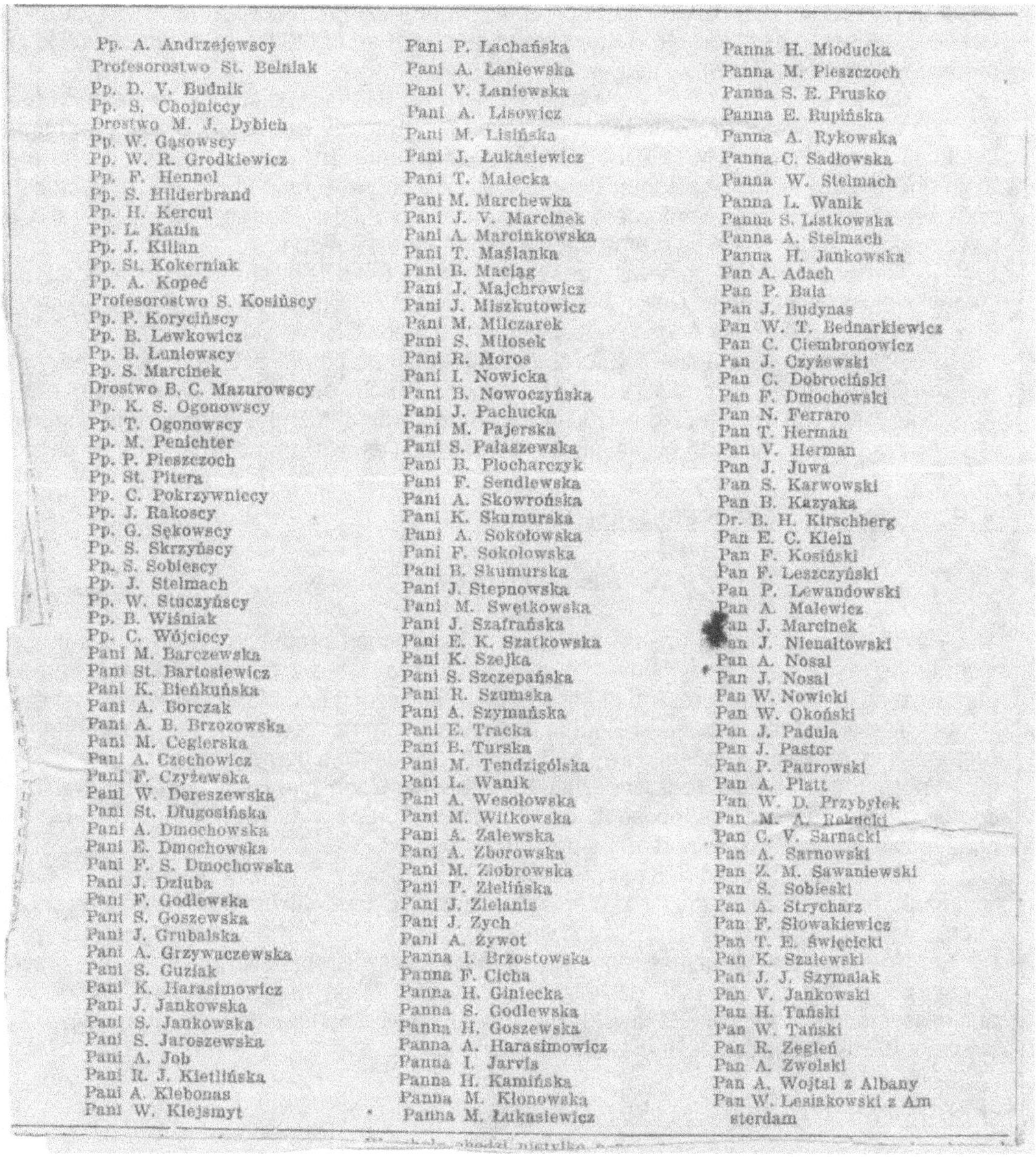

Pp. A. Andrzejewscy
Profesorostwo St. Belniak
Pp. D. V. Budnik
Pp. S. Chojniccy
Drostwo M. J. Dybich
Pp. W. Gąsowscy
Pp. W. R. Grodkiewicz
Pp. F. Hennel
Pp. S. Hilderbrand
Pp. H. Kercul
Pp. L. Kania
Pp. J. Kilian
Pp. St. Kokerniak
Pp. A. Kopeć
Profesorostwo S. Kosińscy
Pp. P. Korycińscy
Pp. B. Lewkowicz
Pp. B. Laniewscy
Pp. S. Marcinek
Drostwo B. C. Mazurowscy
Pp. K. S. Ogonowscy
Pp. T. Ogonowscy
Pp. M. Penichter
Pp. P. Pieszczoch
Pp. St. Pitera
Pp. C. Pokrzywniccy
Pp. J. Rakoscy
Pp. G. Sękowscy
Pp. S. Skrzyńscy
Pp. S. Sobiescy
Pp. J. Stelmach
Pp. W. Stuczyńscy
Pp. B. Wiśniak
Pp. C. Wójciccy
Pani M. Barczewska
Pani St. Bartosiewicz
Pani K. Bieńkuńska
Pani A. Borczak
Pani A. B. Brzozowska
Pani M. Cegierska
Pani A. Czechowicz
Pani F. Czyżewska
Pani W. Dereszewska
Pani St. Długosińska
Pani A. Dmochowska
Pani E. Dmochowska
Pani F. S. Dmochowska
Pani J. Dziuba
Pani F. Godlewska
Pani S. Goszewska
Pani J. Grubalska
Pani A. Grzywaczewska
Pani S. Guziak
Pani K. Harasimowicz
Pani J. Jankowska
Pani S. Jankowska
Pani S. Jaroszewska
Pani A. Job
Pani R. J. Kietlińska
Pani A. Klebonas
Pani W. Klejsmyt
Pani P. Łachańska
Pani A. Łaniewska
Pani V. Łaniewska
Pani A. Lisowicz
Pani M. Lisińska
Pani J. Łukasiewicz
Pani T. Malecka
Pani M. Marchewka
Pani J. V. Marcinek
Pani A. Marcinkowska
Pani T. Maślanka
Pani B. Maciąg
Pani J. Majchrowicz
Pani J. Miszkutowicz
Pani M. Milczarek
Pani S. Miłosek
Pani R. Moros
Pani I. Nowicka
Pani B. Nowoczyńska
Pani J. Pachucka
Pani M. Pajerska
Pani S. Pałaszewska
Pani B. Plocharczyk
Pani F. Sendlewska
Pani A. Skowrońska
Pani K. Skumurska
Pani A. Sokołowska
Pani F. Sokołowska
Pani B. Skumurska
Pani J. Stepnowska
Pani M. Swętkowska
Pani J. Szafrańska
Pani E. K. Szatkowska
Pani K. Szejka
Pani S. Szczepańska
Pani R. Szumska
Pani A. Szymańska
Pani E. Tracka
Pani B. Turska
Pani M. Tendzigólska
Pani L. Wanik
Pani A. Wesołowska
Pani M. Witkowska
Pani A. Zalewska
Pani A. Zborowska
Pani M. Ziobrowska
Pani P. Zielińska
Pani J. Zielanis
Pani J. Zych
Pani A. Żywot
Panna I. Brzostowska
Panna F. Cichа
Panna H. Giniecka
Panna S. Godlewska
Panna H. Goszewska
Panna A. Harasimowicz
Panna I. Jarvis
Panna H. Kamińska
Panna M. Kłonowska
Panna M. Łukasiewicz
Panna H. Mioducka
Panna M. Pieszczoch
Panna S. E. Prusko
Panna E. Rupińska
Panna A. Rykowska
Panna C. Sadłowska
Panna W. Stelmach
Panna L. Wanik
Panna S. Listkowska
Panna A. Stelmach
Panna H. Jankowska
Pan A. Adach
Pan P. Bala
Pan J. Budynas
Pan W. T. Bednarkiewicz
Pan C. Ciembronowicz
Pan J. Czyżewski
Pan C. Dobrociński
Pan F. Dmochowski
Pan N. Ferraro
Pan T. Herman
Pan V. Herman
Pan J. Juwa
Pan S. Karwowski
Pan B. Kazyaka
Dr. B. H. Kirschberg
Pan E. C. Klein
Pan F. Kosiński
Pan F. Leszczyński
Pan P. Lewandowski
Pan A. Malewicz
Pan J. Marcinek
Pan J. Nienaltowski
Pan A. Nosal
Pan J. Nosal
Pan W. Nowicki
Pan W. Okoński
Pan J. Padula
Pan J. Pastor
Pan P. Paurowski
Pan A. Platt
Pan W. D. Przybyłek
Pan M. A. Rakocki
Pan C. V. Sarnacki
Pan A. Sarnowski
Pan Z. M. Sawaniewski
Pan S. Sobieski
Pan A. Strycharz
Pan F. Słowakiewicz
Pan T. E. Święcicki
Pan K. Szalewski
Pan J. J. Szymalak
Pan V. Jankowski
Pan H. Tański
Pan W. Tański
Pan R. Zegleń
Pan A. Zwolski
Pan A. Wojtal z Albany
Pan W. Lesiakowski z Amsterdam

Figure 18: Page of the Scrapbook listing Maska Supporters.

1936 – December 7, *Schenectady Gazette*

Zych to Head Maska Group

The Maska Dramatic Club at its recent annual meeting at the P. N. A. community home, Crane street, re-elected Stanley J. Zych as president of the club. Mathew Ozarowski was chairman of the election. Mr. Zych has been an active leader of the organization for the past three years. During this time he has shown great acting ability. He ranks as one of the most convincing actors

of the organization and has the greatest number of major roles of the past season to his credit. He is also an instructor in the Polish youth training organization, "Harcestwo," sponsored by the Polish[1] National Alliance. This summer Mr. Zych was sent to Poland by the Gmina for a course in advanced Harcestwo training.

Lucyan J. Sekowski, vice president, is also an energetic member of the club, holding the office of publicity manager. He has been active in promoting production affairs of the group and has also appeared as actor. Mr. Sekowski will be chairman of the board of directors. He is also a member of the Conrad Literary Fellowship.

Others elected to office were Miss Genevieve Stelmach, recording secretary; Miss Nellie Pitera, treasurer; Victor W. Platt, business manager; Anthony Kopec, sergeant-at-arms; Bernard Deptula, press manager; Miss Alice Nowicki, parliamentarian; Zygmunt Kilian, stage manager; Zygmunt Brzozowski, art manager; John Laniewski, property manager; Misses Sophie Hojnicki and Agnes Pieszczoch, wardrobe and make-up; Both Miss Agnes Pieszczoch and Joseph Czyzewski will again serve as drama directors for the next season.

The board of directors will consist of Lucyan Sekowski, chairman; Stanley Zych, Miss Genevieve Stelmach, Miss Nellie Pitera, Miss Alcie Nowicki, Victor W. Platt, Zygmunt Kilian, Zygmunt Brzozowski, Miss Agnes Pieszczoch and Joseph Czyzewski.

Rehearsals are in full swing for the presentation of a three-act mystery comedy, *Straszna Noc*, on Sunday in the second scheduled presentation of the season in the auditorium of the P. N. A. Scenery is being constructed by Kilian and Brzozowski. This play is under the directorship of Miss Agnes Pieszczoch, with Miss Genevieve Stelmach as assistant director.

1936 – December 12, *Schenectady Gazette*

Polish Club to Offer Comedy

The Polish Dramatic Club "Maska" will present the second production of the season tomorrow night in the Polish community home. The play, *Straszna Noc* is a three act mystery comedy. The performance is under the direction of Miss Agnes Pieszczoch and Miss Genevieve Stelmach.

The action takes place at Paul Mankiewicz's summer residence in the Adirondacks. Jan Bagdan, his nephew, is on his way to his uncle's summer home to receive some important information from his aunt regarding valuable papers. Upon his arrival he is met with serious complications. The uncle, supposedly on his way to Europe, has been killed in his high-backed chair in the room where the rest of the party are revealed.

The cast includes Misses Frances Harasimowicz, Agnes Dmochowski, Genevieve Stelmach, Messers John Laniewski, Leon Marcinek, Thadeus Kilian, Mathew Ozarowski, Stanley Zych, Zygmont Kilian and Joseph Czyzewski.

The general committee consists of Miss Pieszczoch, director, Miss Stelmach, sub-director, Zygmont Brzozowski, art director, Zygmont Kilian stage manager, Victor W. Platt, business manager, Lucyan Sekowski, publicity, Misses Sophie Chojnicki, Irene Nowicki, Alice Nowicki, Wilma Dombkowski, Irene Witkowski, make-up.

1937 – February 9, *Dziennik dla Wszystkich*

From Schenectady N.Y. Walter Sekowski Takes an Oath from the New Administration of the Maska Dramatic Circle

A varied installation program was presented at the Polish Home--Fine speeches during the banquet- Many guests
The ranks of the Circle is increased with some new members

With the help of many members and guests, February 4th was a very nice day for the installation of the new officers of the Maska Dramatic Circle, with a very beautiful and varied program. The oath for the new officers was taken by Walter Sekowski, after which there were speeches appropriate to the circumstances, and they were interspersed with songs and music.

---

[1] The original uses the word "Police" in error.

Honored guests of the Circle were the president of the Council 53 Z. N. P. – Mr. M. Rekucki, Mr. Stefan Skoczynski, Mr. and Mrs. W. Grodkiewicz and Mr. and Mrs. H. Lewkowicz.

Eleven year old Peter Lewandowski sang beautifully, Miss Irene Witkowska played some songs beautifully on the piano, - a piano and saxophone duet was presented by Richard Drewczynski and Alicia Drewczynska – a piano solo by Mateusz Tyborowski. All these numbers received plentiful applause. Mr. Rekucki, president of Council 53 ZNP, Mr. S. Skrzynski and Mr. Grodkiewicz spoke.

New Officers of the Circle Who Were Sworn In

The new officers of the Circle are as follows:
President – Stanley Zych
Vice-President – Lucian Sekowski
Secretary prot. – Genevieve Stelmach
Treasurer – Nellie (P)itera
Marshal – Anthony Kopec
Directors – Agnes Pieszczoch, Joseph Czyzewski
Stage Marshal – Henry Klejsmyt
Artistic Manager – Zymunt Brzozowski
Finance Manager – V. D. Platt
Parliamentarian – Alice Nowicki
A recreation committee was formed: L. Sekowski, chairman,
Helen Kilian, Mary Dziuba and Sophie Hojnicka.
The following were received into the Circle:
Sophie Korycinska, Zygmunt Wisniewski, Matthew Ozarowski and Stanley Plocharczyk.

Figure 19: Maska at a Banquet in the Polish Home, clipping from *Dziennik dla Wszystkich*, Scrapbook.

1937 – February 9, *Dziennik dla Wszystkich*

Remaining Under Doctor's Care

The President of the Maska Dramatic Circle Mr. Stanley Zych, as well as Mr. John Laniewski, a member of the group, were both ill with colds and remained in bed, under the care of the doctor. Everyone wishes that they quickly return to health

1937 – February 11, _Dziennik dla Wszystkich_

"Maska" Prepares for Polonia
Something Interesting and Merry

They Will Present a Mystery Farce in Three Acts on Sunday, February 21 - Commitment to the Presentation of Our Most Talented Amateur Force

The Maska Dramatic Circle, which not long ago presented the interesting play *Terrible Night*, with great success and recognition from the public, did not rest on their laurels, but are further preparing with even more energy for our countrymen a kind and cheerful surprise from which you can pick sides.

The mysterious farce, in three acts, is full of jokes, laughs and mysterious moments, and will take place in the Polish Home on Sunday, February 21st.

Our brave young women taking part in the play are the following: Helen Kilian, Genevieve Stelmach, Mary Dziuba, Hedwig Woltner, Alice Nowicka, Mary Zborowska and Sophie Korycinska. At the appropriate time for this interesting presentation we will write more details.

1937 – February 19, _Dziennik dla Wszystkich_

Sunday Presentation

Everywhere you turn today, everyone is talking about the Sunday presentation of the Maska Dramatic Circle at the Polish Home. A tragic farce will be presented which holds one's interest from beginning to end. There is no doubt that many of the local Polonia will fill the hall of the Polish Home to the brim this coming Sunday, February 21st. And also it should be so because the Maska Dramatic Circle absolutely deserves sincere support.

1937 – February 20, _Schenectady Gazette_

Maska Players Will Give 3-Act Farce at P.N.A.

The Maska Dramatic Club, now in its fifth year in the civic life of the Polish community, will present its third program of the season tomorrow at the P. N. A. home at 7:30 o'clock.

The program comprises a three-act farce, *Kobieta Znikła [A Woman Disappears]* by J. C. Zawistowski, produced under the direction of Joseph Czyzewski. Zigmond Brzozowski and Henry Klejsmyt designed the sets.

The cast includes Miss Helen Kilian, Miss Mary Dziuba, Miss Genevieve Stelmach, Mrs. Hedwig Woltner, Miss Alice Nowicka, Miss Sophie Korycinska, Miss Mary Zborowski, Messrs. Stanley Zych, Mathew Ozarowski, Lucyan Sekowski, Bernard Deptula and Joseph Czyzewski. Miss Sophie Korycinska and Miss Mary Zborowska will appear for the first time in the Maska presentation.

The technical personnel include Mr. Czyzewski, director; Zigmond Brzozowski, art manager; Henry Klejsmyt, stage manager; Victor Platt, financial manager; Bernard Deptula, publicity. The general committee consists of Misses Agnes Dmochowska, Wilma Dombkowska, Irene Witkowska, Irene Nowicka, Messrs Willian Bonczyk and Anthony Kopec.

Between acts there will be a musical interlude featuring Miss Alice Drewczynska at the piano and Richard Drewczynski, saxophone. Guests from Albany, Amsterdam and Cohoes are expected.

1937 – February 24, *Dziennik dla Wszystkich*

From Schenectady N. Y. More than 500 People Attended "Maska" Circle's Presentation Stan Zych and M. Ozarowski Played Like Professional Actors. The Entire Presentation Went off with General Satisfaction – To the Great Merit of Director Mr. Joseph Czyzewski

The final presentation of the "Maska" Dramatic Circle was held in the Polish Home on Sunday, February 21st, the largest audience in the history of the organization was gathered – close to 500 people were in the audience, many coming from out of town, to admire the excellent play given by the amateurs taking part in *Woman Disappears*, which fared well in every aspect.

Stan Zych, in the role of Konstanty S. Piernik, as the police inspector, played like a professional actor – also excellent was M. Ozarowski in the role of colonel. These two gathered deserved laurels and the audience did not spare their applause. Mary Dziuba, Sophie Korycinska, Genevieve Stelmach, Helen Kilian, Hedwig Woltner, Alice Nowicka and Mary Zborowska performed famously in the roles assigned to them. Bernard Deptula and Lucian Sekowski play excellently, so that the whole fell together unexpectedly well. The main credit goes to director Joseph Czyzewski.

The "Maska" Dramatic Circle sincerely thanks Polonia for attending the plays and for their sincere support. The next presentations will take place on April 18th and will be the last of the season.

1937 February 26, Report in the Scrapbook

Sophie Korycinski gave a party described in Chapter 1.

1937 – June, Report in the Scrapbook (See Example 20 on the next page)

Lucian Sekowski Selected as "Maska" Circle President

Last week elections were held for the new officers of the "Maska" Dramatic Circle. The results were as follows: Lucian Sekowski, president; Zygmunt Kilian, vice-president, Sophie Chojnicka, secretary; Nellie Pitera, treasurer.

The new officers have already sincerely gone to work, - so the audience again in the fall will have a good opportunity to admire the beautiful presentations the new officers have for which the "Maska" Circle is famous for arranging

SCHENECTADY, N.Y. – The whole square around St. Adalbert's Polish church on Crane Street, is splendid, thanks to the strong effort of Miss Mariana Fajdowska, who has revealed outstanding ability in beautifying the square around the parish buildings.

1937 - July 2. *Schenectady Gazette* (Page 3)

Lucyan J. Sekowski was installed president of the Maska Dramatic Club at the installation ceremonies Thursday night at the P. N. A. community home, Crane street. Stanley Zych, past president, was installing officer.

Sekowski has been active in various club activities and is vice president of the Conrad Literary Fellowship. Zygmunt Kilian was seated as vice president. He will also serve as chairman of the board of directors.

Other officers installed were Miss Sophie Chojnicka, recording sercretary; Miss Nellie Pitera, treasurer; Leo Marcinek, business manager; Bernard Deptula, sergeant-at-arms; John Laniewski, press manager; Miss Sophie Korycinska, art manager; Miss Mary Zborowska, stage managers; Miss Alice Nowicka, parliamentarian; Miss Agnes Dmochowski, wardrobe and make-up. Both Miss Agnes Pieszczcoch and Joseph Czyzewski will again serve as drama directors for the next season.

The board of directors will include Zygmunt Kilian, chairman; Lucyan Sekowski, Miss Sophie Chojnicka, Miss Nellie Pitera, Miss Alice Nowicka, Leo Marcinek, Miss Agnes Pieszczoch, Miss Sophie Korycinska, Miss Mary Zborowska and Joseph Czyzewski.

Figure 20: Clipping about elections of the new Board from the Scrapbook (see the translation in the first paragraph on the previous page).

Chapter 6
The 1937 – 1938 Season
November 28, 1937 – April 3, 1938

Fig. 21: Headline: "Hitler Proclaims Union of Austria and Germany,"
Weekly Gazette, March 17, 1938 Scrapbook.

The season opening play was indeed a first! *Devil With a Monocle [Djabeł z Monoklem]* was written by Maska member Zygmunt Brzozowski, under the pen name Zigmont Antony [aka Sigmond Antony]. The plot includes references to Nazi Germany, indicating that Maska members were well aware of events in Europe. The second presentation, *Comical Goofiness [Śmieszna Głupota]*, a farce, was an adaptation from the American stage; the playwright is unknown. The season closed with *Cares & Worries [Trudy i Troski]*, [playwright unknown], again an American stage adaptation. This presentation undoubtedly reflected current events: "the financial and social worries of a WPA [Works Progress Administration] worker and his family."

1937 – November 15, *Schenectady Gazette* (Page 8)

Maska Club to Stage Mystery

Rehearsals are under way by the Maska Dramatic Club players for the presentation of a three-act mystery drama on Sunday, November 28, in the first scheduled subscription play season to be staged in the auditorium of the P. N. A. community home, Crane street, according to Director Agnes Pieszczoch.

Four new members will make their stage debut in this presentation.

A cast of 13 will take part. The stage setting will represent a castle and a dungeon scene.

The mystery *Djabeł Z Monoklem*, *Devil with a Monocle*, by Sigmund Antony, a story dealing with the ill doings of an international dope smuggling ring, begins with a violent electrical storm raging about the Castle of Count Volstoya when the large transport plane is forced down within the castle grounds with six passengers. Seeking protection from the storm, the passengers gain admittance to the castle – literally speaking, they step from out of the frying pan into the fire. Once in the castle they are forced to cope with the villainous count and a walking dead man.

It is an interesting melodrama that pages the gamut of human emotions, skillfully intermingling romance, comedy, horror and adventure into a lively, comic-mystery play enacted in a castle in the desolate Polish moors.

The cast includes Bernard S. Deptula as Count Volstoya; Stanley J. Zych, the count's faithful, hunchbacked servant; Lucyan J. Sekowski as Jon Bonarek and Miss Genevieve Stelmach as Halina Balecka; Edward Kwiecinski, a new member in the club, a playwright, Ryszard Marcin and Walter Zoladz in the role of Teofil Dudek; Thaddeus Kilian as the mystery man, Stefan Sikorski; Frank Dzierwa, a newcomer, as Josef Banaski, the pilot; Miss Helen Kilian, Wanda Walska, a popular actress; Miss Frances Harasimowicz, Jadzia Majewicz, her companion. The monster will be played by Zygmunt Kilian.

1937 – December 21, *Schenectady Gazette* (Page 21)

Subscriptions Listed by Club

Miss Agnes Pieszczoch and Stanley Plocharczyk, captains of the teams in the recent subscription campaign held by the Maska Dramatic Club players have announced the following subscription list for the fall and winter series of plays.

Mr. and Mrs. Stanley Korkosz, Mrs. And Mrs. John Kilian, Mr. and Mrs. Wadsworth Grodkiewicz, Mr. and Mrs. Daniel Budnik, Mr. and Mrs. Stanley Lazinski, Mr. and Mrs. Henry Lewkowicz, Dr. and Mrs. B. C. Mazurowski, Mr. and Mrs. Gustav Sekowski, Mr. and Mrs. Bernard Luniewski, Mr. and Mrs. John Morawski, Mr. and Mrs. A. B. Brzozowski, Mr. and Mrs. Peter Pieszczoch, Mr. and Mrs. Walter Klejsmyt, Mr. and Mrs. Peter Korycinski, Mr. and Mrs. C. S. Ogonowski, Mr. and Mrs. J. F. Stelmach, Mr. and Mrs. Chester Strenkowski, Mr. and Mrs. Stanley Tytko, Mr. and Mrs. F. S. Witkowski, Mr. and Mrs. Benjamin Jakubowski, Mrs. Nicholas Marcinkiewicz, Mrs. Arthur Onisk, Mrs. Anthony Ruszkowski, Mrs. Edward Wisiomierski, Mrs. Peter Szumski, Mrs. John Deptula, Stasia Sobieski, Mrs. Katherine Palaszewska, Mrs. J. J. Sobel, Mrs. Ann Wiśniewski, Mrs. Walter Kaulska, Mrs. Roman Kidalowski, Mrs. Joseph Prewenski, Mrs. John Chociej, Mrs. J. W. Pietrzykowski, Mrs. Vincent Cicha, Mrs. Vincent Kulczyk, Mrs. John Pentkowski, Mrs. Lottie Wojs, Mrs. Anna Zalucka, Mrs. Helen Tanski, Mrs. Michael Galka, Mrs. Veronica Kwiatkowska.

Also Mrs. Mary Hilderbrand, Mrs. Mary Pajerski, Mrs. Nancy Jankowski, Mrs. Stasia Gasowski, Mrs. Mary Milczarek, Mrs. Anastasia Peszel, Mrs. Katherine Styczynski, Mrs. Winifred Nowicki, Mrs. Jean Kietlinski, Mrs. Anna Wanik, Mrs. Allen Kostek, Mrs. Betha Olender, Mrs. Alfred Grzywaczewski, Mrs. Joan Skiba, Mrs. John [?Joseph] Zych, Mrs. Theresa Jaroszewski, Mrs. Jane Wesolowski, Mrs. Mary Goszewski, Mrs. Mildred Popiel, Mrs. Mary Pitera, Mrs. Bernard Plocharczyk, Mrs. Stanley Plocharczyk, Mrs. Alberta Parsley, Mrs. Anna Lalak, Mrs. Frank Chojnicki, Stanley Bartosiewicz, John Sammler, Peter Lewandowski, Blase Lewkowicz, W. D. Przybylek, Thaddeus Noskowiak, K. C. Sarnowski, Edward Trojakowski, W. J. Lillis, Casper Wojcicki, Casimer Hibnew, John Pastor, C. T. Zurn, Frank Tadeusiak, J. A. Monaco, Oswalkd D. Heck, Joseph Gzyms [my maternal grandmother's brother], William Daszewski, Jan Myszkolowicz, Michael Penichter, Edward Morawski, John Riddervold, Michael Rekucki, Frank Surowicz, Charles Sarnacki, Frank Sasinowski, Frank Semrad, Anthony Zwolski, Zygmunt Sawaniewski, Frank Kosinski, Henry Zdrodowski.

Also Anthony Nosal, Frank Smith, Michael Marcheski, John Laniewski, Mathew Trojanowski, Leo Marcinek, Nickolas Marcinkiewicz, Daniel Zmyslowski, John Witkowski, Frank Godlewski, Miss Josephine Stelmach, Miss Mary Krempa, Miss Helen Klarman, Miss Anna Konieczna, Miss Mary Azaula, Miss Anna Rykowski, Miss Veronica Kania, Miss Jean Wesolowski, Miss Mary Pieszczoch, Miss Jean Dwojakowski, Miss Winifred Stelmach, Gmina 53, Z. N. P., Swoboda Lodge, 509, Postep Lodge, 878, Jednosc Lodge, Mloda Polska Lodge, Wolnosc Lodge, Prawda and Praca Lodge, May Lodge, Zgoda Lodge, Veterans of Polish Army.

1938 – February 9, *Schenectady Gazette* (Page 8)

Maska Players Slate Comedy

The Maska Dramatic Club will present *Śmieszna Głupota*, a three-act comedy at the second scheduled performance of its current subscription season Sunday, March 6, in the auditorium of the P.N.A. community home on Crane street. Rehearsals by the cast of 10 are progressing under direction of Joseph Czyzewski and Lucyan Sekowski.

The farcical drama, *Śmieszna Głupota*, has all the requisites of ideal humorous entertainment. In the cast are Miss Alice Drewczynski, Miss Nellie Pitera, Frank Dzierwa, Bernard Deptola, Edward Zoladz, Edward Kwiecinski, Mathew Ozarowski, Joseph Czyzewski and Alexander Dzierwa.

Stage requirements are being made ready by the production staff including Mary Zborowski, stage manager; Miss Sophie Korycinski, art manager; Stanley Plocharczyk, business manager; Misses Genevieve Stelmach, Helen Kilian, Sophie Chojnicki and Agnes Pieszczoch, make-up; Walter C. Sekowski, publicity, Zygmunt Brzozowski, Henry Klejsmyt, Zygmunt Wisniewski and Ignatius Kalinowski are also included.
Comment: Mom: Art Manager and pianist

1938 – March 5, *Schenectady Gazette* (Page 8)

Maska Club to Offer Comedy For 2nd Play

Presenting the second play of the subscription season, the Maska Dramatic Club players will enact the three act comedy, *Śmieszna Głupota*, tomorrow at 7:30 p.m. in the auditorium of the P. N. A. community home, Crane street, under direction of Joseph Czyzewski and Lucyan J. Sekowski.

Śmieszna Głupota is a rollicking comedy in three acts portraying the whims of a middle aged business man whose chief pleasure is in making others miserable. Zdzisław Bladoklepski is certain that he has convulsions and his behavior in order to prevent recurring attacks is most ridiculous. His wife, Laura, thinks her crabby spouse has lost his mind and has become a dangerous maniac. She treats him accordingly. The climax of the play is most unusual and it seems that nothing can cure Zdzisław of his crabbiness.

Settings have been designed and built by Zygmunt Brzozowski with the assistance of Miss Mary Zborowski, Lucyan J. Sekowski, Stanley Zych and Walter C. Sekowski.

The cast includes Joseph Czyzewski, Miss Nellie Pitera, Miss Alice Drewczynska, Frank Dzierwa, Walter Zoladz, Miss Mary Zborowski, Lucyan Sekowski, Edward Kwiecinski, Mathew Ozarowski, Stanley Zych.

The production staff is Miss Agnes Pieszczoch, Miss Sophie Chojnicka, Miss Genevieve Stelmach, Miss Agnes Dmochowska, Miss Alice Nowicka, Stanley Plocharczyk and Zygmunt Wisniewski.

The program will be supplemented by musical selections by Miss Sophie Korycinski, Pianist.

1938 March 9 *Schenectady Gazette* (Page 3)

Big Audience Sees Play by Maska Group

Three hundred and fifty persons attended the second production of the cycle of three presentations scheduled for the season by the Maska Dramatic Club players Sunday night in the auditorium of the P. N. A. community home, Crane street.

This performance of the gay and diverting three-act comedy, *Śmieszna Głupota*, drew forth enthusiastic applause from the large audience. Colorful settings were designed by Zygmunt Brzozowski with the assistance of Lucyan Sekowski. The comedy was under the direction of Joseph Czyzewski and Lucyan Sekowski.

The cast included Miss Nellie Pitera, Miss Alice Drewczynski, Miss Mary Zborowski, Joseph Czyzewski, Frank Dzierwa, Lucyan Sekowski, Edward Kwiecinski, Mathew Ozarowski, Stanley Zych.

The general committee consisted of Miss Agnes Dmochowski, Miss Alice Nowicki, Miss Agnes Pieszczoch, Miss Genevieve Stelmach, Miss Sophie Chojnicki, Miss Wanda Korycinski, Mrs. J. Czyzewski, Zygmunt Wisniewski, Henry Klejsmyt, Walter C. Sekowski, Michael Tytko and Stanley Plocharczyk, financial manager.

The program was supplemented by musical selections by Miss Sophie Korycinski, pianist.

The third and final presentation of the current season will be staged April 8.

1938 – April 2, *Schenectady Gazette* (Page 8)

Maska Club to Close Season – Players Present Comedy Tomorrow Night; Sekowski Will Direct

Completing a season of three play performances, the Maska Dramatic Club will present its final stage production, a comedy, *Trudy-i-Troski* tomorrow at 7:30 p. m. in the auditorium of the P. N. A. community home, Crane street.

The enactment of *Trudy-i-Troski*, directed by Lucyan J. Sekowski will be in three acts and has a cast of nine.

This comedy is a portrayal of the everyday doings of a typical average American family. Jozek Miedoszyty, a WPA worker, is well represented by Mathew Ozarowski. Lucia is his eldest daughter, an office worker. Her mother's one anxiety is to get her married, while father's ambition is to get his son to work. Sister Kasia has one passion, and that is getting out of doing her piano lessons. Later Lucia announces that a young man is calling on her. The sensation of it all is that Lucia has never had a young man "caller" before. Filip Kukulka, a fine upstanding young fellow is left alone with Lucia after embarrassed introduction. Mother puts her finger in the domestic pie. She drops hints and tells Filip that her daughter is accustomed only to the best of everything. She tells the neighbors what a wonderful fellow Lucia has won and that he is a big banker and the game of bluff goes on. Having heard all this "propaganda," Filip begins to wonder what sort of family he is getting into.

The cast includes Miss Mary Dziuba as the mother; Miss Genevieve Stelmach as Lucia; Lucyan J. Sekowski as Filip Kukulka; Kasia, Miss Sophie Korycinski, and Walter Sekowski as Stachu, her brother; Miss Agnes Dmochowski, a dress-maker, Miss Kluska. And Miss Alice Nowicki, Filip's mother, Mrs. Kukulka. Zygmont Brzozowski supervised renovation of the stage and the building of new scenery

1938 – April 6 *Schenectady Gazette* (Page 14)

Maska Drama Club Finishes Fifth Season

The Maska Dramatic Club recently completed its fifth successful subscription season of plays in the auditorium of the P. N. A. community home, Crane street. The season comprised three presentations and the various casts engaged 23 players.

The play productions were under the direction of Miss Agnes Pieszczoch, who directed the first; Joseph Czyzewski and Lucyan Sekowski jointly directed the second, and Lucyan Sekowski directed the third.

The plays presented were *Djabeł z Monoklem*, or *Devil with a Monocle*, Sigmund Antony; *Śmieszna Głupota*, [Comical Goofiness, author unknown] and *Trudy i Troski* [*Cares & Worries, author unknown*]. The selected three-act plays consisted of a mystery and two comedies.

The casts of the productions included Misses Genevieve Stelmach, Helen Kilian, Frances Harasimowicz, Nellie Pitera, Alice Dremozynski, Mary Zborowski, Sophie Korycinski, Alice Nowicki, Agnes Dmochowski; also, Bernard S. Deptula, Stanley J. Zych, Lucyan J. Sekowski,

Edward Kwiesinski, Walter Zoladz, Thaddeus Kilian; Zygmunt Kilian, Frank Dzierwa, Henry Klejsmyt; Joseph Czyzewski, Mathew Ozarowski, Walter C. Sekowski and Joseph Stelmach.

The members of the production staff in charge of scenic requirements, properties, make-up, wardrobe and general business management were Misses Sophie Chojnicki, Helen Kilian, Wanda Korycinski, Nellie Pitera, Mary Zborowski, Genevieve Stelmach, Agnes Dmochowski, Alice Nowicki; also Zygmond Kilian, Zygmunt Wisnieski, Michael Tytko. Lucyan Sekowski, Henry Klejsmyt; Andrew Podbielski, Zygmont Brzozowski, Stanley Plocharczyk.

Plans for the coming season are being arranged tentatively by the board of directors.

The Maska club will meet tomorrow at 8 o'clock in the P. N. A. hall.

1938 – May 11 *Schenectady Gazette* (Page 17)

Maska Players To Hold Mardi Gras May 26th

The Maska May mardi-gras being arranged by the members of the Maska Dramatic Club under the sponsorship of the Gmina 53, P. N. A., will be a novel affair. The event will take place in the auditorium of the P. N. A. home, Crane street, Thursday, May 26.

The features include dancing from 8 to 1 o'clock, amusements, Polish food, floor show and a $5 prize. Several weeks of planning and preparation for the occasion have been spent by a crew of club members. The committee has worked out an elaborate scheme of decorations and special lighting effects.

The committee is headed by Walter C. Sekowski with the assistance of Helen Kilian, Mary Zborowski, Mary Dziuba, Alice Drewczynski, Agnes Dmochowski, Mary Kilian, Alice Nowicki, Sophie Chojnicki, Genevieve Stelmach, Nellie Pitera, Agnes Pieszczoch, Sophie Korycinski, Wanda Korycinski, Stanley Plocharczyk, Henry Klejsmyt, Zygmunt Wisniewski, Andrew Podbielski, Zygmunt Brzozowski, Frank Dzierwa, Mathew Repka, Lucyan J. Sekowski, Joseph Czyzewski, Stanley Zych, Mathew Ozarowski, Bernard Deptola, Ted Kilian and William Barczyk.

Chapter 7
The 1938 – 1939 Season
October 9, 1938 – July, 1939

Legionnaire on the Field of Honor [Legjonista na Polu Chwały] by Antoni Jax, is the first of 3 offerings this season. The play is based on the Polish Legions on the European Eastern Front in 1916, commemorating the 29th anniversary of the Declaration of Polish Independence by the Warsaw Committee. Several pages from the recently discovered manuscript are shown in Appendix 6. There is little information on the next play, *Quick Work [Prędka Robota]*, a three act comedy, listed as adapted from the American stage; the playwright is unknown.

Pazura [The Claw – aka Trapped] a second play by Maska member Zygmunt Brzozowski, under the pen name Zigmont Antony [aka Sigmond Antony], concludes the season's offerings. The entire manuscript was discovered along with the *Legionnaire..* text. The story centers on six young potential heirs, summoned by a lawyer to the estate of a wealthy relative who had died 20 years previous, to hear his will. Billed as a comedy / mystery, the play is apparently set in Schenectady. Stage directions are in English; dialogue in Polish. Initial pages of each chapter are shown in Appendix 6. Brzozowski's father founded a funeral home in 1904 in the Mont Pleasant community. Zygmunt later studied at the Simmons Institute of Funeral Service and continued to run the family business. His sense of humor shines through the years in the autograph found in the program for the February 3, 1935 presentation in Chapter 3. See Appendix 4 for complete program.

The May 1939 Maska Buletyn [Newsletter], Appendix 5, encourages members to attend the semi-formal dance in late June at the Bohemian Tavern. Another social event, the July Jamboree on July 27, is also promoted in this newsletter. The last page is difficult to read but the location at the "PNA Enclosed Fairgrounds" and "Free Dancing." can be deciphered.

<u>1938 – October 8, *Schenectady Gazette* (Page 8)</u>

Maska to Open Drama Season
The Maska Dramatic Club will open its sixth subscription season tomorrow at the Polish home on Crane street. Its first production, *Legionista na Polu Chwały*, is the story of the action of the Polish Legion during 1916, and also includes a love angle. The plot centers about a young legionnaire, son of a wealthy and aristocratic family, who has fallen in love with the daughter of a poor village schoolmaster. According to the old tradition among the Polish nobles, their children cannot marry one beneath their class. That tradition persists to this day. In Maska's play the father of the young legionnaire absolutely forbid his son to marry the daughter of the village schoolmaster, and as a result that obstinacy precipitated a deeper tragedy than even the war could bring. Maska is positive that the scenes of this play will bring back vivid memories to those Polish-American Schenectadians who saw service in the Polish Legion, or who lived in Poland in 1916.
    The cast is as follows:Anzelm Zapolski, wealthy Polish aristocrat, Matthew Ozarowski; Karol, his Legionnaire son, Walter Zborowski; Wasala, veteran of the 1863 Polish revolution,

Joseph Czyzewski; Zytnicki, village schoolmaster, Henry Klejsmyt; Marta, schoolmaster's wife, Wanda Korycinski; Wanda, schoolmaster's daughter, Genevieve Stelmach; Sosnowski, young teacher from neighboring village, Walter Zolad; Aurora Misenko, Russian baroness, Sophie Korycinski; Slomka, right hand man of the baroness, Stanley Bachleda; Mosiek Pinkeles, Russian spy, Henry Ausfeld.

Directors of the play are Joseph Czyzewski and Stanley Zych. The committee in charge of the production comprises Mary Zborowski, art director; Matthew Ozarowski, Property manager; Zygmund Brzozowski, stage designer; Andrew Podbielski, assistant; Matthew Repka, William Bonczyk and Casimir Laniewski, stage hands; Stanley Plocharczyk, business manager; Sophie Chojnicki and Genevieve Stelmach, make up; Jane Borowski, Helen Kilian, Mary Czyzewski, Mary Ausfeld, Irene Nowicki, reception committee.

The sound effects will be produced by Paul Gurzenski and Anthony Kopec. Nellie Petera is furnishing the shrubbery and outdoor effects.

The officers of Maska Dramatic Club for this season are Lucian Sekowski, president; Zygmund Wisniewski, vice president; Sophie Korycinski, secretary; Nellie Petera, treasurer; Alice Nowicki, parliamentarian

1939 – May 9, *Schenectady Gazette* (Page 8)

Maska Circle To Give Play

The Maska Dramatic Circle will conclude its fifth subscription season next Sunday at the Polish home with the presentation of a mystery-comedy entitled *Pazura*. The plot of the play centers about a will left by an eccentric old man who had made a fortune here in America and then had no one to whom to leave his estate. So he made a most extraordinary will that becomes a bone of contention among his distant relations. The person who finally inherited the fortune of Horacyjusz Burak also inherited a pack of trouble because she aroused the ill will of the other claimants. Zosia Burak a very distant relative of the old man became the target of a murder plot and various other unpleasant surprises. The play is fast moving and is packed with action.

Rehearsals are being staged every day during these last few days and Stanley Zych and Joseph Czyzewski are co-operating in preparation for next Sunday. An entirely new set of scenery is being made especially designed to add chills to the play. The stage work is being supervised by Mary Zborowski, Zygmunt Brzozowski and Zygmund Kilian.

Sunday's play will conclude Maska's fifth successful subscription season.

1939 – May 17, *Schenectady Gazette* (Page 8)

Mystery Drama Is Presented by Maska Players

Maska closed its fifth subscription season Sunday night with a comedy-mystery entitled *Pazura* (*The Claw*). The play was packed with laughs and chills. The receptive audience was kept in suspense until the very end of the play. The revealing of the villain was a shock to all. Genevieve Stelmach as Tosia Burak, the plucky young heiress, had enough will power to overcome the assaults of her mental capacity.

Lucian Sekowski as the hero, Stas Chmurka was the very picture of shyness, hesitancy and fright. Leo Marcinek as the villain, Pawel Polonowicz was so smooth and sly that he escaped detection until the very end. Helen Kilian as Broncia Cukierek was the sarcastic relative of the deceased, bitterly disillusioned because she did not inherit the Burak fortune. Her biting sarcasm placed the finger of guilt on her more than once in the play, Sophie Korycinski as Klara Makowka, another disappointed relative, did a good job of her role, Stanley Zych as Marek Syaka, the executor of the Burak estate and also the victim of the villain's diabolic plot, admirably portrayed the role, Casimir Laniewski as the unsuccessful lover showed his disappointment in no uncertain terms. Thaddeus Kilian as Grzegorz Kapuscisk was instrumental in revealing the villain. His role was excellent. Mary Czyzewski as Kunnegunda Pirog, the spiritualistic medium, gave every one the creeps by her trances. Joseph Czyzewski as the mysterious Dr. Dionyzy Galareta added to the mystery of the play. The play was under the direction of Stanley Zych and Joseph Czyzewski.

Zygmunt Brzozowski did a remarkable job in preparing the odd sets of scenery for the mystery-comedy and his innovations added many more chills. Stanley Bachleda and Bernard Szumachowski aided during the evening's work on the stage. Celia Boroski and Regina Chantnicki took care of the makeup. Michael Tytko was prompter as usual.

Maska is now making final plans for a June jamboree, details of which will soon be ready. To top off Maska activities for the 1938-39 season, there will be a semi-formal social and dance during the closing days of June.

Sunday marked the successful close of Maska's fifth subscription season, and Maska wishes to take this occasion to thank those patrons who have been loyal throughout. Plans are already afoot for a better and bigger sixth subscription season, the 1939-40 season.

1939 – June 1 *Schenectady Gazette*

Maska Club Will Select Officers

The annual meeting of the Maska Dramatic Club will be held tonight at 7 o'clock at the P.N.A. home. Plans for the annual semi-formal dance and the club's "June Jamboree" will be made.

Present officers of the club are as follows: Lucyan J. Sekowski, president; Zygmunt Wisniewski, vice president; Sophie Korycinska, secretary; Nellie Petera, treasurer; Stanley Plocharczyk, business manager; Stanley Zych and Joseph Czyzewski, play directors; Mary Zborowska, stage manager; Alice Nowicka, parliamentarian; Helen Kilian, entertainment chairman.

Chapter 8
The 1940 Season
December 1939 – August 1940

Germany invaded Poland from the west on September 1, 1939, marking the beginning of World War II. The Soviet Union invaded Poland from the east on September 17th. Belgium, France, Luxembourg and the Netherlands were taken by Germany the following May. The Soviet Union incorporated Lithuania, Latvia and Estonia in early August 1940. The Schenectady immigrant community had many ties to these countries and were undoubtedly deeply concerned for the families and friends left behind. Therefore, the Maska season offerings were probably selected to bring a bit of diversion from the cares and worries of the day.

The picture (Fig. 22) of the many smiling young Maska members was taken in this period. The people, listed in Sophie Korycinski Zych's handwriting, include Stanley Zych and Sophie's younger brother Alexander Korycinski.

A melodrama and three comedies were staged this season. There is little information on the first offering, *On Our Soil [Na Naszej Glebie]*, by Anna Karwatowa, nee Bardzka. Its theme is Polish village life in the early 20th century. The program is found in the Maska Buletyn [Newsletter], Appendix 5.

The headline of the news article of February 17, 1940 [below] adds a bit of confusion. The two plays given on February 18 were the second offerings of Maska's 8th year, not the first; this is the 7th subscription season, not the 8th. [See below, April 29, 1940.]. *Lend Me Your Wife [Pożycz Mi Swej Żony]*, a two act farce by Maurice Desvallieres, is set in Warsaw in the summer of 1939. *The Horse Cure [Końska Kuracja]* by Cyril Danielewski, a one act comedy, concerns a medical mixup, set in Poznan in 1938.

The final plays of the season were two comedies: *Soliwoda Runs for Alderman [Kandydatura Soliwody]*, and *The Bitter and the Sweet [Słodkie i Pierne]*, by Maska member and play director Joseph Czyzewski. *Soliwoda's* plot concerns the trials and tribulations of a Polish-American citizen who runs for local office.

"The Bitter and the Sweet," described in the articles of April 1 and April 6 below, is the most intriguing of all Maska offerings. Based on the daily life of a Mont Pleasant family, the small cast includes both Sophie Korycinski and Stanley Zych. At that time, Sophie was a saleswoman for a downtown Schenectady women's clothing store and Stanley, who had had various retail jobs, was working at the General Electric Co. Unfortunately, no script has been found to date.

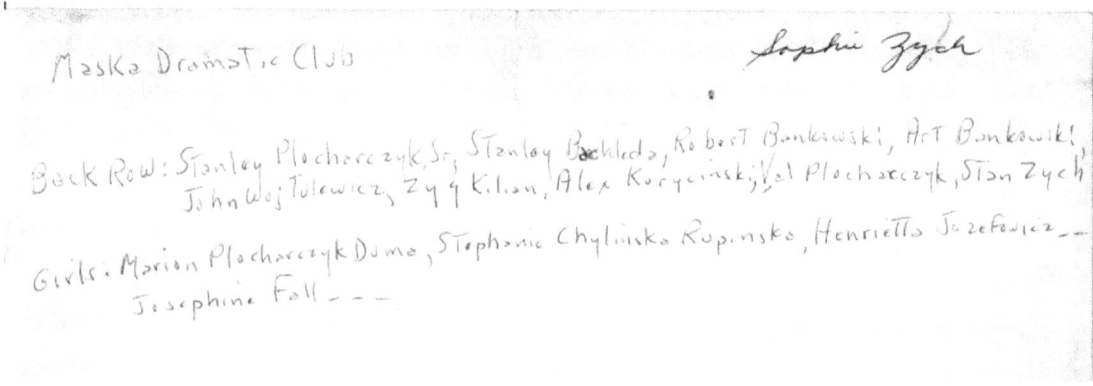

Figure 22: Scrapbook Maska Dramatic Club ~1940. Back Row: Stanley Plocharczyk, Sr., Stanley Bachleda, Robert Bankowski, Art Bankowski, John Wojtulewicz, Zyg Kilian, Alex Korycinski, Val Plocharczyk, Stan Zych. Girls: Marion Plocharczyk Duma, Stephanie Chylinska Rupinska, Henrietta Jozefowicz, and Josephine Fall.

1940 – February 17, *Schenectady Gazette* (Page 6)

First program of 8th season
Maska Circle To Present 2 Plays Sunday

Maska Dramatic Circle will present the second program of the season tomorrow at the Polish home on Crane street. The curtain will go up at 7:30 p.m.

The program will consist of two plays, a two-act farce written by Maurice Desvailers and entitled *Pożycz Mi Swej Żony,* or *Lend Me Your Wife,* and the other a one-act comedy written by Cyril Danielewski and entitled *Końska Kuracja,* or *The Horse Cure.*

The action of the first play takes place in Warsaw in the summer of 1939. The plot revolves around the antics of the younger set of Warsaw. The cast includes Leon Marcinek as Commandant Tabakiewicz, the uncle; Arthur Bankowski as the ungrateful nephew; Casimira Gorski as the wife that was borrowed; Stanley Bachleda as the best friend; Mary Juba as the uncle's daughter; Regina Chantnicki as the nursemaid; Alexander Korycinski [My mother's younger brother] as John, the butler; Stefania Chylinski as the maidservant; and Edward Repka as the county attorney of Rypin.

The one-act play, *Końska Kuracja* tells the story of an incident in the life of a family in the City of Poznan in 1938. The plot revolves around the fact that the father of the family and the family horse fall ill at the same time. A veterinary is called for the horse Hektor but the wife gives the veterinary's prescription to her husband.

The cast includes Joseph Czyzewski as the father, Bonifacy; Stefania Chylinski as the mother, Aurelia; Sophie Korycinski as the daughter; Zygmont Wiśniewski as the young veterinary, Dr. Morski; Regina Chantnicki as the maid; and Aleksander Korycinski as Philip the butler. Both plays are under the direction of Joseph Czyzewski.

The Krakowiak Trio will play musical selections in the intermissions. The trio is composed of Boleslaus Dondalski, trumpet; Edward Wajda, accordion, and Richard Snyder, violin. The trio will be accompanied at the piano by Sophie Korycinski.

The following committee will be in charge of the program: Lucian Sekowski, president; Henry Ausfeld, vice-president; Celia Borowski, secretary; Aniela Petera, treasurer; Stanley Plocharczyk, financial manager; Casimer Laniewski, stage manager; Zygmunt Brzozowski, scenery designer; Stanley Bachleda, art director; Genevieve Ausfeld and Mary Zborowski make-up artists, and Walter Zolad, Mary Budka, Henrietta Jozefowicz and Stanley Zych [my father], stage assistants.

The Sunday program will inaugurate the eighth year of Maska's existence as a Polish dramatic circle.

1940 - April 1, *Schenectady Gazette* (Page 6)

Maska Drama Circle to Close Season Sunday

Maska Dramatic Circle will conclude its seventh subscription season next Sunday. The final presentation of the season will consist of two one-act comedies, one an original scene written by Maska's director, Joseph Czyzewski, so-called *Słodkie i Pierne,* or *The Bitter and the Sweet.*

In putting on the original play, Maska will try an experiment. The play is based on the daily life a of a Polish-American family in the Mont Pleasant area. The comedy is full of local color and incidents with which the local Polish-American society comes into contact almost daily. Prominent local citizens of Polish extraction enter into the dialogue of the play. Those taking part in this play include Sophie Koryciński, Celia Borowski, Mary Czyzewski, Stanley Zych, and Stanley Bachleda.

The other play is *Kandydatura Soliwedy,* or *Soliwoda Runs for Alderman,* a farce based on the complications involved in a local campaign for the city council in which an American citizen of Polish extraction runs for the position of alderman in a ward made up of American citizens of various foreign extractions. This play has been streamlined from a play by the late Count Skorupka entitled *Wybory do Rady Miejskiej* [*Elections to the City Council*]. The rearrangements

were made by Mr. Czyzewski. The cast includes Henry Ausfeld, Stanley Plocharczyk, Henrietta Josefowicz, George Mozejko, and Mr. Czyzewski. Both plays are under the direction of Helen Kilian and Joseph Czyzewski. The scenery effects are under the direction of Zygmunt Brzozowski, designer; Alexander Korycinski, stage manager; Arthur Bankowski, assistant stage manager and Stanley Bachleda, art direction.

The orchestra that scored at Maska's last presentation is again preparing for Sunday's program. The orchestra is composed of William Dondalski, trumpet; Richard Snyder, violin; Walter Swarczewski, accordion and Arthur Bankowski, drums.

The following Polish societies cooperated with Maska Dramatic Club during the season: Młoda Polska, Postęp, Prawda and Praca, Swoboda, Wolność, and Zgoda societies.

1940 – April 6, *Schenectady Gazette* (Page 8)

Maska Players Close Seventh Season Sunday

Maska Dramatic circle will present its last plays of the seventh subscription season at the Polish community home on Crane street tomorrow. Sunday's presentation will be Maska's 40th program.

The program will consist of two one-act comedies. One of them, *Słodkie i Pierne* is based on the everyday life of a Polish-American family of Mont Pleasant. The comedy is full of local roles, replete with humorous incidents of the Polish-American community. This play has been written at the request of many of Maska's patrons during the past seven years. The cast of the play includes Stanley Zych, Mary Czyzewski, Sophie Korycinski, Celia Hojnicki, Stanley Bachleda.

The other play is *Kandydatura Soliwody*, or *Soliwoda Runs for Alderman,* a farce based on the trials and tribulations of a Polish-American citizen who is a candidate in a municipal election. It is satire on local politics and especially on local politicians. The cast includes Joseph Czyzewski, Henry Ausfeld, Henrietta Jozefowicz, Stanley Plocharczyk and George Mozejko. Both plays are under the direction of Joseph Czyzewski and Helen Kilian.

The scenery and stage effects are under the direction Zygmunt Brzozowski scenery designer; Alexander Korycinski, stage manager; Arthur Bankowski, assistant stage manager; Stanley Bachleda, art director; and stage hands Zymunt Wisniewski, Joseph Romanowski, Chester Baranowski, and Frank Baranowski.

The "Krakowiaki" orchestra will play during the evening and will play during the evening and also furnish musical background for one of the plays. The orchestra is composed of William Dondalski, trumpet; Richard Snyder, violin; Walter Swarczewski, accordion, and Arthur Bankowski, drums.

The committee in charge of production includes Lucian Sekowski, president; Henry Ausfeld, vice president, Nellie Pitera, treasurer, Celia Bo?, secretary, Stanley Plocharczyk, financial manager, Genevieve Ausfeld, Mary Zborowski and C[?] Ko..ki, make-up, Michael Tytko, prompter. The general committee is composed of Louis Okonsky, Pearl Okonsky, [?]Lemanski, Mary Budka, Stephen Kacinski, Stephania Chylinska and Zygmunt Kilian.

As Maska members joyfully list their members and patrons on the page of the *Schenectady Gazette*, the adjacent image of Nazi troops is a stark reminder of the times.

1940 – April 29, *Schenectady Gazette* (Page 9)

Maska Dramatic Circle, the oldest Polish dramatic club in upper New York state, recently completed the seventh season. During the seven subscription seasons the following members have contributed to 44 Maska productions.

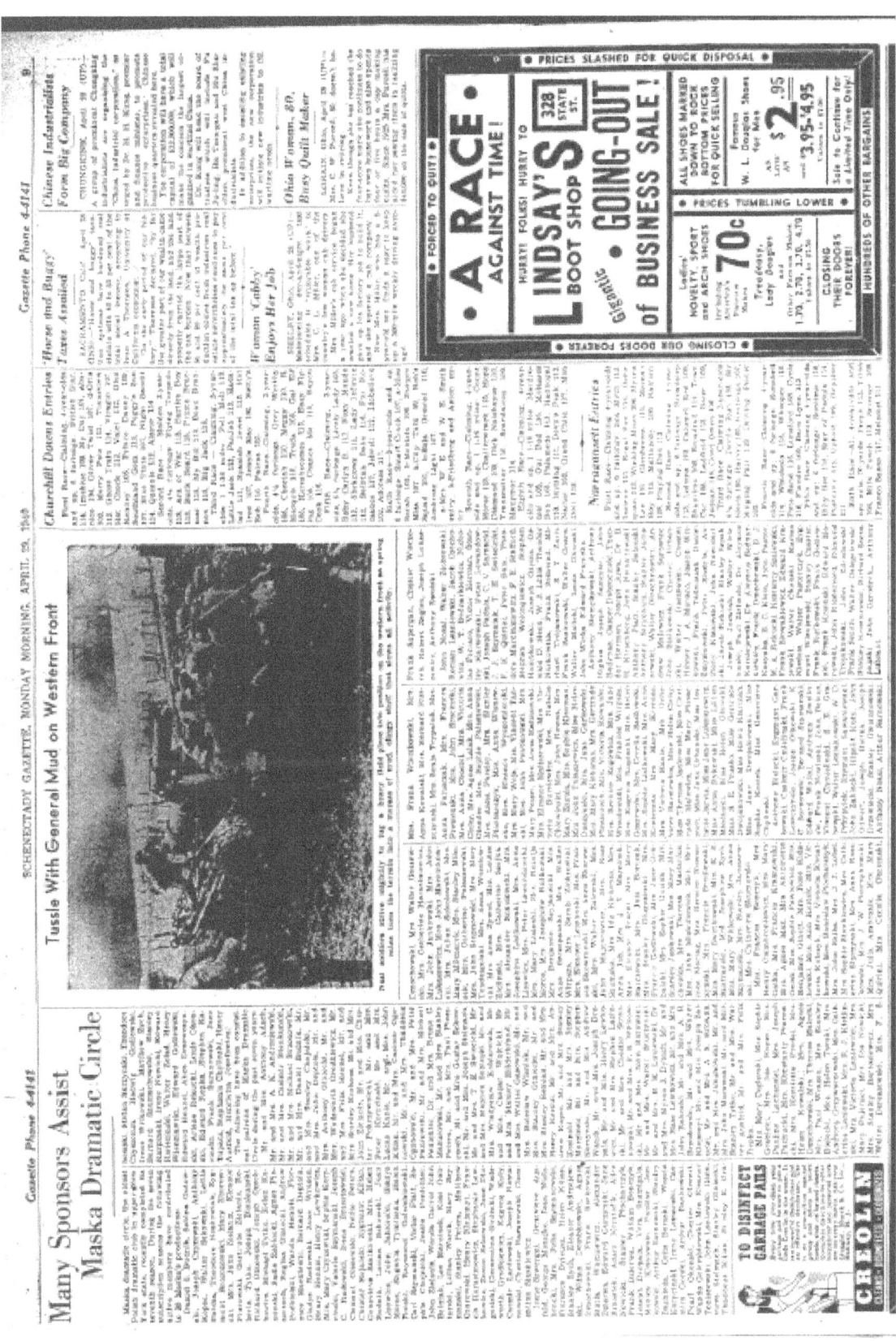

Figure 23: Press clipping from the Scrapbook, *Schenectady Gazette*, April 29, 1940 (Page 9)

1940 – June 15, *Schenectady Gazette* (Page 6)

Maska Players Select Officers - Sekowski is Renamed Head for 4th Time; Installation Planned

The Maska Dramatic Club at the annual meeting of the P. N. A. home reelected Lucyan J. Sekowski president for the fourth consecutive time. Mr. Sekowski has been an active leader of the organization for the past seven years.

Henry Ausfeld, re-elected vice president for the second time, will act as chairman of the board of directors.

Others elected were Mrs. Mary Czyzewski, recording secretary; Miss Sophie Korycinski, treasurer; Stanley Plocharczyk, business manager; Joseph Czyzewski, press manager; Alexander Korycinski, stage Manager; Stanley Bachleda, art manager; Arthur Bankowski, property manager; Misses Stephanie Chylinski, Mary Czyzewski, Mary Dziuba, make-up artists; Joseph Czyzewski and Stanley Zych, drama directors.
    Stanley Zych was chairman of the elections with the assistance of Louis Okonski and Chester Baranowski. Miss Stephanie Chylinski was secretary of elections.
    The board of directors will consist of Henry Ausfeld, chairman; Lucyan J. Sekowski and Miss Sophie Korycinski, Mrs. Mary Czyzewski, Miss Mary Dziuba, Miss Stephanie Chylinski, Stanley Zych, Joseph Czyzewski, Stanley Plocharczyk, Arthur Bankowski, Stanley Bachleda.
    The induction of officers and a celebration marking the close of the seventh season will be held on Saturday, June 22.
    The committee is Misses Sophie Korycinski, Stephanie Chylinski, Henrietta Jozefowicz, Stanley Zych and Lucyan Sekowski

1940 – August 1, *Schenectady Gazette* (Page 3)

Forum Service Will Show Film Tonight

The Forum service will sponsor two motion picture programs tonight at 9 o'clock at Riverside park and at the Polish home on Crane street. Members of the Maska Dramatic club will meet at the home at 8 o'clock preceding the picture program.
    John Barbieri will represent the Forum and Miss Syd McGregor, Mick Rieg and Ron Budynas, the park bureau, at Riverside park. The following educational pictures will be shown.
    Making Modern Man o' Wars men, *Submarine Service*, *Neptune's Realms*, and *Gateway of the Pacific*, all U. S. Navy productions and *First Century of Baseball*, a Fisher Body division of General Motors film.
    Joseph Czyzewski will represent the Forum at the Polish Home. Several shorts and a Westinghouse picture, *The Middleton Family At the World's Fair*, will be shown by Maska Dramatic club in co-operation with the Forum service. No admission is charged at either place.

Chapter 9
November 1940 – June 1941

The Maska season opens as Germany continues to bomb London, the US rearms and The Great Depression finally begins to lift. Information on Maska events in this period is sparse and presents a puzzle. *Catherine Goes to Court [Katarzyna w Sądzie]*, by Jakub Stefan Zieliński, a three act comedy published in 1938, was given on Sunday, December 1st. This was followed on February 2nd, by *Borrowed Feathers [Cudze Piórka]*, by Józef Jarem-Mirski, a three act folk comedy of Polish village life in the summer of 1938 and *Jealousy [Zazdrość]*, [Author unknown], a one act novelty sketch that includes an imaginary trip to a radio studio.

The news article of February 4 mentions that the "next Maska presentation will be given on April 6." No information on the April play was found either in the scrapbook or in the fultonhistory.org resource of old New York State newspapers. Only two Maska Buletyns were found in that period, December 1940 and June 1941 [See Appendix 5]; there is no mention in either one of an April play date. The June Buletyn as well as the news article of June 11 (See below) mention the "annual" semi-formal to be held at the Circle Inn.

Was there an April performance? Perhaps not. Joseph Czyzewski, Maska stalwart and frequent director, was preparing to leave for a job downstate. Under "Social Gossip" in the June 1941 Buletyn [Appendix 5] is found the following:

> Our farewell party for Joseph Czyzewski was quite a success. Joseph was presented with a military case from all his friends of the Maska CIUB. To those who have not heard, Joseph has accepted a position in Newburgh, N. Y. where he will be in charge of a N.Y.A. Center. We all wish you lots of luck, Joseph.

Figure 24: Entry from Maska Buletyn Scrapbook

The National Youth Administration (NYA) was a New Deal agency that focused on providing work and education for Americans between the ages of 16 and 25.[2]

1940 – November 23, *Schenectady Gazette* (Page 16)

Maska Dramatic Club Lists Season's Patrons

Maska Dramatic club has announced its preliminary list of patrons and patronesses for the 1940-1941 season, which begins Sunday, Dec. 1, with a three-act comedy entitled, *Katarzyna w Sądzie*, or *Catherine Goes to Court*. The play will be presented at the Polish community home on Crane street.

---

[2] https://en.wikipedia.org/wiki/National_Youth_Administration accessed on February 26, 2016.

Taking part will be Helen Dziuba, Marion Plocharczyk, Mary Czyzewski, Stanley Plocharczyk, Lucyan Sekowski, Stanley Zych, Daniel Klimas, Eugene Kopec, Joseph Godlewski, Joseph Czyzewski and Arthur Bankowski. Stanley Zych is director.

Officers of Maska for the 1940-1941 season are Lucyan Sekowski, president; Henry Ausfeld, vice president; Mary Czyzewski, secretary; Sophie Zych, treasurer; Chester Baranowski, property manager; Stephanie Chylinski, Celia Borowski and Jeanna Dziuba, make-up artists; Stanely Plocharczyk, financial manager; Stanley Zych and Joseph Czyzewski, play coaches and Stephen Kaczynski, assistant art manager.

Mrs. Antonia Szatkowska, Mrs. and Mrs. Alexander Godlewski, Mrs. Sophie Wajda, Mr. and Mrs. Walter Klejsmyt, Mrs. Adam Wisniewski, Dr. and Mrs. August Korkosz, Mrs. Mary Wojs, Mrs. And Mrs. Peter Korycinski, Miss Irene Borowska, Mr. and Mrs. Bernard Luniewski, Miss Sophia Grzywna, Mr. and Mrs. Walter Okonski, Miss Wanda Mankiewicz, Mr. and Mrs. Henry Przybylek, Miss Bertha Marcinkiewicz, Mr. and Mrs. Gustaw Sekowski, Miss Gladys Justin.

Mr. and Mrs. Anthony Wroblewski, Walter Andrzejewski, Mrs. Antonia Bartkowska, Wallace Armour, Mrs. Wladyslawa Borowska, Dr. Ignatius Bednarkiewicz, Mrs. Antonia Chylinska, Joseph Bietka, Mrs. Agnes Dziengielewska, Charles A. Brundage, Mrs. Eva Dziuba, Paul Christian, Mrs. Julia Dziuba, John Cieplinski, Mrs. Stanislawa Gasowska, Morris Marshall Cohn, Mrs. Mary Jankowska, David Cohn, Mrs. Joseph Jarozelska, Dr. Edmund Colby, Mrs. Mary Jozefowicz, Joseph Daszewski, Mrs. Benjamin Kaszubska, Lewis B. Dewk, Mrs. Antonia Kopec, Joseph A. Dick, Mrs. Anna Klimas, Joseph D'Jimas, Mrs. Catherine Palaszewski, Dr. Myron J. Dybich, Mrs. Mary Pajerska, Walter Dziengielewski, Mrs. Josephine Rutkowska, Leo Florkiewicz, Mrs. Antonia Saniewska, John Falkowski, Mrs. Josephine Stelmach, Joseph A. Gallup.

Walter Galkiewicz, Andrew Makowski, John Golembiowski, John Matson, Carroll A. Gardner, Chester Marcinkiewicz, Walter Gnara, Edward Murowski, Stanley Grabicki, Joseph Nusbaum, George A. Graves, Frank Odasz, Joseph Gzyms, Adam Ogonowski, Carl Heisler, Thaddeus Ogonowski, Joseph Holland, Adolf Pachucki, William Jackson, Walter Patton, Benjamin Jakubowski, Paul Perkowski, Benjamin Kazyaka, Matthias P. Poersch, Adam Klimowicz, Stanley Pokrzywnicki, Frank Kosinski, Benjamin Predel, Anthony Kozlowski, Ralph J. Ury, Ted Kostyniak, John Sauls, Charles Krasucki, Joseph Sammler, Stanley Krasnowski, K. C. Sarnowski, Benjamin Kuczynski, Arthur Sarnowski, Frank Leszczynski, Sigmon Sawaniewski.

Roman Lesniewski, Richard Levy, Samuel Schein?, Stanley Szczepanski, Blazej Lewkowicz, Peter Siudyla, Henry Lewkowicz, Joseph Snyder, Peter Lewandowski, Anthony Szpak, Charles Lynch, John Szwantkowski, James C. MacDonald, Michael J. Rekucki, Edward Malik, Jacob Rekucki, Walter Malicki, Frank Rosiak.

Anthony Ricciardi, Edward K. St. Louis, Mills Ten Eyck, George Voris, Charles Wagoner, Thomas Wallace, Carl Weiss, Anthony H. Wise, Frank Wierzbowski, Joseph Whitney, Daniel Zmyslowski, Anthony Zwolski, Walter Zytkowski, Gmina 53 ZNP, Tow. Postep ZNP, Tow. Swoboda ZNP, Tow. Zgoda ZNP, Tow. Mloda Polska ZNP, Tow. Prawda I Praca ZNP, Tow. Wolnosc ZNP.

1940 – November 30, *Schenectady Gazette* (Page 6)

Maska Club Opens Drama Season Sunday

The Maska Dramatic club will present the first play of the eighth season tomorrow night at 7:30 o'clock at P. N. A. hall. The vehicle, *Katarzyna w Sądzie*, or *Catherine Goes To Court*, is an elegant musical comedy.

The play portrays scenes from the life of two average Polish American families in a large community facing the "Roaring Twenties." In the cast are Mary Czyzewski, Stanley Zych, Helen Dziuba, Stanley Plocharczyk, Joseph Czyzewski, Lucyan Sekowski, Marian Plocharczyk, Daniel Klimas, Joseph Godlewski, Edward Repka, and Arthur Bankowski. The play is under the direction of Stanley Zych.

Mrs. Sophie Zych will accompany members of the cast in several of the scenes. Chester Baranowski, Zygmunt Brzozowski and Joseph Godlewski have designed and constructed the scenery. Stephanie Chylinska will take care of the make-up. Members of the general committee Frank Baranowski, Louis Okonski, Pearl Okonski, Celia Borowski, Regina Godlewski, Henrietta

Jozefowicz, Helen Wiezbowski, Victor Deptola, Zygmunt Wisniewski, Thaddeus Kilian, Mary Budka, Stanley Bachleda, Henry Ausfeld, George Macejka and Nellie Petera.

1941 – January 6, *Schenectady Gazette* (Page 10)

Maska Club Tryouts Tonight

Tonight at 7:30 o'clock in the Polish community home, Maska Dramatic club will hold tryouts for its second program of the 1940-1941 season.

The program for the second presentation will consist of two comedies, one a short three-act play based on a scene of peasant life in a Polish village in 1936 and the other a one-act sketch of an aristocratic Polish family. The three-act play is entitled *Cudze Piórka*, or *Strange Feathers* while the one-act play is entitled *Dyament z Wioski* or *A Diamond in the Rough*.

The second Maska presentation of the 1940-1941 season will be given Feb. 2. Rehearsals will be directed by Joseph Czyzewski. The scenery effects will be handled by a committee composed of Chester Baranowski, Zygmunt Kilian, Zygmunt Brzozowski, Stanley Bachleda. Arthur Bankowski will prepare the properties and accessories.

Tonight's tryouts are open to anyone who has a reading knowledge of the Polish language regardless whether he or she be a member of Maska or not. Rehearsals will be in full swing right after tonight's tryouts.

1941 – February 1, *Schenectady Gazette* (Page 7)

Maska Club to Give Program Tomorrow

Maska Dramatic club will present its second program of the season tomorrow at the Polish National home on Crane street. The curtain will go up at 7:30 p.m.

The program will consist of a three-act folk comedy and a novelty one-act sketch. The three act comedy is entitled *Cudza Piórka* or *Borrowed Feathers*. It is a story of Polish village life immediately preceding the present war. In fact the action takes place in the summer of 1938. The author was Joseph Jarem-Mirski, one of Poland's best post-war dramatists. He was killed in action when the Nazis invaded Poland in September 1939. He wrote most of his plays during the years 1925-1939.

Cudza Piorka is the story of an orphan girl left to the none too tender mercies of her aunt. This unscrupulous aunt was determined to marry her to a city fop who would like nothing better than to waste away the dowry left the girl by her mother. The girl has her heart set on a soldier who had come home on a leave of absence. Despite the machinations of the aunt and the city dandy the story turns out the way theater-goers prefer.

In the cast are Marian Plocharczyk, Celia Boroski, Stanley Bachleda, Robert Bankowski, Arthur Bankowski and Valentine Plocharczyk. The play is under the direction of Joseph Czyzewski.

The novelty one-act sketch is entitled *Zazdrość* or *Jealousy*. Maska club will take its audience on an imaginary trip to a radio studio. Those taking part are Joseph Czyzewski, Mary Czyzewski and Josephine Fall.

The following are in charge for the preparations for the Sunday presentations: Lucyan Sekowski, Stanley Plocharczyk, Chester Baranowski, Zygmunt Brzozowski, Zygmunt Kilian, Mary Czyzewski, Sophie Zych, Arthur Bankowski, Stephanie Chylinski, Jean Dziuba and Celia Borowski.

The following general committee will cooperate in the program: Louis Okonski, Misses Pearl Okonski, Eugenia Kilian, Mary Budka, Henrietta Jozefowicz, Helen Dziuba, Helen Wiśniewski, Julia Cygan, Regina Godlewski, Stefan Kaczynski, Zygmund Wisniewski, Thaddeus Kilian, Eugene Kopec, Daniel Klimas, Francis Baranowski, Victor Deptola and Miss Catherine Dereski. Maska will also pass out another issue of the *Maska Buletyn* which serves as a program and also contains interesting notes by Maska members.

1941 – February 4, *Schenectady Gazette* (Page 8)

Maska Gives Two Dramas At Polish Home

A sketch entitled *Jealousy* and a three act folk comedy, *Borrowed Feathers*, were presented by Maska Dramatic club Sunday at the Polish National home on Crane street.

Acting in the sketch, which took the audience on an imaginary trip to a radio studio, were Stanley Bachleda, Arthur Bankowski, Joseph Czyzewski, Mary Czyzewski and Josephine Fall.

The comedy play called in Polish *Cudze Piórka*, starred Robert Bankowski, Cecilia Borowski and Mr. Bachleda. Others in the cast were Marian Plocharczyk, Valentine Plocharczyk and Arthur Bankowski. It was directed by Mr. Czyzewski.

Chester Baranowski, Zygmunt Brzozowski and Zygmunt Kilian directed the scene designing, lighting and sound effects.

The next Maska presentation will be given on April 6. [3]Members of the club will meet at the Polish home at 7:30 p.m. Thursday.

1941 – June 11, *Schenectady Gazette* (Page 8)

Maska Club Re-elects Sekowski

Lucyan J. Sekowski was re-elected president of the Maska Dramatic club at the PNA community home, the club reported, last night. John Wojtulewicz was chairman during the elections.

Mr. Sekowski, who is beginning his fifth term, has been active in the organization for eight years. He has served on various committees in plays and has directed two productions.

Alexander Korycinski, newly elected vice president, will also serve as chairman of the board of directors.

Others elected to office were Miss Marian Plocharczyk, recording secretary; Miss Eugenia Kilian, treasurer; Stanley Plocharczyk, re-elected business manager; Stanley Zych and Mary Czyzewski, drama directors; Walery Plocharczyk, stage manager; John Wojtulewicz, art manager; Arthur Bankowski, property manager; Misses Stephanie Chylinski, Julia Cygan, Josephine Fall and Pearl Okonski, make-up.

The board of directors consists of Korycinski, chairman; Miss Sekowski, Miss Marian Plocharczyk, Miss Kilian, Mr. Plocharczyk, Mr. Zych, Mrs. Czyzewski, Miss Walery Plocharczyk, Mr. Wojtulewicz and Mr. Bankowski.

The Maska Dramatic Club will hold its annual semi-formal together with the installation of officers Saturday June 21s at the Circle Inn at 7:30 p.m.

Heading the committee are Miss Stephanie Chylinska, Sophie Zych, Stanley Plocharczyk and Lucyan Sekowski.

Maska's monthly meetings are held every first Thursday.

---

[3] There is no record of this performance.

Chapter 10
December 1941 – March 1942

Japan's attack on Pearl Harbor brings the United States into World War II. Employment at Schenectady's American Locomotive Company and The General Electric Company swells as these companies contribute to the war effort.

A careful reading of the Maska Play List [Appendix 5], brings the realization that the only two offerings of the season are repeats from the past. *Difficulties and Concerns [Trudy i Troski]* was performed on April 3, 1938; *An Eye for an Eye [Wet za Wet]* was originally presented on March 4, 1935.

My sister, Elizabeth Zych Kislinger, recalls our mother telling her that our parents were at a Maska performance when someone ran in and told them that Pearl Harbor had been bombed, Sunday, December 7, 1941: *Difficulties and Concerns [Trudy i Troski]*, indeed!

An Eye for an Eye was presented on March 29, 1942. When the curtain came down, this was truly the end of Maska.

1941 – December 1, *Schenectady Gazette* (Page 4)

Maska Club's Initial Play Slated Dec. 7

Trudy i Troski will be the first production of the ninth season of the Maska Dramatic club players to be presented Dec. 7 in the auditorium of the P.N.A. community home on Crane street.

The comedy is under the direction of Stanley Zych. A cast of nine has been chosen for the roles in the story of an average family.

The cast includes Mr. Zych, Miss Marion Plocharczyk, Miss Stefany Chylinska, Stanley Plocharczyk, Miss Josephine Fall, Robert Bankowski, Mrs. Stanley Zych, Tommy Dwojakowski and Miss Helen Wisniewska.

The stage is being renovated by Walery Plocharczyk, stage manager, and John Wojtulewicz, art manager.

1942 – March 28, *Schenectady Gazette* (Page 7)

Maska Slates Final Play

Maska dramatic club will present its last play of the current season at the Polish Community Home on Crane street tomorrow. A two-act comedy will be featured. It is entitled *Wet Za Wet* or *Eye for an Eye*. The story takes place in the early 1930s and revolves around a family scene wherein the husband and wife are on the verge of divorce. The cause of the difference between the two is the husband's primary interest in his laboratory as a research chemist.

In the cast are Miss Josephine Fall, Robert Bankowski, Miss Helen Wisniewski, Carl Gurzenski, Miss Alfred Dwojakowski, Zygmunt Kilian and Joseph Czyzewski.

The stage effects have been prepared by Zygmunt Brzozowski, Valentine Plocharczyk, Arthur Bankowski and Zygmunt Kilian.

On the general committee Sunday are Miss Pearl Okonski, Louis Okonski, Miss Helen Sokolowski, Miss Irene Siudyla, Daniel Klimas, Victor Deptola, Zygmunt Wisniewski, Joseph Godlewski and Miss Regina Godlewski.

In charge of make-up are Mrs. Jean Sekowski, Miss Stephanie Chylinski and Miss Josephine Fall.

Each member of the audience will receive a special copy of Maska Buletyn, a program. The committee working on the bulletin consists of Lucian Sekowski, Zygmunt Kilian, Zygmunt Brzozowski, Mrs. Sophie Zych, Mrs. Mary Czyzewski and Joseph Czyzewski.

The curtain will go up at 7:30 p.m.

* * *

Chapter 11
1946 – 1980 Reorganization and Reunions

The end of World War II brings with it the hope for a return to normalcy. Marriages, children and busy lives conspire to keep the Maska Dramatic Circle from being revived. While former Maska members speak Polish occasionally to their own parents, few children of the next generation are able to converse in Polish.

The articles below cite two different counts for the total number of plays performed by the Maska group: 57 and 75. Counting the plays performed only by Maska, identified in Appendix 3, the total number is 50 between 1933 and 1942.

Why this discrepancy? It is possible that not all plays have been identified. Perhaps the performances repeated in two other cities with two other local Polish performing groups were during May 1934 were also counted.

1946 - April 4, *Schenectady Gazette* (Page 17)

Maska Drama Club Will Be Reorganized

The Maska Dramatic club, discontinued during the war, will resume its activities with a meeting in PNA hall tonight at 7:30 o'clock, according to Lucyan J. Sekowski, club president.

Plans for the 1946-1947 season will be formulated. It is expected that a series of three-act plays, most of them by Polish authors, will be presented, although the group hopes to obtain suitable translations of some American plays.

Purpose of the organization is the preservation of Polish customs and traditions and the entertainment of Schenectady's approximately 12,000 Polish-American citizens.

Organized in 1932 [sic 1933], the Maska Dramatic club presented 57 plays before becoming inactive during the war, when many of its members left to serve with the armed forces.

Persons having knowledge of stage maintenance of the Polish language have been invited to apply for membership at tonight's meeting.

A program of social activities for the coming year has been outlined by the board of directors and will be announced in the near future.

1962 – February 6, Reunion Report in the Scrapbook

Maska Club Players to Have Reunion

Plans for a reunion of former members of the Maska Dramatic Club, which presented more than 75 stage productions in the PNA home on Crane street for a decade, are under way.

Lucyan J. Sekowski, president of the group during its last year, 1942, is general reunion chairmen.

The Maska players, as an integral part of the cultural activities at the PNA home, staged plays by some of the outstanding Polish dramatists, including several written and produced by Zygmont Anthony, pseudonym for Zygmont Brzozowski of Schenectady, who was a stage director for the group. Mrs. Agnes Pieszczoch Chmielinski of Colonie and Joseph Czyzewski, a Schenectady school teacher, served as directors during the regular fall and winter subscription seasons.

Included on the reunion committee are Mrs. Gene Olwert, Stanley Zych, Leo Marcinek, Mrs. Sophie Korycinski Zych, Mrs. Nellie Petera Tomaszewski, Czyzewski and Mrs. Chmielinski. Former members interested in the reunion may call Stanley Zych or Gene Olwert.

1980 – Report in PNA News

The Maska Dramatic Club ReUnion, held recently at the Galway Lake residence of Mr. and Mrs. Stanely Zych, was attended by Mr. and Mrs. Henry Ausfeld, Mr. and Mrs. Walter Zolad, Mr. and Mrs. Leo Marcinek, Mr. and Mrs. Chester Olwert, Mr. and Mrs. John Olwert, Mr. and Mrs. Richard Olkowski, Dr. Michael Tytko, Miss Mary Jane Tytko, Mr. and Mrs. Frank Kozak, Mr. and Mrs. Andrew Podbielski, Mr. and Mrs. Peter Tomaszewski, Mr. and Mrs. Joseph Czyzewski, Mrs. Jane Koryciński and Mrs. Regina Mitchell.

Plans were formulated for another such re-union for next year.

Additional reunions of the Maska Dramatic Circle members were held in 1962 and 1980. Sophie Korycinski Zych was a driving force behind the Maska Reunions of these years, as shown in the photos and notes in the Maska Scrapbook.

Figure 25: Scrapbook - 1962 Maska Reunion. The text is transcribed below.

Maska Reunion Planned

The Maska Dramatic Club of Schenectady, which ceased operations in 1942, will observe its 20th anniversary of disbandment with a reunion of former members April 28 at PNA hall. The reunion planning committee, composed of, seated from the left, Mrs. John Olwert, Stanley Zych and Lucyan Sekowski, and standing, Leo Marcinek, is shown at PNA hall leafing through several scrapbooks of the club, which from 1932 [sic] to 1942 presented approximately 55 plays in the Schenectady area.

Thespians' Reunion Slated Tonight

Dr. Michael Tytko will speak at the 20-year reunion of the former Maska Dramatic Club dinner which will be held at 6:30 tonight at the PNA Hall. Also, on the program, speakers will include Lucyan Sekowski, former president of the club and Joseph Czyzewski and Stanley Zych former directors of the numerous plays and productions put on by the organization.

An exhibit of play programs, pictures, news articles, bulletins, and scrapbooks will be on display for the former members to glance through.

The committee planning the events are Lucyan Sekowski, chairman, Leon Marcinek, Stanley Zych, Joseph Czyzewski, Mrs. John Olwert and Mrs. Stanley Zych.

1980 – Report in the Scrapbook

The following page shows a report written by Sophie Korycinski Zych; apparently prepared for a newspaper. It is not known if a reunion was held the next year.

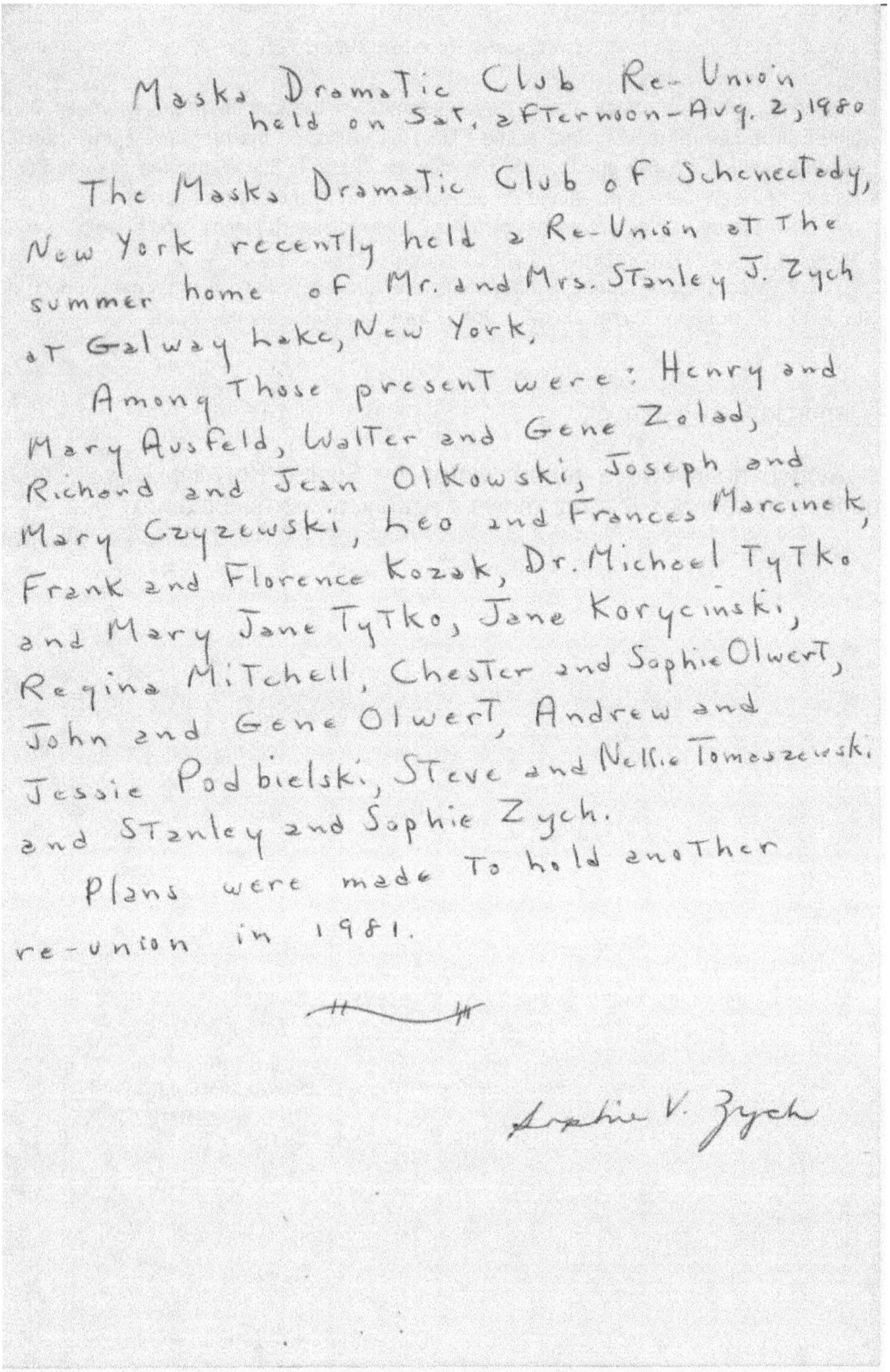

Maska Dramatic Club Re-Union
held on Sat. afternoon - Aug. 2, 1980

The Maska Dramatic Club of Schenectady, New York recently held a Re-Union at the summer home of Mr. and Mrs. Stanley J. Zych at Galway Lake, New York.

Among those present were: Henry and Mary Ausfeld, Walter and Gene Zolad, Richard and Jean Olkowski, Joseph and Mary Czyzewski, Leo and Frances Marcinek, Frank and Florence Kozak, Dr. Michael Tytko and Mary Jane Tytko, Jane Korycinski, Regina Mitchell, Chester and Sophie Olwert, John and Gene Olwert, Andrew and Jessie Podbielski, Steve and Nellie Tomaszewski, and Stanley and Sophie Zych.

Plans were made to hold another re-union in 1981.

Sophie V. Zych

Figure 26: Report from the 1980 reunion of Maska, Scrapbook.

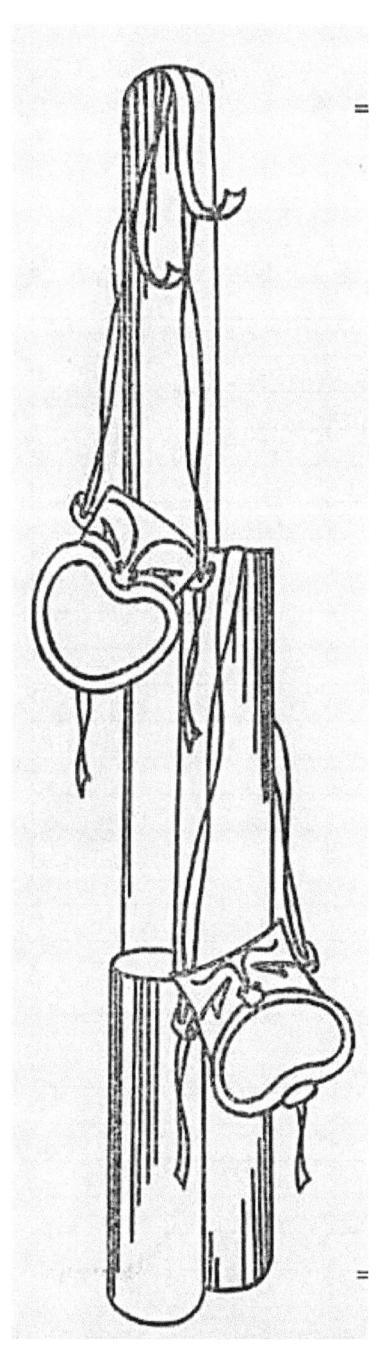

APPENDIX 1

LIST OF

MASKA

MEMBERS

Appendix 1: List of Maska Members

Note that the Polish last and first names do not use Polish diacritical signs, that were lost after the immigration to the U.S. For instance, the spelling of Sękowski was changed to Sekowski in most, but not all source documents.

Andrzejewski	Eleanor
Ausfeld	Genevieve
Ausfeld	Henry
Bachleda	Stanley
Balska	L.
Bankowski	Arthur
Baranowski	Chester
Baranowski	Frank
Beleusz	Florentyna
Belniak	John
Bienkuski	Joseph
Bojarski	Chester
Bonczyk	William
Borkowski	Frank
Borowski	Celia
Briskie	George W. Jr.
Brzostek	Jane
Brzostowski	Irene
Brzozowski	Zygmunt
Budka	Mary
Budnick	Daniel V.
Budnick	Mrs.
Byleusz	Florence
Chantnicka	Regina
Chatnicka	Virginia
Chmielinski	Vincent
Chojnicki	Sophie
Chylinski	Stephanie
Czechowicz	Joseph
Czyszczon	J.
Czyszczon	Theodore
Czyzewski	Joseph
Czyzewski	Mary
Deptola	Victor
Deptula	Bronislaw / Bernie
Dlugosinski	Jane
Dmochowski	Agnes
Dombkowski	Wilma

Drapala	Joseph
Drzewczynski	Alice
Dzierwa	Aleksander / Alexander
Dzierwa	Frank
Dziuba	Jean
Dziuba	Marianna / Mary / Marja
Dziuba	Helen
Fall	Josephine
Garrut	Miss J.
Garrut	Wanda
Giniecka	Mrs. S.
Giniecka	Regina
Giniecki	Clementine
Giniecki	Stanley
Godlewski	Edward
Godlewski	Joseph
Godlewski	Jadwiga / Hedwig
Godlewski	Reggie
Golembiowski	Raymond
Golembiowski	Stanley
Golembiowski	Wanda
Gontarski	Rozalia / Rose
Gorski	Casimira
Grabowski	Stanley
Grodkiewicz	Wadsworth
Gurzynski	Edward
Gutowska	Sabina
Harasimowicz	Francis
Hennel	Edward
Hennel	Henry
Hennel	Wanda
Jablonski	John
Jankowski	Pauline
Józefowicz	Henrietta
Kacinski/Kaczynski	Stephen
Kaminski	Helen
Karpinski	Stanley
Kilian	Helen
Kilian	Thaddeus
Kilian	Zygmunt
Kleysmyt	Henry
Klimas	Daniel
Klonowski	Monica
Kopec	Anthony
Kopec	Eugene
Korycinski	Alexander
Korycinski	Sophie

Korycinski	Wanda
Krystofik	Adam
Kuty	Eugene
Kwiecinski	Edward
Kwiecinski	Steven
Lake	Patricia
Laniewski	Casimir
Laniewski	John
Lemanski	Helen
Lemanski	Irene
Lewkowicz	Henry
Lewkowicz	Stefania / Stephanie
Lisowicz	Joanna / Joan
Mackiewicz	Agnes
Mackiewicz	Florence
Marcinek	Leo
Moros	Wladyslawa / Gladys
Mozejko	George
Nisiobencki	Jean
Noskowiak	Theodore
Nowicki	Alice
Nowicki	Irene
Okonski	Louis
Okonski	Pearl
Olkowski	Ryszard / Richard
Olszewski	Klement / Clement
Olwert	Chester
Ozarowski	Matthew
Patka	Stefania
Penichter	Jessie
Penichter	Miss C.
Petera	Stanley
Petera / Peters/Pitera	Nellie
Pieszczoch	Agnes
Piurowska	Eleonora
Plath	V.W.
Platt	Wladyslaw / Victor
Plocharczyk	Marion
Plocharczyk	Stanley
Plocharczyk	Val
Podbielski	Andrew
Rekucki	Arlene
Repka	Edward
Roiski	
Romanowski	Joseph
Rudowski	Gladys
Rudowski	J. Czeslaw / Chester / Joseph C.

Sarnowski	Arthur
Sekowski	Lucian
Sekowski	Walter
Sekowski	Zenon
Siaskiewicz	Clementine
Skrzynski	Stefan
Stelmach	Genevieve
Szatkowski	Genowefa / Genevieve
Szumachowski	Bernard
Szumigala	Vera
Szwergel	Irene
Szymanowski	Julia
Szymanska	Waleria / Valerie
Szymanski	Carl
Szymanski	Karol
Szymanski	Marja / Mary
Toniszewski	Mrs. Eleanor
Tupacz	Jane
Tyminska	Eugenia
Tytko	Michael
Tytko	Roberta
Wanik	Liljanna / Lillian
Wienclawski	Henry
Wisniewska	Helen
Wisniewski	Zygmunt
Witkowski	Irena / Irene
Wojtulewicz	John
Wojtulewicz	Stanislawa / Statia
Wrazen	Jane
Zablocki	Sadie
Zborowski	Mary
Zielanis	Gertrude
Zielanis	John
Zielanis	Mrs. R.
Zielinska	Irene
Zolad	Walter
Zych	Matthew
Zych	Stanley

APPENDIX 2

LIST OF

MASKA

PATRONS

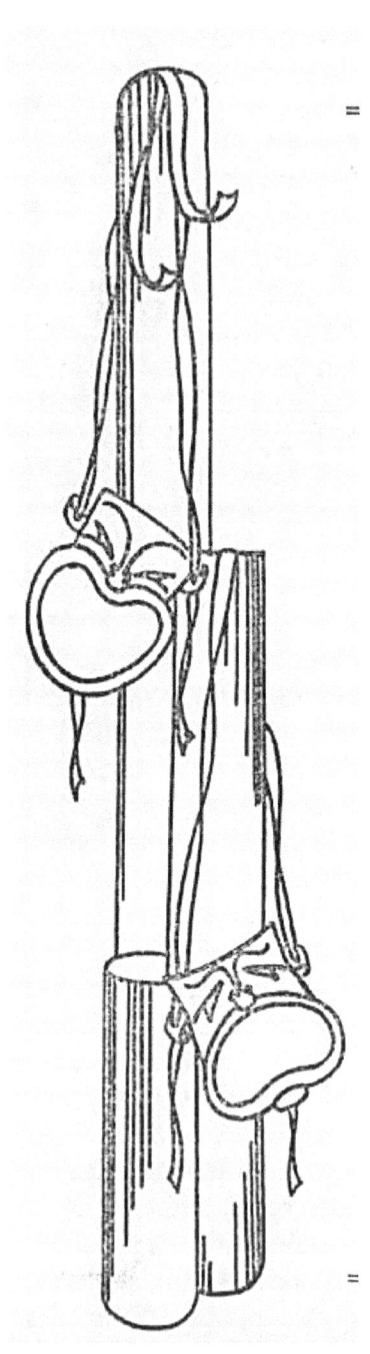

Appendix 2
List of Maska Patrons, 1933-1942

Mr. & Mrs.	Anthony	Adach
Mrs.	Julia	Ambrozik
Mr. & Mrs.	A.K.	Andrzejewski
	Wallace	Armour
Mr. & Mrs.	Walter	Ausfeld
	Peter	Bala
Mrs.	Mary	Barczewski
Mrs.	Antonia	Bartkowska
Mrs.	Stanley	Bartosiewicz
Dr.	Aloysius	Bednarkiewicz
	W. T.	Bednarkiewicz
	John	Beleuz
Mr. & Mrs.	Stanley	Belniak
	John	Bialkowski
	Anthony	Bielecki
Mrs.	Stanley	Bielecki
Mr. & Mrs.	Casimir	Bienkunski
	Joseph	Bietka
Mrs.	Frances	Bonczyk
Mrs.	Julia	Borczak
Miss	Irene	Borowska
Mrs.	Wladyslawa	Borowska
Mr. & Mrs.	John	Borowski
Mr. & Mrs.	A. S.	Browka
	Charles A.	Brundage
Mr. & Mrs.	A. B.	Brzozowski
Mr. & Mrs.	Michael	Brzozowski
Mr. & Mrs.	Daniel	Budnik
	John	Budynas
Mrs.	Genevieve	Bursiewicz
Mrs.	Victoria	Bursiewicz
Mrs.	Mary	Ceglersk
Mrs.	Natalie	Chlewinski
	Vincent	Chmielinski
Mrs.	Anna	Chociej
Mrs.	F.	Chojnicka
Mr. & Mrs.	Stanley	Chojnicki
	Paul	Christian
Mrs.	Antonia	Chylinski
Miss	Genevieve	Chylinski
Miss	Helen	Cichy
Mrs.	Victoria	Cichy

Mrs.	Henry	Ciembroniewicz
	John	Cieplinski
	Casimir	Cmielinski
	David	Cohn
	Morris Marshall	Cohn
Dr.	Edmund	Colby
Mr. & Mrs.	Robert	Cox
	Stanley	Czaster
	Jacob	Czechowicz
	J.	Czyzewski
	Walter	Daszewski
Mr. & Mrs.	John	Deptula
Mrs.	Walter	Dereszewski
	Lewiss B.	Dewk
	Joseph A.	Dick
	Joseph A.	D'Jimas
Mrs.	Stanley	Dlugosinski
Mrs.	Agnes	Dmochowski
Mrs.	F. S.	Dmochowski
	Frank	Dmochowski
	Casper	Dobrocinski
Mr. & Mrs.	Joseph	Drapala
		Drewczynska
	Joseph	Drzewiecki
Miss	Helen	Duszynski
Miss	Gertrude	Dwojakowski
Miss	Jane	Dwojakowski
Dr. & Mrs.	Myron J.	Dybich
	Walter	Dziegelewski
Mrs.	Agnes	Dziengielewski
	Wladyslaw	Dziengielewski
Mrs.	Eva	Dziuba
Mrs.	Julia	Dziuba
	John	Falkowski
Mrs.	Anna	Faluszczak
	Nicholas	Ferraro
	Leon	Florkiewicz
	Edward	Frantzke
Mrs.	Mary	Galka
	Wladyslaw	Galkiewicz
	Joseph A.	Gallup
	Zygmunt	Garbowski
	Carroll A.	Gardiner
Mrs.	Jane	Garkowski
Mrs.	Stanislawa	Gasowska
Mr. & Mrs.	Walter	Gasowski
Mrs.	Benjamin	Ginejt

Mr. & Mrs.	Anthony	Giniecki
Mr. & Mrs.	Stanley	Giniecki
Miss	Helen	Ginteski
	Wladyslaw / Walter	Gnara
	Alexander	Godlewski
Mrs.	Francis	Godlewski
	Frank	Godlewski
	John	Golembiewski
	?	Gorecka
Mrs.	Helen	Goszewski
Mrs.	Walter	Goszewski
Mrs.	Sophie	Grabicki
	S. E.	Grabowski
	George A.	Graves
Mr. & Mrs.	Wadsworth	Grodkiewicz
Mrs.	Jane	Grubalski
Mrs.	Anthony	Grzywaczewski
Miss	Sophie	Grzywna
Mrs.	Sophie	Guziak
	Stanley	Gwiazdowski
	Joseph	Gzyms
Mrs.	Catherine	Harasimowicz
	Oswald D.	Heck
	Carl	Heisler
Mr. & Mrs.	Felix	Hennel
	Theodore	Herman
	Victoria	Herman
	Chester	Hibner
Mr. & Mrs.	Stanley	Hilderbrand
	Joseph	Holland
	Stephen	Hombkowski
	Anthony	Hughes
	William	Jackson
Mr. & Mrs.	Benjamin	Jakubowski
	Stanley	Janiszewski
Mrs.	John	Jankowski
Mrs.	Stanley	Jankowski
Miss	Theresa	Jankowski
Mrs.	Stanley	Jaroszewski
	T.	Jaroszewska
Miss	Isabelle	Jarvis
Mrs.	Jozefa	Jerozalska
Mrs.	Anna	Job
Mrs.	Marya	Jozefewicz
	Joseph	Jozwiak
Miss	Wladyslawa	Justin
	Joseph	Juwa

Mrs.	Anna	Kalinowski
Miss	H.	Kaminska
Mr. & Mrs.	Lucas	Kania
Mrs.	Victoria	Kania
	Stanley	Karwowski
Mrs.	Benjamin	Kaszubska
	B. J.	Kazyaka
Mr. & Mrs.	Henry	Kercul
Mrs.	Rose	Kidalowski
	Marion	Kiedzis
Mrs.	R. J.	Kietlinski
Mr. & Mrs.	John	Kilian
Dr.	B. H.	Kirschberg
	Anthony	Kislowski
Miss	Helen	Klarman
Mrs.	Sophie	Klarman
Mrs.	Mary	Klebonas
Mrs.	Uda	Klebonas
	F. C.	Klein
Mr. & Mrs.	Walter	Kleismyt
Mrs.	Anna	Klimas
	Adam	Klimowicz
Mr. & Mrs.	Wladyslaw	Kokierniak
Mrs.	Anna	Konieczna
Mr. & Mrs.	Andrew	Kopeć
Mrs.	Ida	Kopeć
Mr. & Mrs.	Stanley	Korkosz
Dr.	Aloysius	Korniejewski
Mr. & Mrs.	Peter	Korycinski
	Frank	Kosinski
Mr. & Mrs.	Stanley	Kosinski
Mrs.	Anna	Kostek
Miss	Jane	Kostek
	Tadeusz	Kostyniak
Mrs.	Anna	Kowalski
Mrs.	Helen	Kowalski
Mrs.	Victoria	Kowalski
	Antoni	Kozlowski
	Edward	Krajewski
Mrs.	Frances	Krasnowski
	Stanley	Krasnowski
	Kazimierz	Krasucki
Mrs.	Mary	Krempa
	Benjamin	Kuczynski
Mrs.	Victoria	Kulczyk
	Hipolit	Kuty
Mrs.	Hipolit	Kwiatkowski

Mrs.	Pauline	Lachanski
Mrs.	Agnes	Lalak
Mr. & Mrs.	Bernard	Laniewski
Mrs.	Catherine	Laniewski
Mrs.	Victoria	Laniewski
Mrs.	Sophie	Lastkowski
Mr. & Mrs.	Stephen	Lazinski
Mrs.	Eleanor	Lemanski
	Frank	Leszczynski
	Walter	Lesiakowski
	Roman	Lesniewski
	Frank	Leszczynski
	Richard	Levy
Mrs.	Peter	Lewandowski
	Peter	Lewandowski
Mr. & Mrs.	Blazej	Lewkowicz
Mr. & Mrs.	Henry	Lewkowicz
	W. J.	Lillis
Mrs.	Mary	Lisinski
Mrs.	Anna	Lisowicz
Mrs.	Josephine	Listkowski
Mrs.	J. J.	Lobel
	Anthony	Lubrant
Miss	Jane	Lukasiewicz
Mrs.	John	Lukasiewicz
	Joseph	Lukasiewicz
Mr. & Mrs.	B. K.	Luniewski
	Charles	Lynch
	James C.	MacDonald
Mrs.	Bernice	Maciag
Mrs.	John	Majchrowicz
	Andrzej	Makowski
Mrs.	Theresa	Malecki
	Andrew	Malewicz
Miss	Gertrude	Malewicz
	Walter	Malicki
	Edward	Malik
Mrs.	Eleanor	Maliszewski
Miss	Wanda	Mankiewicz
Mrs.	Mary	Marchewka
Mrs.	J. V.	Marcinek
Mr. & Mrs.	Stanley	Marcinek
Miss	Berta	Marcinkiewicz
	Czeslaw	Marcinkiewicz
	Theodore	Marcinkiewicz
Mrs.	John	Marcinkowski
Mrs.	Theresa	Maslanka

	John	Matson
Mrs.	Agnes	Max
Dr. & Mrs.	Bruno C.	Mazurowski
Mrs.	Mary	Milczarek
Mrs.	Stanley	Milosek
Miss	Lillian	Mioducki
Mrs.	John	Miszkutowicz
		Mloda Polska - Society
	J. A.	Monaco
	Edward	Morawski
Mr. & Mrs.	John	Morawski
Mrs.	Rozalja	Moros
	Edward	Murawski
	John	Nienaltowski
	Anthony	Nosal
	John	Nosal
	Theodore	Noskowiak
Mrs.	Ida	Nowicki
	Frank	Nowinski
	John	Nowobielski
Mrs.	Bernice	Nowoczynski
	Joseph	Nusbaum
Mrs.	Cecelia	Obremski
	Franciszek	Odasz
	Adam	Ogonowscy [Plural]
Mr. & Mrs.	Casimir	Ogonowski
Mr. & Mrs.	Thaddeus	Ogonowski
	John	Ogrodnik
	Louise	Okonski
	Walter	Okonski
	Walter	Olechnowicz
Mrs.	Anna	Olender
	Joseph	Olkowski
	John	Olwert
Mrs.	Antoinette	Onisk
Mrs.	Joseph	Pachucki
	Joseph	Padula
Mrs.	Mary	Pajerski
Mrs.	Catherine	Palaszewski
Mrs.	Sophie	Palaszewski
Mrs.	Anna	Parsley
	John	Pastorczyk
	Walter	Pastorczyk
	Walter	Patton
Mr. & Mrs.	Michael	Paurowski
Mrs.	Sophie	Pawlowicz
Mr. & Mrs.	Michael	Penichter

Mrs.	John	Pentkowski
	Pawel	Perkowski
Mrs.	Mary	Peszel
Mr. & Mrs.	Stanley	Petera
Mrs.	Gertrude	Pieszczoch
Miss	Mary	Pieszczoch
Mr. & Mrs.	Paul	Pieszczoch
Mrs.	H. W.	Pietrzykowski
	?	Piotrowski
Mrs.	M.	Pitera
Mrs.	Konstanty	Piurowski
	Anthony	Platt
Mrs.	Boleslaw	Plocharczyk
Mrs.	Stanley	Plocharczyk
	Matthias P.	Poersch
Mr. & Mrs.	Chester	Pokrzywnicki
	Stanislawa	Pokrzywnicki
		Prawda i Praca – [Truth and Work] Newspaper
Mrs.	Henrietta	Predel
Mrs.	F.	Prewencka
Mrs.	Frances	Prewenski
Miss	S. E.	Prusko
Mr. & Mrs.	Henry	Przybylek
	W. D.	Przybylek
	F. K.	Quirini
Mrs.	Mary	Quirini
Mr. & Mrs.	John	Rakoski
	Jacob	Rekucki
	M. A.	Rekucki
Mr. & Mrs.	Felix	Repka
	John	Riddervold
	?	Roach
Mrs.	Bernice	Rogowicz
Mrs.	Anna	Roszkowski
Mrs.	John	Rowna
	Mr.	Rudkowski
Mrs.	Eugenia	Rupinski
Mrs.	Bernard	Ruszczynski
	Frank	Rutkowski
Mrs.	Josephine	Rutkowski
Miss	Anna	Rykowski
Mrs.	Cecelia	Sadlowski
	Joseph	Sammler
Mrs.	Antonia	Saniewska
	C. V.	Sarnacki
	Arthur	Sarnowski
	K. C.	Sarnowski

	Frank	Sasinowski
	John	Sauls
	Zygmunt	Sawaniewski
	R.	Szczepanski
Mr. & Mrs.	Gustav	Sekowski
	Frank	Semerad
Mrs.	Francis	Sendlewski
	Peter	Siudyla
Mrs.	John	Skiba
Mrs.	Frances	Skowronski
Mr. & Mrs.	Stephen	Skrzynski
Mrs.	Catherine	Skumurski
	Frank	Slowakiewicz
	Frank	Smith
	Stanley	Sobieski
Mr. & Mrs.	Stephen	Sobieski
Miss	Alexander	Sokolowski
Mrs.	Julian	Sokoaowski
	Z.	Sowaniewski
Mrs.	John	Srocinski
	F. E.	Stafford
Mrs.	Sophie	Stankiewicz
Mr. & Mrs.	Joseph	Stelmach
	Anthony	Stempkowski
Mrs.	John	Stepnowski
Mr. & Mrs.	Chester	Strenkowski
	Anthony	Strycharz
Mr. & Mrs.	Walter	Stuczynski
Mrs.	Catherine	Styczynski
	Frank	Supergan
	Frank	Surowiec
	A.	Swetkowski
Mrs.	Mary	Swetkowski
Mr. & Mrs.	T. E.	Swiecicki
		Swoboda - Newspaper
Mrs.	K. S.	Szafranski
	Konstanty	Szalewski
Mrs.	Helena	Szargiewicz
Mrs.	Antonia	Szatkowska
Mrs.	Anna	Szczepanski
	Richard	Szczepanski
Mrs.	Catherine	Szejka
	Stanley	Szpak
Mrs.	Rose	Szumska
Mrs.	Benjamin	Szyjkowski
	J. J.	Szymalak
Mrs.	Anna	Szymanski

	Bernard	Szymanski	
	Frank	Tadeuszak	
Mrs.	Vincent	Tanski	
Miss	Mary	Tendzigolski	
Mrs.	Eleanor	Tracki	
	Edmund	Trojanowski	
	Michael	Trojanowski	
Mrs.	Sonja	Trypaluk	
Mrs.	John	Tulaszewicz	
Mrs.	Helen	Turski	
Mr. & Mrs.	Stanley	Tytko	
	Chester	Urbanski	
Miss	Jane	Urbanski	
	Ralph J.	Ury	
Mrs.	Zofia	Wajda	
Mr. & Mrs.	Andrew	Wanik	
Mrs.	Anna	Wesolowski	
Mrs.	Jane	Wesolowski	
	John	Wicks	
	Chester	Wieczorek	
	Walter	Wielebinski	
Mrs.	Frank	Wierzbowski	
Mrs.	Frances	Wirpsza	
Mrs.	Walter	Wirpsza	
Mr. & Mrs.	Boleslaw	Wisniak	
Mrs.	Adam	Wisniewska	
Mrs.	Anna	Wisniewski	
	Zygmunt	Wisniewski	
Mr. & Mrs.	F. S.	Witkowski	
	Joseph	Witkowski	
Mrs.	Mary	Witkowski	
Mr. & Mrs.	Caspar	Wojcicki	
Mrs.	Mary	Wojs	
	Edward	Wojtal	
	Stephen	Wolongiewicz	
Mrs.	Paul	Wrazen	
Mr. & Mrs.	Antoni	Wroblewski	
Mrs.	Eleanor	Wyszomierski	
	John	Zablocki	
Mrs.	Walter	Zalewski	
Mr. & Mrs.	J.	Zalucey (Zalucki?)	
Mr. & Mrs.	Joseph	Zalucki	
Mrs.	Mary	Zazula	
Mrs.	Anna	Zborowski	
	John	Zdrodowski	
	Robert	Zeglen	
		Zgoda - Newspaper	

Mr. & Mrs.	John	Zielanis
Mrs.	Louise	Zielinski
	Paul	Zielinski
Mrs.	Sarah	Ziobrowski
	Walter	Ziobrowski
	Daniel	Zmyslowski
	G. T.	Zurn
	Anthony	Zwolinski
	Anthony	Zwolski
	Joseph	Zych
Mrs.	Rozalia	Zych
Mrs.	Anna	Zywot

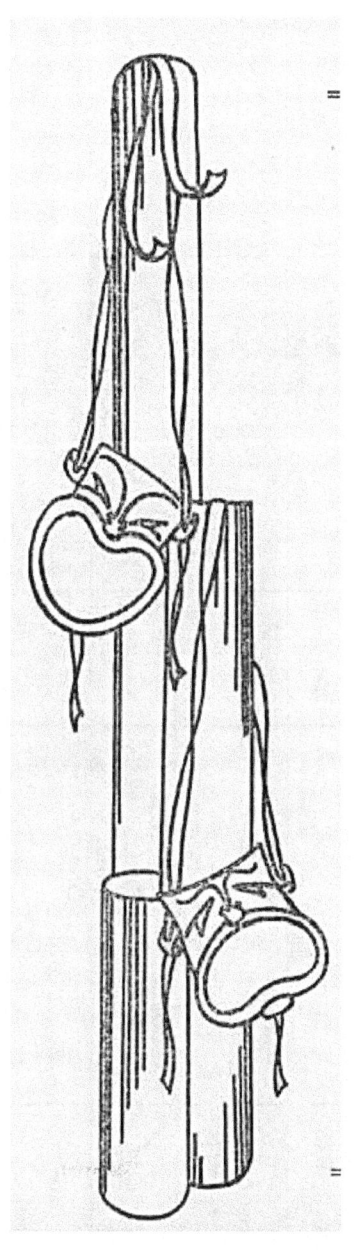

APPENDIX 3

CHART OF

MASKA

PLAYS &

TIMELINE

Appendix 3

MASKA DRAMATIC CIRCLE – LIST OF PLAYS AND TIMELINE

Season	Date	Polish Title	English Translation	Number of Acts & Play Type	Playwright	Comments
1933	April 1933	Gra Karciana	The Card Game	Two skits		First program, Szczerpanski's Hall, performed by Maska members
1933-1934 *1	Sunday, November 1, 1933	Znawca Kobiet	Connoisseur of Women	One Act	Zygmunt Przybilski (Przybylski; 1856-1909), prolific Polish author of popular comedies	First performance at PNA Hall – Polish Home
1933-1934 *	Sunday, November 1, 1933	Słowiczek	Nightingale	One Act Operetta	A. Belzy	
1933-1934	Sunday, December 10, 1933	Cacusia	Plaything	One Act Operetta	Stanislaw (Stanley) Zenon Wachtel (1887-1959) a very prominent actor and playwright[2]	Cacusia Operetka w jednym akcie. Published in 1915 with music by M.A. Rozycki, 46p.
1933-1934	Sunday, December 10, 1933	Preludium Chopina	Chopin's Prelude in C Minor	One Act Drama		
1933-1934	Sunday, December 10, 1933	Stryj Przyjechał	Uncle Arrived	One Act Comedy	Count Władysław Koziebrodzki (1839-1893), Polish writer, politician, and community activist from Galicia.[3]	The play was published in 1900, 80p.[4]

[1] Program marked with an asterisk * is in Appendix 4 and the Program marked with a pound sign # is in one of Maska Buletyns, Appendix 5.
[2] Information from Dr. Karen Majewski, email of February 19, 2016. For additional information and Wachtel's biography, see: http://www.poles.org/db/w_names/Wachtel_SZ.html
[3] Information from Dr. Karen Majewski, email of February 19, 2016.
[4] Information from Dr. Karen Majewski, email of February 19, 2016.

1933-1934	Non-Maska Program		Vaudeville	WGY Players "Skip Step and Anna"	First program of the year followed by dance
1933-1934	Gruby Szkandal	Great Scandal	Three Acts Comedy		Included two older actors
1933-1934	Title Unknown	Title unknown	Skit		Portrays the domestic differences in a family where the husband is inclined to be a partaker of strong beverages
1934		Historical drama in honor of the late Marshal Pilsudski	One Act Drama		"Poles to Honor Joseph Pilsudski"
May 27, 1934; Play contest *	Pierwszy Bal	The First Ball	One Act	Zygmunt Przybylski	Three group contest; performed in 3 cities
May 27, 1934 Play contest *	O.S.S., Or The Marriage Portion	The Marriage Portion	One Act		Three group contest; performed in 3 cities
May 27, 1934; Play contest *	Kokusia	Fledgling	One Act	Pobratym	Three group contest; performed in 3 cities
1934-1935 *	W Zielonym Gaiku	In the Dell	One Act	Zygmunt Przybylski	
1934-1935 *	Tatuś Pozwolił	Papa Permits	One Act	Gustaw Mozer, [in Polish translation by A. Walewski]	Popular play translated from German, published in 1882, reprint 1889 in Lwów, Galicia; in a series Library for Amateur Theaters, no. 23; published by Gazeta Narodowa
1934-1935 *	Żywy Nieboszczyk	The Live Ghost	One Act	Gustaw Belly	Stanley Zych's first play

_{dates column note:} Maska Sunday May 27, 1934 / Literary Circle of Albany, NY Sunday May 27, 1934 / Amateur Circle of Amsterdam, NY Sunday May 27, 1934 / Sunday, September 16, 1934 (rows 5–10 respectively — January 14, 1934; March 4, 1934; March 4, 1934; March ~19, 1934 for rows 1–4)

1934-1935 *	Sunday, November 18, 1934	*Radcy Pana Radcy*	Councilor of Mr. Councilman	Three Act	Michał Bałucki (1837-1901), well-known Polish playwright, novelist, and poet, author of 12 novels and over 10 comedies and satirical plays	Written in 1867
1934-1935 *	Sunday, December 16, 1934	*W Pułapce*	Trapped	One Act	Alfa = Joseph Czyzewski, Maska member	Original by a Maska member
1934-1935 *	Sunday, December 16, 1934	*Przygody Małżeńskie w Podróży Poślubnej*	Adventures on a Honeymoon	One Act	Antoni Jax (1850-1926), popular Polish-American playwright, based in Chicago since 1889	
1934-1935 *	Sunday, December 16, 1934	*Błazen*	The Jester	One Act	Aleksander Świętochowski (1849-1938), famous Polish novelist and playwright, leader of the Positivism movement	
1934-1935 *	Sunday, February 3, 1935	*Małżeństwo na Probę*	Marriage on Trial (Trial Marriage)	Three Act	Francis Wysocki, contemporary Polish playwright who is a master of comedy.	
1934-1935 *	Sunday, March 24, 1935	*Wet za Wet*	An Eye for An Eye	One Act	Marja Finklówna	Full title: *Małżeński spisek, czyli Wet za wet, komedja w 1 akcie*, adapted from a French play; performed in Poland in 1922 and 1935
1934-1935 *	Sunday, March 24, 1935	*Kalosze*	Galoshes	One Act Comedy	Aleksander Fredro (1793-1876), the greatest comedy writer of the 19th century in Poland	Fredro's masterful plays and poems form the core of Polish literature: comedy and poems for children
1934-1935 *	Sunday, March 24, 1935	*Straszna Ciotunia*	The Terrible Aunt	Three Act	Ary Jawycz	End of first subscription season; 11 plays, 38 players; majority were "comedies of a farcical nature." 4/12/35

	Date	Polish Title	English Title	Type	Author	Notes
1935-1936 *	Sunday, October 6, 1935	*Krewniak z Ameryki*	*Relative from America*	One Act Comedy	Marja Gerson Dąbrowska (1869-1942), Polish writer, painter and sculptor; author of many plays for youth	
1935-1936 *	Sunday, October 6, 1935	*Generalna Próba*	*Dress Rehearsal*	One Act Farce	W. Roart	
1935-1936 *	Sunday, November 17, 1935	*Na Bezrybiu i Rak Ryba*	*Catching Fish without Fishing*	One Act	Karol N. Wachtel, Polish-American playwright, based in Chicago, editor of *Dziennik chicagoski*, brother of writer Stanisław.[5]	Over 400 attend Maska's first plays; Stage Personality Contest begins
1935-1936 *	Sunday, November 17, 1935	*Szpytal Warjatów*	*Hospital for the Insane*	One Act	Eugène Scribe (1791 – 1861) French playwright and librettist of operas; with Auguste Augustin, popular Romanticist dramatists of the early 19th century; Adapted from the French	Acrobatic Act; Contest continues
1935	Sunday, December 1, 1935	*Cud na Jasnej Górze*	*Miracle on Clear Mountain*		Jakub Stefan Zieliński, a Polish playwright, also widely performed in Polonia.[6]	Dramatic Circle of St. Mary's Church presents its first play, *Miracle on Clear Mountain*
1935-1936 *	Sunday, December 15, 1935	*Peruka Professora*	*Professor's Wig*	Comedy, Farce	Anthony Jax	350 spectators witness Polish Plays
1935-1936 *	Sunday, December 15, 1935	*Pokój Do Wynajęcia*	*Room To Rent*	Comedy, Farce	Popławski and Golański, the latter probably Wacław Golański, a prominent actor and radio personality active in Detroit.[7]	
1935-1936 *	Sunday, February 2, 1936	*Ciotka Karola*	*Charlie's Aunt*	Three Acts; Comedy	T. Brandon	

[5] Information from Dr. Karen Majewski, email of February 19, 2016.
[6] Ibidem.
[7] Ibidem.

1936	February 1936				A Card Party and Entertainment is planned for St. Valentine's Day.	First newsletter as gift at card party
1935-1936 *	March 29, 1936	*Koszyk Kwiatów or Los Sieroty*	*A Basket of Flowers or Fate of the Orphan*	Three Acts Melodrama	Adapted from a story by X Schmider by Joseph Chociszewski	Polish village life; Tense drama of human faith and suffering occurring in Poland in 1858.
1936	May 21, 1936	N/A	*N/A [General Electric Jubilee Parade]*			General Electric Jubilee Parade; Maska float was entered by the Polish Welfare Council; won the first prize.
1936-1937	October 25, 1936	*Niewinność Zwycięża*	*Innocence Conquers*	Five Acts		Translated from English into Polish; based on Polish village life.
1936-1937 *	Sunday, December 3, 1936	*Straszna Noc*	*Terrible Night*	Three Acts Mystery / Farce	ZAZ	Polish adaptation of an American mystery farce; Tajemnica Komedja;
1936-1937 *	February 21, 1937	*Kobieta Znika*	*A Woman Disappears*	Three Acts Farce	J. Zawistowski	Adaptation from an American Farce; Sophie Korycinska's first appearance; Stanley Zych also in play; cat in cast; 500 people attend.
1937-1938	November 28, 1937	*Djabel z Monoklem*	*Devil With a Monocle*		Written by Maska member Zygmort Brzozowski aka Zigmont / Sigmond Artoni.	The plot centers around an ingenious method of smuggling contraband into Poland from Nazi Germany.
1937-1938	March 6, 1938	*Śmieszna Głupota*	*Comical Goofiness*	Farce		Adaptation from the American stage
1937-1938	April 3, 1938	*Trudy i Troski*	*Cares & Worries*			A true to life adaptation from an American play portraying the financial and social worries of a WPA worker and his family.
1938-1939 *	October 9, 1938	*Legjonista na Polu Chwały*	*Legionnaire on the Field of Honor*	Six Acts; Tragedy	Antoni Jax	Based on the action of the Polish Legions on the Eastern Front in 1916. Commemoration of the 29th anniversary of

					Declaration of Polish Independence by the Warsaw Committee.
1938-1939 #	Sunday, December 4, 1938	*Prędka Robota*	*Quick Work*	Three Acts Comedy	Adaptation from the American Stage
1938-1939	April 23, 1939	*Pazura*	*The Claw*	Comedy-mystery	Playwright Maska member Zygmont Brozowski a.k.a. Zygmort / Sigmond Antoni
1939	June 25, 1939				Maska Semi-Formal at the Bohemian Tavern
1939	July 27, 1939				Maska Jamboree PNA enclosed fairgrounds.
1939-1940 #	Sunday, December 10, 1939	*Na Naszej Glebie*	*On Our Soil*	Two Acts Melodrama	Anna Karwatowa, nee Bardzka (1854-1932), a Polish poet and playwright, author of many educational plays, staged by amateur theaters in Poland and abroad[8]	2 comedies of Polish urban life on the 1920s in Warsaw and in Poznań. Full title: *Na naszej glebie Obrazek ludowy w dwóch aktach ze śpiewami*, published in 1894, reprinted in 1908, 1909, and 1928.
1939-1940	Sunday, February 18, 1940	*Pożycz Mi swej Żony*	*Lend Me Your Wife*	Two Acts Farce	Maurice Desvallières (1857–1926), French author of comedies, used in many film scripts in the 1930s	
1939-1940	Sunday, February 18, 1940	*Końska Kuracja*	*The Horse Cure*	One Act Comedy	Cyril Danielewski	
1939-1940	Sunday, April 6, 1940	*Słodkie i Pierne*	*The Bitter and the Sweet*	One Act Comedy	Joseph Czyzewski, Maska member	Daily life of a family in the Mont Pleasant area of Schenectady.
1939-1940	Sunday, April 6, 1940	*Kandydatura Soliwody*	*Soliwoda Runs for Alderman*	Farce		Trials and tribulations of a Polish-American citizen who is a candidate in a municipal election.
1940-1941	Sunday,	*Katarzyna w*	*Catherine Goes*	Three	Jakub Stefan Zieliński, a Polish	Published in 1938, 64 pages.

[8] Information added by Dr. Maja Trochimczyk, email of February 19, 2016.

#		Sądzie	to Court	Acts	playwright, popular in Polonia communities.[9]	
1941		Tryouts		Comedy		Open to anyone with a reading knowledge of Polish language.
1940-1941	Sunday, February 2, 1941	Cudze Piórka	Borrowed Feathers	Three Acts Folk Comedy	Józef Jarem-Mirski, Polish author of patriotic plays published in Poland in late 1930s.	Polish village life before the present war – summer 1938.
1940-1941	Sunday, February 2, 1941	Zazdrość	Jealousy	One Act Novelty sketch		
1941-1942	Sunday, December 7, 1941	Trudy i Troski	Difficulties and Concerns	Comedy		Story of an average family. **NOTE: Someone came into the auditorium and announced that Pearl Harbor had been bombed.**
1941-1942	Sunday, March 29, 1942	Wet za Wet	An Eye for an Eye		Marja Finklówna	Full title: *Małżeński spisek, czyli Wet za wet, komedja w 1 akcie*, adapted from a French play.

---

[9] Information from Dr. Karen Majewski, email of February 19, 2016.

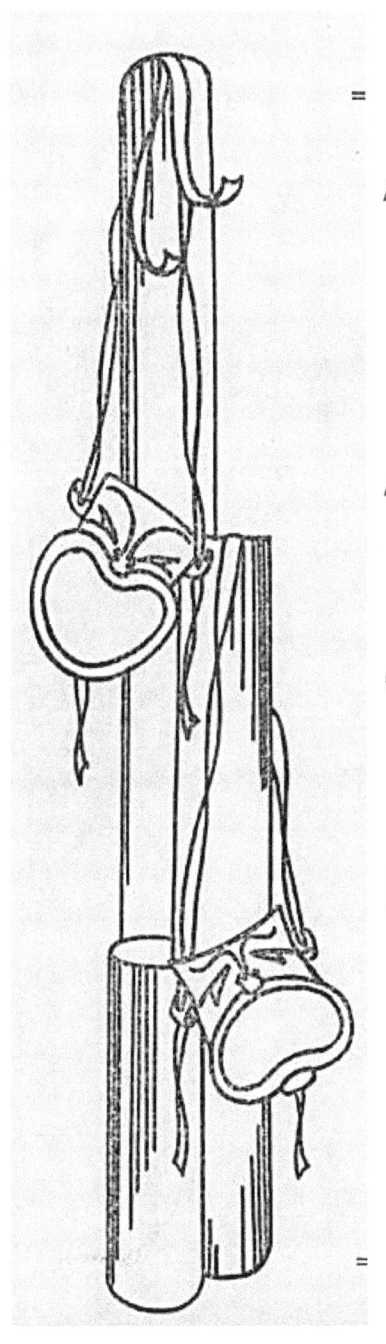

Appendix 4

A Sample of Maska Programs

1933, November 1

First Performance

"Maska"
Dramatic Circle
Presents Two One Act Plays

In the auditorium
of the Polish Home
Council No. 53

Sunday, November 1st, 1933

Pierwsze Przedstawienie

"MASKA"
KÓŁKO DRAMATYCZNE
WYSTAWIA DWIE JEDNOAKTÓWKI

W AUDYTORJUM DOMU POLSKIEGO
Gminy No. 53 Z. N. P.

NIEDZIELA, 1GO PAŹDZIERNIKA, 1933 ROKU

Z. K.

Zygmunt Kilian

1933, November 1

CONNOISSEUR OF WOMEN
One Act Play – by Z. Przybylski

CAST

Landowner
His daughters
Their cousin

Servant

Things happen and the scene
Takes place in the drawing room
of Mr. Borowinski's home.

Director Mr. Daniel Budnik

NIGHTINGALE
One Act Play – by A. Belza

CAST
Nightingale
Her beloved
Wealthy Englishman
His servant

Things happen and the scene
Takes place in Slowiczek's florist workshop
Vice-Director
Miss Agnieszka Pieszczoch

Program

"ZNAWCA KOBIET"
Jednoaktorka – Z. Przybylskiego

OSOBY:

Pan Borowiński, obywatel ziemski .... Michał Tytko
Zofja   } jego córki .... Walerja Szymańska
Malwina   .... Sabina Gutowska
Panna Helena, ich kuzynka .... Helena Kamińska
Edmund Weszyński .... J. Czesław Rudowski
Wiktor Ruczyński .... J. Czyżewski
Kasia .... Irena Brzostowska
Służący .... Antoni Kopeć

Rzecz dzieje się i scena przedstawia salonik w domu pana Borowińskiego

Reżyser – p. Daniel Budnik

"SŁOWICZEK"
Jednoaktówka – A. Belzy

OSOBY:

Zosia, Słowiczek .... Stanisława Zabłocka
Antoś, jej kochanek .... Klemens Olszewski
Lord Lilburn, bogaty Anglik .... Władysław Sękowski
John, jego służący .... Michał Tytko

Rzecz dzieje się i scena przedstawia warsztat kwiaciarski Słowiczka

Wice-reżyserka – panna Agnieszka Pieszczoch

Po Przedstawieniu Zabawa Taneczna – Orkiestra p. C. Zeltman'a

---

After the presentations, there will be a dance – Mr. C. Zeltman's Orchestra

1933, November 1

The entr'act and accompaniment to "Slowniczek" played by C. Zeltman's Orchestra.

FURNITURE was donated by Mr. Stanislaw Bartosiewicz

FLOWERS were donated by Miss Aniela Pitera

BACKDROPS AND SCENERY – a gift to the Polish Home from the firm, "Community Garage," Railroad St., Brothers Korkosz and Wrazen, Proprietors. The Polish-Artistic Society "Polart" built and installed the scenery

BOARD OF THE MASKA SOCIETY

D.W. BUDNIK	J. CZYZEWSKI	
President	Recording Secretary	
MRS. R. ZIELANIS	MISS ANIELA PITERA	
Vice President	Treasurer	

W antraktach i jako akompanjament do sztuki "Słowiczek" przygrywa orkiestra p. C. Zeltman'a.

MEBLE: dostarczył bezinteresownie p. Stanisław Bartosiewicz

KWIATY dostarczyła bezinteresownie panna Aniela Pitera

KULISY I SCENERJE—dar dla Domu Polskiego przez firmę "Community Garage", Railroad St., Bracia Korkosz i Wrażeń, właściciele. Budowa i ustawienie scenerji przez Polsko-Artystyczne Tow. "Polart"

KOMITET PRZEDSTAWIENIA:

Reżyser	Daniel S. W. Budnik
Wice-reżyserka	Agnieszka Pieszczoch
Zarządca własności	J. Czesław Rudowski
Dyrektor dochodu	Michał Tytko
Wicedyrektorka i charakteryzatorka	Agnieszka Pieszczoch
Dyrektor ogłoszeń	J. Czyżewski
Wicedyrektorki	L. Balska i R. Giniecka
Elektrotechnik	T. Noskowiak
Asystenci elektrotechniczy	C. Bojarski, A. Podbielski
Dyrektor scenerji	Zygmunt Kiljan
Asystent dyrektora scenerji	Zygmunt Brzozowski
Dyrektorka artystyczna	Wanda Hennel
Asystentka dyrektorki artystycznej	Genowefa Szatkowska
Upiększenie sceny	M. Zborowska, W. Balska, F. Mackiewicz

ZARZĄD TOW. "MASKA"

D. W. BUDNIK	J. CZYŻEWSKI
Prezes	Sekretarz Protok.
PANI R. ZIELANIS	PANNA ANIELA PITERA
Wice Prezeska	Kasjerka

PROGRAM COMMITTEE
Stage Manager
Vice Stage Manager
Property Manager
Revenue Manager
Vice Director and Makeup
Advertising Director
Vice Directors
Electricians
Assistant Electricians
Scenery Director
Assistant Scenery Director
Artistic Director
Assistant Artistic Director
Scenery Decoration

1934, May 27

FIRST CONTEST
OF AMATEUR CIRCLES

Participating Groups

Literary Circle of Albany, NY
Amateur Circle of Amsterdam, NY
Dramatic Circle of Schenectady, NY

Sunday, May 27th, 1934
At the Polish Home,
Schenectady, NY

1934, May 27

"MASKA" Dramatic Circle presentation
THE FIRST BALL
By Zygmunt Przybylski

Program

Kółko Dramatyczne "Maska" przedstawia

"PIERWSZY BAL"
Zygmunta Przybylskiego

OSOBY:

Pan Wodiński, urzędnik bankowy .... Józef Czyżewski
Pani Wodińska, żona .... Helena Kilian
Edia, córka .... Regina Gibiecka
Antoś, kochanek .... Bronisław Dąstek
Pani Pukalska, szwagrowa .... Marjanna Dutsba
Rozunia, jej córka .... Florentyna Baksas
Pani Zawitka, pobożna stryjenka .... Aniela Fitera
Anusia, służąca .... Irena Brzostowska

Reżyserka .... panna Agnieszka Pleszczoch
Skrzypek .... Józef Czechowicz
Zarząd własności i kostiumer .... Czesław Badowski

CAST

Bank clerk
Wife
Daughter
Lover
Sister in law
Her daughter
Pious aunt
Servant

Director
Violin
Property Manager and Costumer

The Literary Circle presents
"O.S.S.", OR "THE MARRIAGE PORTION"

Kółko Literackie przedstawia

"O. S. S.", CZYLI "WYPRAWA MAŁŻEŃSKA"

OSOBY:

Pan Cycero Schusert, przemysłowiec .... Edward Wojtal
Paul Schusert, żona .... panna Maria Albrecht
Stanisława, córka .... panna Helena Chmielińska
Onufry Schwamm, pokrzywny, fact .... Wincenty Chmielewski
Otton Schambert, kochanek .... Allan Skiziński
Ottmar Senkenberg .... Kazimierz Chmieliński

Reżyser .... Edward Wojtal

CAST: Industrialist; Wife; Daughter; Guy; Lover
Director

1934, May 27

Amateur Circle of Amsterdam
FLEDGLING KOKUSIA
Written by Pobratymiec

CAST

Wealthy townsman
His wife

Clerk
Factor

Director

THE BOARD OF THE MASKA
DRAMATIC CIRCLE

President
Vice-President
Secretary
Treasurer
Marshal

The "Maska" Circle orchestra during the entr'acte and dance is under the direction of Mr. Zych. **My father**

This Evening's Contest Committee

Furniture through the kindness of the Knickerbocker Furniture Co.

Kółko z Amsterdam przedstawia
"KOKUSIA PODLOTKIEM"
Napisana przez Pobratymca

OSOBY:

Bonifacy Nekaś, zamożny mieszczanin .... Lawik Dziubiński
Eleonora, jego żona .... panna Florentyna Kawczyńska
Kokusia .... panna Józefa Grzebień
Lalicki, urzędnik konceptowy .... Piotr Laszkiewicz
Wąchocki, faktor .... Antoni Sitka
Posługacz .... Leon Clonek

Reżyser .... W. Lesiakowski

ZARZĄD KÓŁKA DRAMATYCZNEGO "MASKA"

Józef Czyżewski, ... prezes
Panna Agnieszka Pieszczoch .... wice-prezeska
Panna Wanda Hennel .... sekretarka
Panna Aniela Pitera .... kasjerka
Antoni Kopeć .... marszałek

W antraktach i podczas tańca przygrywa orkiestra Kółka
"Maska" pod kierownictwem p. Zycha.

Komitet Dzisiejszego Wieczora Kontestu:
Józef Czechowicz, zarządca dochodu; Antoni Kopeć, panna
A. Giniecka, panna Roberta Tytko, panna Joanna Lesowicz

Meble przez grzeczność firmy Knickerbocker Furniture Co.

1934, September 16

"MASKA"

presents

Three One-Act Plays

In the Auditorium of the Polish Home

Sunday, September 16, 1934
Starting at 7:30 PM

"MASKA"

—Wystawia—

TRZY JEDNO-AKTÓWKI

W AUDYTORJUM DOMU POLSKIEGO

W NIEDZIELĘ, 16-GO WRZEŚNIA, 1934 ROKU

Początek o 7:30 wieczorem

1934, September 16

IN THE DELL

Play written by Zygmunt Przybylski

Townsman
Townswoman
Young peasant
Peasant

Director
Director

Violin solo by Professor Stanislaw E. Grabowski
Accompanied on the piano by
Mrs. S. E. Grabowski

PAPA PERMITS

Play written by Gustaw Mozer

Writer
Wife
Nephew
Writer
Cattle dealer
Servant

Director

1934, September 16

THE LIVE CORPSE

Play written by Gustaw Belly

Apolinary	
Wife	
Daughter	
Vinegar maker	
Servant	

Orchestra conducted by Stanley Zych
Members:
Orchestra will play during the presentation and for the dance.
Program Committee

COMMITTEE OF THIS PERFORMANCE

Stanley Zych's first play

CIRCLE ADMINISTRATION
President
Vice-President
Secretary
Treasurer
Marshal
General Director
Director

Furniture provided by Knickerbocker Furniture Co.

Decorations, sets, lighting and all scenery were by the "POLART" Circle

Director of Ornamentation
Assistant
Scenery Decorator
Property
Manager
Assistant
Makeup

III

"ŻYWY NIEBOSZCZYK"
Sztuka napisana przez Gustawa Belly'ego

Apolinary Strachajło	Michał Tytko
Aurelja, żona	Helena Kilian
Marja, córka	Zofja Chojnicka
Celestyn Fic	Władysław Sękowski
Kwaśnicki, fabrykant octu	Stanisław Zych
Służąca	Florentyna Beleusz
Reżyserka	panna Agnieszka Pieszczoch

Orkiestra pod kierownictwem p. Stanisława Zycha
Członkowie: T. Vilamo, Jan Laniewski, L. Marcinak, Stefan Patka, J. Slachtowski, J. Guerra
Orkiestra będzie przygrywać podczas przedstawienia i do tańca

KOMITET PRZEDSTAWIENIA:
Panna Wanda Hennel, Zygmunt Brzozowski,
Józef Czechowicz, zarządcy dochodu

OGÓLNY KOMITET ZABAWY:
Stanisław Gimiecki, przewodniczący; panna Joanna Lisowicz, panna Czesława Penichter, panna Leonora Andrzejewska, Tadeusz Kilian, panna Janina Wrażeń, Karol Szymański

Panna Wanda Hennel	dyrektorka upiększenia
Panna Marja Zborowska	asystentka
Czesław Rudowski	dekorator scenerji
Jan Zielanis	zarządca własności
Lucjan Sękowski	asystent
Panny Agnieszka Pieszczoch i Gertruda Zielanis, charakteryzatorki	

ZARZĄD KÓŁKA:

Prezes	Józef Cayżewski
Wice-prezeska	panna Agnieszka Pieszczoch
Sekretarka	panna Wanda Hennel
Skarbniczka	panna Aniela Pitera
Marszałek	Karol Szymański
Generalny reżyser	Daniel Budnik
Reżyserka	panna Agnieszka Pieszczoch

Meble dostarczone przez firmę Knickerbocker Furniture Co.
Upiększenie, ustawienie, oświetlenie oraz wszelkie przygotowania scenerji przez Kółko "POLART"

1934, November 18

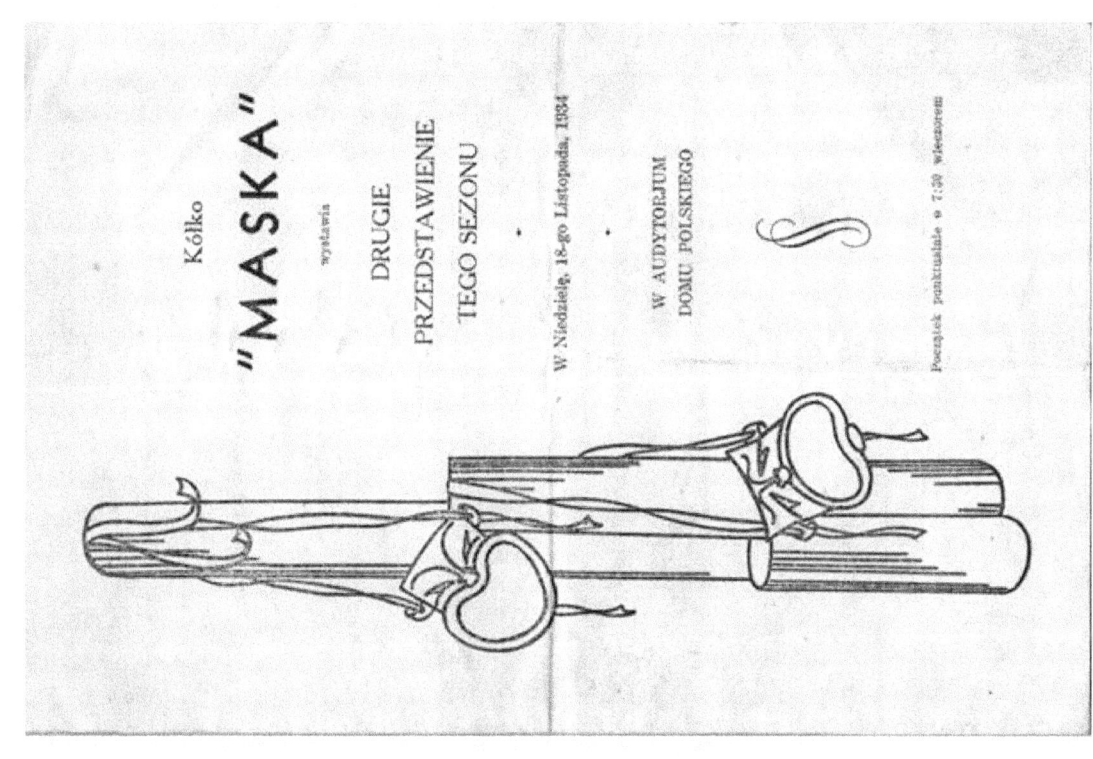

The "MASKA" Circle

Presents

Second Performance of The Season

Sunday November 18, 1934

In the Auditorium of the Polish Home

Starting promptly at 7:30 PM

1934, November 18

COUNCILORS OF MR. COUNCILMAN
By Michał Bałucki

A Play in three acts

A town citizen
His wife
Their daughter

Set in a small town in Poland

ACT ONE - A room in the Dziszewski home
SECOND AND THIRD ACTS – Dziszewskis' salon

The "Violin Choir," under the direction of S. E. Grabowski, will accompany the play as well as the entr'acte.

Miss Stasia Malinowska, soprano, will perform the following

There will be a general dance following the presentation.
The dance orchestra will be under the direction of Mr. S. E. Grabowski

---

"RADCY PANA RADCY"
Michała Bałuckiego

Sztuka w trzech aktach

Piotr Dziszewski, obywatel miejski	Józef Czyżewski
Ewa, jego żona	Marjanna Dziuba
Helenka, ich córka	Florentyna Bełeusz
Eufrozyna *Kowalec Hradecki*	Genowefa Stelmach
Zdzisław	Stanisław Zych
Karol	Jan Łaniewski
Służący	Karol Szymański

Rzecz dzieje się w małem mieście w Polsce

AKT PIERWSZY—Pokój w domu Dziszewskich
AKT DRUGI I TRZECI—Salonik u Dziszewskich

"Chór Skrzypistów", pod kierownictwem p. S. E. Grabowskiego, będzie przygrywał do sztuki oraz w antraktach

Panna Stasia Malinowska, sopran solo odśpiewa:

"HISZPANKA" — Chiari
"THE NIGHT" — S. E. Grabowski

PO PRZEDSTAWIENIU TANIEC OGÓLNY

Orkiestra do tańca pod kierownictwem p. S. E. Grabowskiego

1934, November 18

PROGRAM COMMITTEE
Income Managers
Music Director
Scenery Manager
Assistant Scenery Manager
Artistic Director
Assistant Artistic Director
Property Manager
Decorator
Makeup
Costume Manager
Costume Manager

GENERAL COMMITTEE OF THIS ENTERTAINMENT

CIRCLE ADMINISTRATION
President   Vice-President
Secretary   Treasurer
Historian   Marshal
General Director   Director

External Advisors to the "Maska" Circle
The Honorable Mr. Roman Kwiecien, Consul;
Mr. Jerzy Orzarzewski, New York
The Honorable Professor Stefan P. Mierzwa;
Mr. Wladyslaw Lesiakowski

KOMITET PRZEDSTAWIENIA:

Panna Helena Kamińska i p. Józef Czechowicz — zarządcy dochodu
Pan S. E. Grabowski — dyrektor muzyki
Pan Zygmunt Kilian — zarządca scenerji
Pan Zygmunt Brzozowski — asystent zarządcy scenerji
Panna Wanda Hennel — dyrektorka artystyczna
Panna Marja Zborowska — asystentka dyrektorki artystycznej
Pan Lucjan Sękowski — zarządca własności
Pan Czesław Rudowski — dekorator
Panny Agnieszka Pieszczoch i Regina Giniecka — charakteryzatorki
Panna Helena Kilian — zarządzyni garderoby
Pan Henryk Lewkowicz — zarządca garderoby

OGÓLNY KOMITET ZABAWY:

Pan Stanisław Giniecki, przewodn.
Pani S. Giniecka
Panna J. Lisowicz
Panna W. Garrut
Panna W. Domiakowska
Panna C. Penichter
Panna A. Dmochowska

Pan S. Skrzyński
Pan T. Kilian
Pan L. Marcinek
Pan F. Borkowski
Pan J. Belniak
Pan J. Czyszczun
Pan W. Platt

ZARZĄD KÓŁKA:

Józef Czyżewski, prezes—Agnieszka Pieszczoch, wice-prezeska
Wanda Hennel, sekretarka—Aniela Pitera, skarbniczka
Marjanna Dziuba, kronikarka—Karol Szymański, marszałek
Daniel Budnik, generalny reżyser—Agnieszka Pieszczoch, reżyserka

POZAMIEJSCOWI DORADCY KÓŁKA "MASKA":

Szan. P. Roman Kwiecień, Konsul; Pan Jerzy Orzarzewski, New York
Szan. P. Prof. Stefan P. Mierzwa; Pan Wład. Lesiakowski

1934, December 16

"Maska" Dramatic Circle

presents

Third Performance of The Season

Three One Act Plays

In the Polish Home

Sunday, December 16, 1934

Starting at 7:30 PM

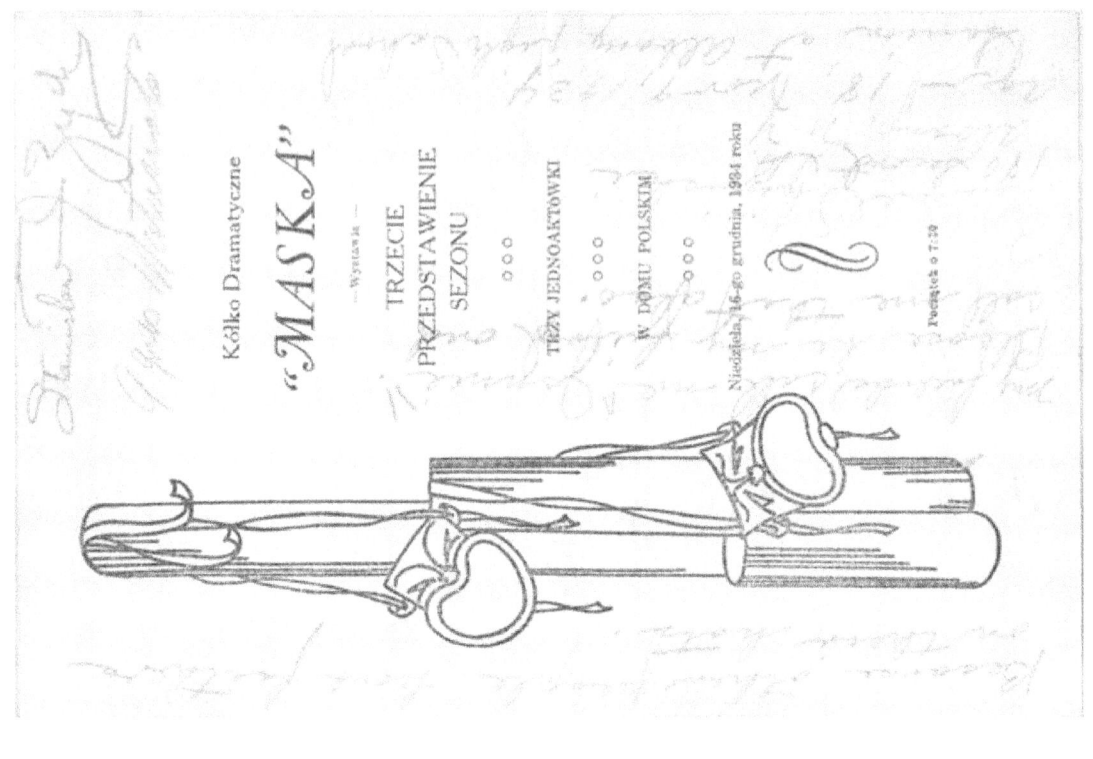

1934, December 16

TRAPPED
By Alfa. Director
Joseph Czyzewski

Citizen
His wife
Doctor
His wife
Daughter
Barber
Watchman

Dialogue in the Entr'acte between
the first and second Plays
Husband
Wife

**MARITAL ADVENTURES
ON A HONEYMOON**
By Antoni Jax
Directed by Agnes Pieszczoch

Arthur
His wife
Laura's father
Manager
Waiter
Maid

President and cashier
All kinds of printed matter

1934, December 16

SECOND DIALOGUE IN THE ENTR'ACTE BETWEEN THE SECOND AND THIRD PLAYS
Husband
Wife

THE JESTER
Written by Alexander Swietochowski
Directed by Joseph Czyzewski
Pielesz
His wife
Blazen
Patron
Governor
Pazdiora

Participants in the musical portions of the program: Miss Agnes Pieszczoch on the piano; Mr. Edward Gurzynski on the accordian; Mr. Joseph Czechowicz on the violin.

PROGRAM COMMITTEE

S. Giniecki, Leader; Z. Brzozowski, scenery; Matthew Zych, electrotechnician; J. Czechowicz, V.W. Platt, business managers; L. Sekowski, Property manager; A. Pieszczoch, R. Tytko, H. Kiljan, character patterns; H. Lewkowicz, wardrobe manager; V.W. Platt, program manager; M. Szymanski, F. Beleusz, J. Brzoset, M. Dziuba, C. Giniecki, G. Stemach, auxiliary committee.

My father's older brother

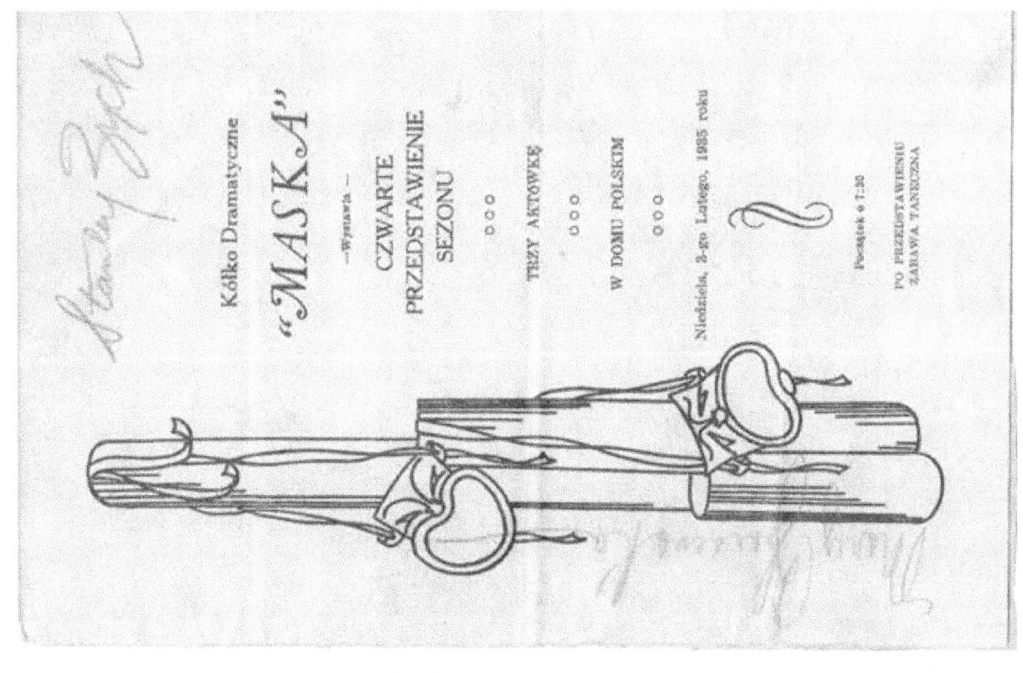

1935, February

Dramatic Circle

"MASKA"

presents

The Fourth Performance of the Season

In Three Acts

At the Polish Home

Sunday, February 3rd, 1935

Starting at 7:30 PM

There will be a dance after the performance.

1935, February

CARLSON'S PAINT and WALL PAPER
515 State Street — 1006 Crane Street

"MAŁŻEŃSTWO NA PRÓBĘ"
FRANCISZKA WYSOCKIEGO

Reżyser: Panna Apolonia Pluskotówna p. Józef Grzewski

OSOBY:

Podpał Beringer .... Jan Lesowski
Rozalja, żona .... Genowefa Stebnach
Józef Basoń, naczelnik straży ogniowej .... Stanisław Żych
Marja Basoń, żona .... Władysława Moroz
Franciszek Brakenhofer, stryj .... Aleksander Dolewa
Zuzanna Brakenhofer, stryjenka .... Marjanna Dziuba
Leopold Brakenhofer, bratanek .... Józef Czajewski
Stefan Połomski, Leopolda rzeźnik .... Lucjan Sękowski
Wentel kurtyzanek, pośrednik czeski .... Franciszek Stańkowski
Paul Sunami, właściciel cukierni .... Edgar Wąsik
Jego Kołb, kelner .... Walerja Szymańska
Małgorzata, siostra Beringera .... Joanna Lesowicz
Kapral straży ogniowej .... Józef Grzechowicz
Listonosz, Kelner .... Antoni Kopeć
Niańka .... Z. Rojnicka

Akt 1 i 2—Pokój u Beringerów: Solo na harmonji, Edward Kurzyński
Akt 3—Kawiarnia w przedmiejskim hotelu

Dr. Samuel S. Feuer
DENTIST
834 Crane Street — Tel. 2-0313

Dr. Samuel Podoloff
824 Crane Street — Schenectady, N. Y.

KNICKERBOCKER FURNITURE CO.

SHOE REBUILDERS	CLEANERS and DYERS

BALL'S Inc.
633 STATE STREET
Phone 2-3456

Compliments of A Friend

PHONE 2-5098

A. B. BRZOZOWSKI FUNERAL HOME
154 CRANE STREET — SCHENECTADY, N. Y.

ZARZĄD KÓŁKA "MASKA"

Prezes, Stanisław Gliniecki
Wiceprezes, Władysław Sękowski
Sekretarka, Wanda Hempel
Skarbniczka, Aniela Pitera
Marszałek, Karol Szymański
Parljamentarze, Roberta Tytko
Zarządcy finansowi, V. W. Plutt, Józef Ciechowicz

Notarka, Agnieszka Plaszczoch
Erdycyt, Józef Czyżewski
Zarządca estrady, Zygmunt Kilijan
Zarządca sceniczny, Zygm. Brzozowski
Zarządca własności, Lucjan Sękowski
Zarządcy garderoby, Lilijana Wąsik
Tadeusz Kilijan
Charakteryzator, Kazim. Gliniecki
Helena Kilijan

KOMITET PRZEDSTAWIENIA

V. W. Plutt, przewodnicy; Mieczysław Żych, elektrotechnik;
J. Rudnik, Aniela Pitera, Czesław Podolsky, Jadwiga
Godlewska, M. Zborowska, Leon Marciniak, Daniel Budnik,
Józef Ciechowicz, Bronisław Deppoia, Stanisław Żych,
W. Sękowski, R. Otkowski, komitet porannicowy.

Życzenia znaku—

PLEASANT VALLEY DAIRY
C. Pokrzywnicki
1125 Van Cortlandt St.
Telefon 2-7853 — Schenectady, N. Y.

1935, February

MARRIAGE ON TRIAL
(TRIAL MARRIAGE)
Francis Wysocki

CAST

Beringer
His wife
Sergeant in the
    fire guard
Sister
Uncle
Aunt
Nephew
Butcher
Czech middleman
Dairy owner
Cashier
Berlinger's servant
Corporal in the
    fire guard
Waiter
Nurse

Acts 1 & 2–A room at
Beringers'
Edward Gurzynski,
accordion solo

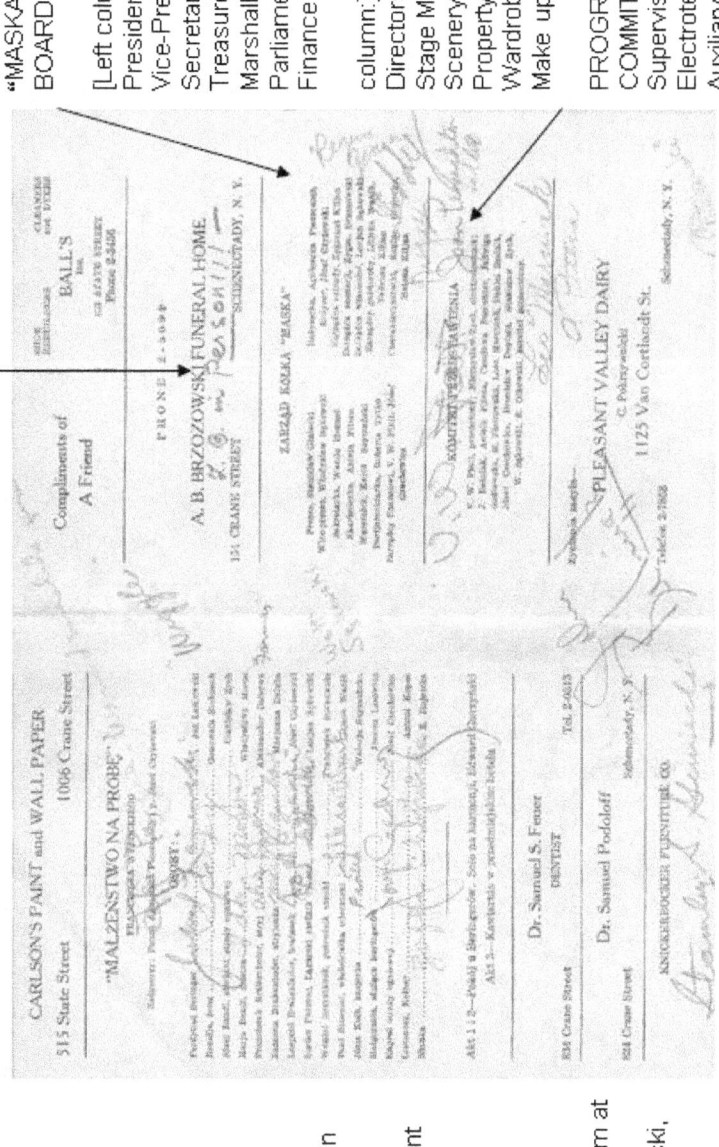

Zygmunt Brzozowski,
Undertaker
"Z.B. in Person!!-"

"MASKA" CIRCLE
BOARD

[Left column]:
President
Vice-President
Secretary
Treasurer
Marshall
Parliamentarian
Finance manager

[Right column:]
Directors
Stage Manager
Scenery Manager
Property Manager
Wardrobe managers
Make up

PROGRAM
COMMITTEE:
Supervisor,
Electrotechnician,
Auxiliary
committee

Sending Congratulations

1935, February

CARLSON'S PAINT and WALL PAPER
515 State Street   1006 Crane Street

"MAŁŻEŃSTWO NA PRÓBĘ"
FRASZKA W WESOŁKIEGO

OSOBY:

Perigard Beringer	Jan Laniewski
Rozalja, żona	Genowefa Stolmach
Józef Bandl, sierżant straży ogniowej	Stanisław Zych
Marja Bandl, żodra	Władysława Moros
Franciszek Brakenfeder, stryj	Aleksander Dzierwa "Wiggle"
Zuzanna Brakenfeder, stryjanka	Marianna Dziuba
Leopold Brakenfeder, bratanek	Józef Czyżewski
Stefan Palomi, laguński taršun	Lajan Sekowski
Wehzel Krzysztalak, podrzędnik czeski	Franciszek Borkowski
Paul Stoessel, właściciela mleczam.	Wakrja Szymańska Lillian Wanik
Jóżia Kolb, kasjerka	Joanna Lisowicz
Małgorzata, służąca Beringerów	Józef Czechowicz
Kapral straży ogniowej	Antoni Kupeć
Listonosz, Kelner	Z. Hojnicka
Studka	

Akt 1 i 2—Pokój u Beringerów. Solo na harmonji, Edward Kurzyński
Akt 3— Kawiarnia w przedmiejskim hotelu

Dr. Samuel S. Feuer
DENTIST
834 Crane Street   Tel. 2-0313

Dr. Samuel Podoloff
824 Crane Street   Schenectady, N.Y.

KNICKERBOCKER FURNITURE CO.

Stanley S. Giniecki

"Wiggle"   Joseph Laniewski
Sparky
Ida Moros
Alex Dzierwa "Farmer"
Mary Dziuba
Joseph Czyzewski
Lou Sekowski
Walt Sekowski
Lillian Wanik
Joseph Czechowicz
Zofia Chojnicka

1935, February

Compliments of A Friend

SHOE REBUILDERS — BALL'S Inc. — CLEANERS and DYERS
643 STATE STREET
Phone 2-3456

PHONE 2-5099

A. B. BRZOZOWSKI FUNERAL HOME
154 CRANE STREET
SCHENECTADY, N. Y.

ZARZĄD KÓŁKA "MASKA"

Prezes, Stanisław Giniecki
Wice-prezes, Władysław Sękowski
Sekretarka, Wanda Hamel
Skarbniczka, Aniela Pitera
Marszałek, Karol Szymański
Parljamentarka, Roberta Tysko
Zarządcy finansowi, V. W. Platt, Józef Czechowicz

Reżyserka, Agnieszka Piaszczoch
Redyser, Józef Czyżewski
Zarządca estrady, Zygmunt Kiljan
Zarządca sceneczk, Zygm. Brzozowski
Zarządca własności, Lucjan Sękowski
Zarządcy garderoby, Liljana Wasyk, Tadeusz Kiljan
Charakteryzatorzy, Kestjan Gniecego, Helena Kiljan

KOMITET PRZEDSTAWIENIA

V. W. Platt, przełożony; Mieczysław Zych, elektrotechnik;
J. Belniak, Aniela Pitera, Czesława Penichter, Jadwiga
Godlewska, M. Zborowska, Leon Marcinek, Daniel Bednik,
Józef Czechowicz, Bronisław Deptuła, Stanisław Zych,
W. Sękowski, R. Olkowski, komitet pomocniczy.

Życzenia zasyła —

PLEASANT VALLEY DAIRY
C. Pokrzywnicki
1125 Van Cortlandt St.
Schenectady, N. Y.

Telefon 2-7858

Regina Genser

Teddy Kugel

Joan Penichter

Leo Marcinek

A. Pitera

V.W Platt

John Belniak

1935, March

Dramatic Circle

"MASKA"

Presents

The Final Offering of the Season

Three One Act Plays

At the Polish Home

Sunday, March 24th, 1935

Starting at 7:30 PM

Thank You Acknowledgment

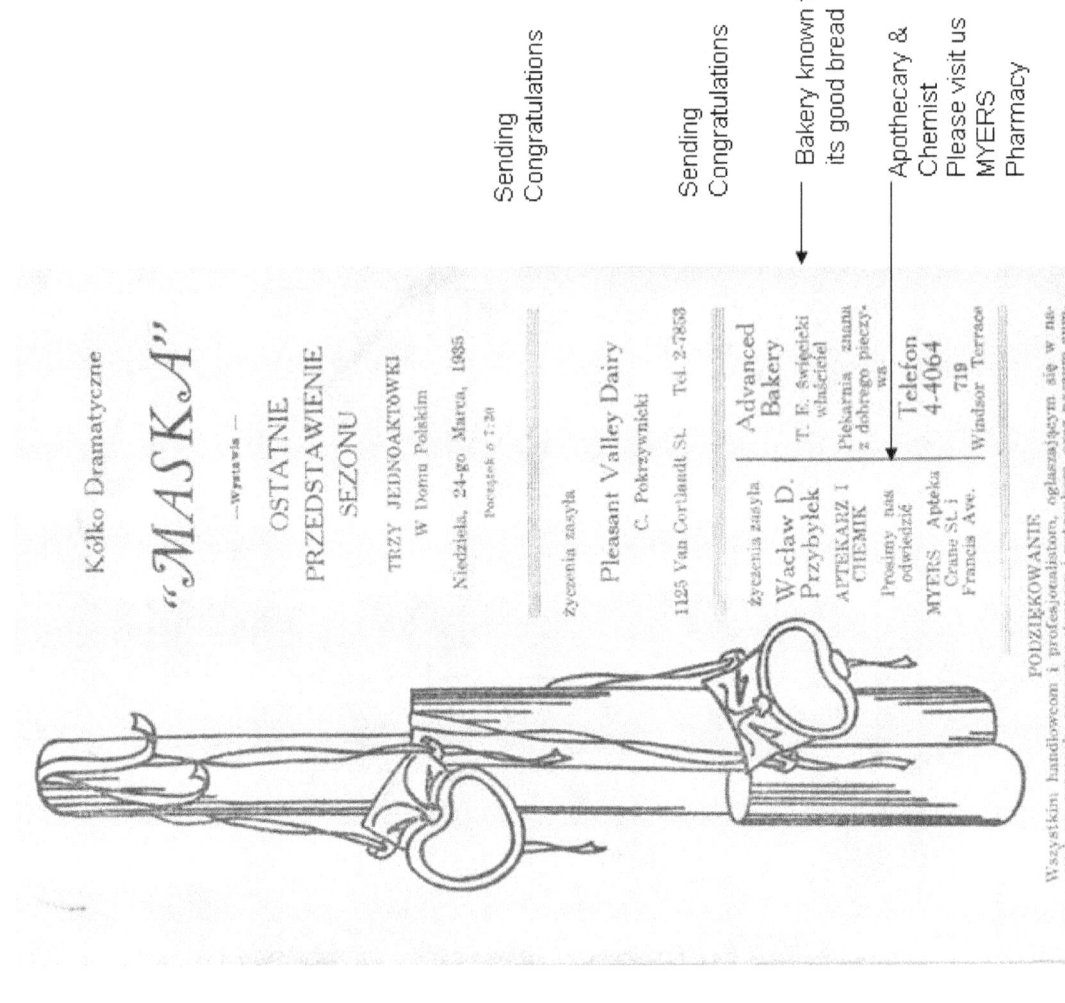

Sending Congratulations

Sending Congratulations

Bakery known for its good bread

Apothecary & Chemist
Please visit us
MYERS Pharmacy

1935, March

EYE FOR EYE
Written by Marja Finklow
Directed by Mr. J. Czyzewski
A ROOM IN A HOME IN A PARIS SUBURB

Chemist
His Wife
Her brother
Sister
Friend
Servant

GALOSHES
Written by Alexander Fredro
Directed by Mr. J. Czyzewski
THE SCENE TAKES PLACE IN A ROOM IN A KRAKOW HOME

Professor
Daughter
Sister
Apprentice
His uncle
Servant
Boy in service Accordionist

Provided various scenery items

CARLSON'S
Wall Paper — Paints — Artists' Materials — Glass
1006 CRANE STREET   515 STATE STREET

"WET ZA WET"
Napisała Marja Finkłowa — Reżyser p. J. Czyżewski
POKÓJ W DOMU NA PRZEDMIEŚCIU PARYSKIEM

Gaston Bardolz, chemik .... Lucjan Sękowski
Madame Bardolz, żona .... Gustowia Siebnach
Ludwik Colombin, jej brat .... Ryszard D. Olkowski
Mlle. Colombin, siostra .... Wanda Gerat
Claud Bacroix, przyjaciel .... Franciszek Borkowski
M. Le Capitane Gabelar .... Jan Laniewski
Marietta, służąca .... Joanna Lisowicz

COMPLIMENTS OF
DISTRICT ATTORNEY'S OFFICE
L. W. BEGLEY, DIST. ATTORNEY

JAMES H. GOULD   STANLEY G. GRABICKI
First Assistant   Second Assistant

"KALOSZE"
Napisał A. Fredro — Reżyser p. J. Czyżewski
SCENA PRZEDSTAWIA POKÓJ W KRAKOWSKIM DOMU

Pan Inicki, profesor .... Stanisław Zych
Emilja, córka .... Irena Witkowska
Balbina, siostra .... Wełma Tamborowska
Karol Butowski, praktykant .... Aleksander Dzierwa
Filberius, jego stryj .... Józef Czyżewski
Zysio, sługus .... Joanna Lisowicz
Chłopiec do usług .... Antoni Kopeć

EDWARD GURZYNSKI — HARMONISTA

A. B. BRZOZOWSKI   Kwiaty, Drzewka, Palmy
Dostarczył drobne rzeczy do   z Oranżerji
upiększenia sceny   ANIELI PITERY
                              1040 Cutler Street

KNICKERBOCKER FURNITURE STORE

Flowers, trees, palms for the Orangerie

1935, March

THE TERRIBLE AUNT

Written by Ary Jawycz
Directed by Miss Agnieszka Pieszczoch
The scene takes place on Boulevard Street Near Karpacki Street

Advisor
His wife
Aniela's aunt
Aniela's fiancé
Sergeant
Attendant
Letter messenger
Cabby
Jew
Milkman
Newspaperman

Program Committee Chairman

Presentation Committee
J. Czechowicz, Chairman

Sending Congratulations

The Brothers Zych

Purveyors of fruits and vegetables

Stanley Zych, my father, and older brother Matthew

1935, March

Korkosz and Wrazen
We install auto glass.

[NOTE: Mr. Wrazen was my Aunt Jane Wrazen Korycinski's father. The family lived on Becker Street. Korkosz was her mother's brother.]

Patrons and
Patronesses of the
Dramatic Circle
[including]:
Pani J. Wrazen – Aunt Jane's Mother
Pani J. Zych – My father's mother

(Image: Maska program page listing "PATRONI I PATRONKI KÓŁK" — Patrons and Patronesses of the Circle — from 120 Railroad Street, with advertisements for Dr. A. F. Korniejewski, Clement F. Olszewski Jeweler, Dr. M. J. Dybich, and Mt. Pleasant Laundry.)

Dr. Myron Dybich, our family doctor who delivered me.

Appendix 4 — Page 139 — Maska Programs

1935, October

EVERYONE NEEDS LAUGHTER

Laugh your heads off
and you will be happy
THIS EVENING

Season Opener
OF THE POLISH DRAMATIC CIRCLE –
"MASKA"

At the Polish Home
On Crane Street
Starting promptly at 7:30

The following plays will be presented
RELATIVE FROM AMERICA
and
DRESS REHEARSAL

These comedies are interspersed with extraordinary humor, not often encountered. There will not be a single moment free of jokes and healthy humor.
A dance after the presentations will complete this pleasant evening for all participants.

Admission is 35c per person
including the dance.
Support the Young Folk!
Come to the Polish Play!

1935, October

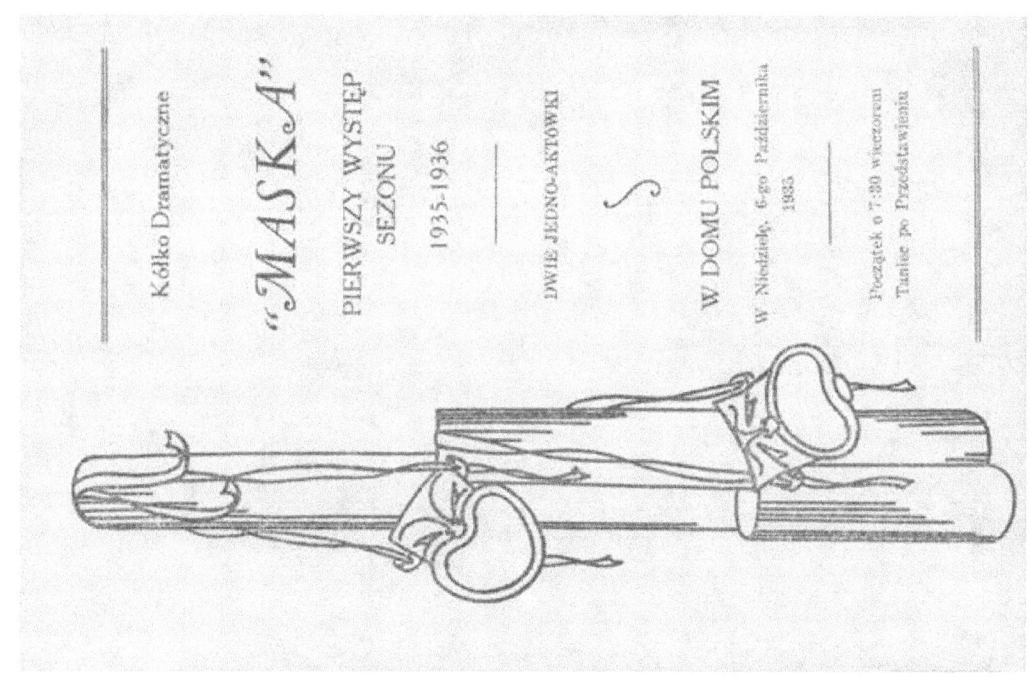

Dramatic Circle

"MASKA"

First Offering of the Season

1935 - 1936

Two One Act Plays

At the Polish Home

Sunday, October 6, 1935

Starting at 7:30 PM
Dance after the Presentation

1935, October

[NOTE: Stage Personality Contest begins]

THE WEEKLY GAZETTE
K. S. Ogonowski, Editor
The only Polish paper in the Capitol District
Printing at modest prices. Union printer.

RELATIVE FROM AMERICA
Marja Gerson Dabrowska

Host
His wife
Daughter

Ploughboy
Sekocki's wench
Widow
Organist
Neighbors

Events take place in the countryside near Warsaw. The scenery portrays the courtyard in front of Simon's cottage. Directed by Miss Agnieszka Pieszczoch

Proprietor

Supplier of milk, cheese and sweet butter. For a courteous and quick milk supply, etc., For which I have a state diploma.

"GAZETA TYGODNIOWA"
K. S. OGONOWSKI, WYDAWCA

Jedyne polskie pismo w dystrykcie stołecznym

Druki po cenach umiarkowanych. Unijna drukarnia.

233 BROADWAY   TEL. 2-2518   SCHENECTADY, N. Y.

"KREWNIAK Z AMERYKI"
Marja Gerson Dabrowska

Szymon Sekocki, gospodarz .... Leon Marcinek
Magdalena, jego żona .... Jadwiga Godlewska
Basia, córka .... Władysława Moros
Wojtek Grzęda .... Stanisław Zych
Walenty Pyrz .... Jan Laniewski
Kuba, parobczak .... Józef Dropeła
Maryśka, dziewucha od Sękockich .... Franciszka Harasimowicz
Katarzyna, wdowa .... Walerja Szymańska
Organista
Sąsiadki:
Maciejowa .... Alicja Nowicka
Mateuszowa .... Zofja Hojnicka
Józefowa .... Irena Witkowska
Sąsiedzi:
Adam .... Antoni Kopeć
Mateusz .... Władysław Sekowski
Josek Żółty, arendarz .... Wiktor Harasimowicz
Dwojra, jego żona .... Joanna Penichter
Grajek .... Edward Gurzyński

Rzecz dzieje się na wsi w okolicy Warszawy. Scena przedstawia podwórze przed chatą Szymona.

REŻYSERIA, PANNA AGNIESZKA PIESZCZOCH

PLEASANT VALLEY DAIRY
C. POKRZYWNICKI, WŁAŚCICIEL

DOSTAWCA MLEKA, ŚMIETANY I SŁODKIEGO MASŁA

Po grzeczną i prędką dostawę mleka itd., za które otrzymałem dyplom stanowy, telefonujcie 2-7853.

1125 VAN COURTLANDT STREET   SCHENECTADY, N. Y.

1935, October

ACKNOWLEDGMENT

The "Maska" Dramatic Circle sends an Old Polish "May God Repay You" to our Patrons for recognizing our work and for their sincere support during this season.
The Committee

DRESS REHEARSAL

By W. Roart, a Farce in one act
The scene takes place at "The Falcon" in the Goat Bullocks on the border in Poland about 1902.

Hurrier
Director
Prompter
Vinegary
Caper

Performance Committee
V. W. Platt, Supervisor

Next Main Attraction
By general request
Belly's "Glossary" and
"Catching Fish without Fishing"
by Wachtel

1935, October

Patrons and Patronesses of the "Maska: Circle

PATRONI I PATRONKI KOŁKA "MASKA"

PAŃSTWO
S. Korkosz
K. S. Ozonowscy
Marciuk
P. Koryciday
W. Gąsowscy
S. Ptera
L. Kaза
C. Pokrzywnicy
G. Sokowscy
W. Grodkiewicz
D. Badsik
S. Hildebrand
P. Pieszpach
M. Prachtler
C. Wójticy
I. Andrzejowscy
B. Lewiowscy
B. Buggsel
S. Sobiesz
J. Kilias
Kokornik
J. Bukoscy

PANOWIE
P. Durchowski
C. Clembroniewicz
Lesiewski
A. Sarnowski
W. Olechowicz
Z. M. Sawaniewski
C. Sarnacki
W. D. Przepylak
P. Kasiński
A. Zwoiski
Dr. M. J. Tydzeh
Dr. H. C. Mazurowski
L. Karnowski
W. Lesiątowski
A. Platt
P. Jura
J. Czyżewski
St. Sobicki
Dożynas
P. Pautrowski
A. Adach
T. Stajęchi
W. Nowicki
Naradowski
Jankowski
A. Kopeć

J. F. Szymniak
J. Pastor
C. Słowakiewicz
C. Dobrociński
W. T. Bednarkiewicz
Prof. S. Belniak
A. Nosal
B. Lasiewski
W. Okolski
N. Ferrano
A. Sarnowski
Józef Nosal
R. Sobut
F. Leszczyński
D. Karyska
C. Szalewski
T. Herman
V. Herman
J. F. Stelmach
H. Tatski
Józef Pedadu
Prof. S. Kostiuki
Wojtal
M. A. Kokucki
A. Strybica

PANIE
A. Pachecka
B. Tuzka
M. Ogrodnika
W. Klejnzyr
J. Irdiaka
J. Maskarewicz
F. S. Pusachowska
B. Stasiurcka
B. Procharczyk
K. Bleszkowska
E. Darecikowska
S. Jankowska
M. Jarocowska
H. Stannia
A. Grzywaczowska
K. Smikowska
K. Lesiewska
A. Marczak
F. Chojnarka
I. Horalimowska
S. Goszewska
M. Mileszek
F. Łukaszewicz
F. Świerkowska
K. Stejka

Stępowska
B. Łaskowska
P. Zielińska
W. Job
A. Szymańska
I. Nowicka
B. Ubicka
S. Dzienęska
Zaborca
Kopeć
B. Wiśniewska
Rywot
St. Kłosek
M. Lisińska
S. Jarunowska
S. Szewciowska
M. Trzcińpolska
M. Maślanka
M. Kaźmaczaka
J. Ziebrowska
J. Miszkniewicz
F. Sokolewska
V. Łomowska
Skowczka
J. Zych
A. Szczepańska
A. Marzinkowska
M. Wilkowska
M. Mardewka
M. Stelmach ← My grandfather
B. Maciąg
R. Bartoshewicz
R. J. Kuźibnita
J. Gwiliowska

PANNY
J. Stelmach
H. Kazińska
Kłobuse
J. Jawin
J. Harakiewicz
J. Łasanlewicz
A. Bykowka
Eugenia Bupińska
Marja Puszaznoch
H. Gostowska
L. Godlewska
H. Moduska
H. Libiecka
F. Cichu
C. Sacrowska
W. Świelmach

1935, November 17

Second Performance of the "Maska" Dramatic Circle On Sunday

See Chapter 5 for translation.

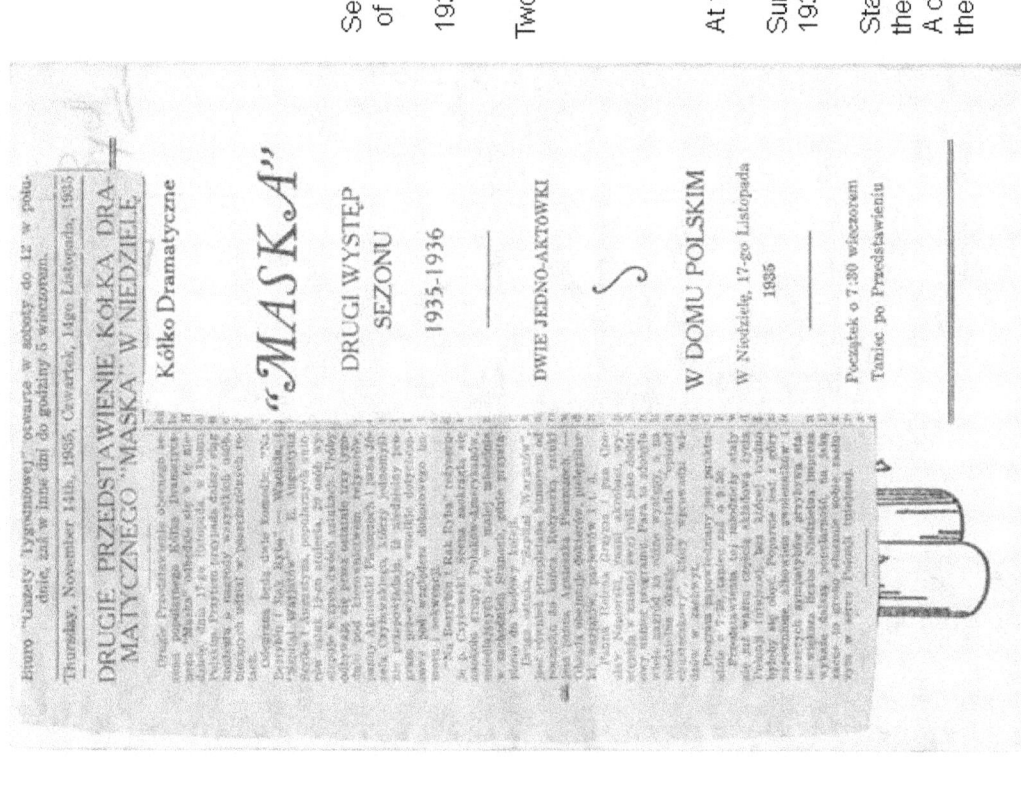

Second Production of the Season

1935 - 1936

Two One Act Plays

At the Polish Home

Sunday, November 17 1935

Starting at 7:30 in the evening
A dance after the performance

Newspaper clipping is tightly glued to the program.

1935, November 17

Sending Congratulations

CATCHING FISH WITHOUT FISHING

Citizen in a provincial city
His daughter
His sister
Officials of a newly built train line
-
Servant

Director

The scene takes place in a provincial town when a rail line is being built.

CIRCLE OFFICERS

President   Property Manager
Vice-Pres.   Costume Managers
Treasurer   Makeup
Marshal   Parliamentarian
Marshal
Finance Board   Auxiliary Committee
Stage Director
Scenery Director

1935, November 17

HOSPITAL FOR THE INSANE

In charge of the hospital for the insane	
His daughter	
Fizik devoid of his sense	
Jadzia's lover	
Intern of the hospital for the insane	
Nurses of the hospital for the insane	
Main insane people	
Hospital maids	
Hospital patients	

The scene takes place in a room in the hospital for the insane, from which a second set of bars can be seen.

Director   Acrobatic act

Judges in the stage personality contest

Sending Congratulations
Publisher of "The Weekly Gazette"

The furniture for today's performance was donated by Mr. S. Bartosiewicz, proprietor of "Mont Pleasant Furniture."

Compliments of
CRANE ST. LIQUOR STORE
"Only One In Mt. Pleasant"
WM. C. SCHOPMAN, PROP.

MT. PLEASANT CAP SHOP
Hats, Shirts, Ties
871 Crane St, opp. Fourth Avenue

COMPLIMENTS
Fred Rakvica

"SZPITAL WARJATÓW"
REG. AUG. SCHLES I ANDRZEJ

Doktor Janczyn, utrzymujący szpital warjatów	Jan Laniewski
Jadzia, jego córka	Agnieszka Dmochowska
Hydrogen, fizyk pozbawiony zmysłów	Stanisław Zych
Edward, kochanek Jadzi	Józef Drapała
Jakób, internista w szpitalu warjatów	Lucjan Sękowski
Pielęgniarki w szpitalu warjatów	F. Harasimowicz, Z. Chojnicka
Główni warjaci	Leon Marcinek i Wiktor Harasimowicz
Słudzy w szpitalu warjatów	Genowefa Stelmach i Wanda Hennel
Pacjenci w szpitalu	Tadeusz Kilian, Antoni Kopeć, Henryk Wienclawski, Bolesław Borczyk i Edward Godlewski

Scena przedstawia sale w szpitalu warjatów, z której widać drugą z kratami.
PANNA AGNIESZKA PISZCZOCH, BEATYSTKA

Panna Helena Grzywna i p. Czesław Napiorski w akcie akrobatycznym

Sędziami kontestu scenicznego "stage personality" są: **Dr. B. H.** Kirschberg, prof. S. Kosiński i Dr. B. C. Mazurowski

życzenia szyle

K. S. OGONOWSKI
Wydawca "Gazety Tygodniowej"

Meble ofiarowane bezinteresownie na dzisiejsze Przedstawienie przez p. S. Bartosiewicza, właściciela firmy "Mt. Pleasant Furniture House", 722 Crane street.

1935, December

DRAMATIC CIRCLE

MOTHER OF

GOD

CZESTOCHOWA

PRESENTING THE FIRST PLAY
"MIRACLE ON CLEAR MOUNTAIN"
J. S. Zielinski

Sunday, December 1, 1935
In the School Auditorium
Our Lady of Czestochowa
At 8 PM

1935, December

Sending Compliments

Water Department Commissioner of the City of Schenectady

Compliments

życzenia nasyła

ADVANCED BAKERY

KNOWN FOR QUALITY PRODUCTS

T. E. Święcicki, prop.

719 WINDSOR TERRACE
PHONE 4-4064

JAN SAWICKI
Piekarnia i Grocernia

17 Jefferson St.
Tel. 2-3969

życzenia nasyła

DR. M. J. DYBICH

809 Crane St.   Tel. 4-6395

Compliments

PROSTACK BROS.

ESSO GAS

NEW LOCATION

Eastern Ave. and
University Place

CLOTHING
For
The Entire Family

Open a charge account today

OSBORNE'S
406 STATE ST.

Schenectady owned and operated

życzenia nasyła

F. L. LESZCZYNSKI

XMAS GIFT
SUGGESTIONS

Fountain Pens and Pencils
Kodaks and Movie Cameras
Stromberg-Carlson Radio

życzenia nasyła

S. GWIAZDOWSKI

J. T. and D. B. LYON

256 State St.   Tel. 4-9647

B. Kowobus, Partner

życzenia nasyła

Waclaw Daniel Przybylek

Komisarz Departamentu Wody Miasta Schenectady

I take this occasion to extend my hearty compliments to the Polish residents of the Sixth Ward

WALTER G. KING

Compliments

McLEOD BROS.

Choice Meats and Groceries

827 Eastern Ave.
Phones 4-4167 and 4-4198

Appendix 4   Page 149   Maska Programs

1935, December

MELODRAMA PERSONNEL

Count
His son
His young daughter
Gamekeeper
Gamekeeper's daughter
Gamekeeper's 4 year old son
Aunt, count's sister
Count's maid
Priest
Doctor from Vienna

Sending Congratulations

Proprietor
Keeps in stock
Fresh and Good Food and Produce
Modest Prices and Polite Service

1935, December, cont.

FRENCH BEAUTY SHOP
Mrs. G. Szewczak

Facials 50c. Long Hair Shampoo 50c. Any other Item 35c; Except Friday and Saturday, 40c.

PERMANENTS $3, $4, $5

We also do Hair Tinting and Bleaching

For appointments phone 1-6548

405 State St., Above Thom McAn's, Bet. Jay and Clinton Sts.

AKT I—W pałacu hrabiego.

AKT II—Odsłona pierwsza; w izbie gajowego; odsłona druga, w izbie gajowego.
Pauza 15 minut. Poczęstunek w tylnym pokoju.

AKT III—W kaplicy Jasnogórskiej przed ołtarzem.

AKT IV—W pałacu hrabiego.

Reżyser .... p. F. G. Halturewicz
Zarządca scenerji .... p. J. Dmochowski
Komitet pomocniczy p. H. Radzewic, p. F. Retajczyk, p. A. Kaczmarek, p. J. Bojczuk.
Dyrektor muzyki .... p. B. G. Warlik
Akomp. na fortepianie (na organach, panna Zofja Witkowska.
Sufler .... p. B. J. Kazyaka

KOMITET PRZEDSTAWIENIA Hieronim Radzewski, przewodniczcy, B. Bar, F. G. Halturewicz, B. G. Warlik, B. J. Kazyaka, H. Rogińska, H. Duszyńska.

MEBLE DOSTARCZONE PRZEZ
Mt. Pleasant Furniture House
720 Crane Street, S. Bartosiewicz, właściciel, Telefon 2-4938

ACT I In the Count's palace

ACT II Scene I Gamekeeper's home; Scene II Gamekeeper's home
A 15-minute pause; Refreshments in the back room

ACT III Before the altar in the Jasna Gora chapel

ACT IV in the Count's palace

Director
Scenery manager
Assistants
Music director
Piano and organ accompanist
Prompter

Committee of the Performance

Furniture provided by

1935, December

Repair of all electrical items, washing machines, vacuum cleaners, radio apparatus, refrigerators, toasters, irons, electric motors, equipment for hairdressing. New and used washing machines and complimentary sales

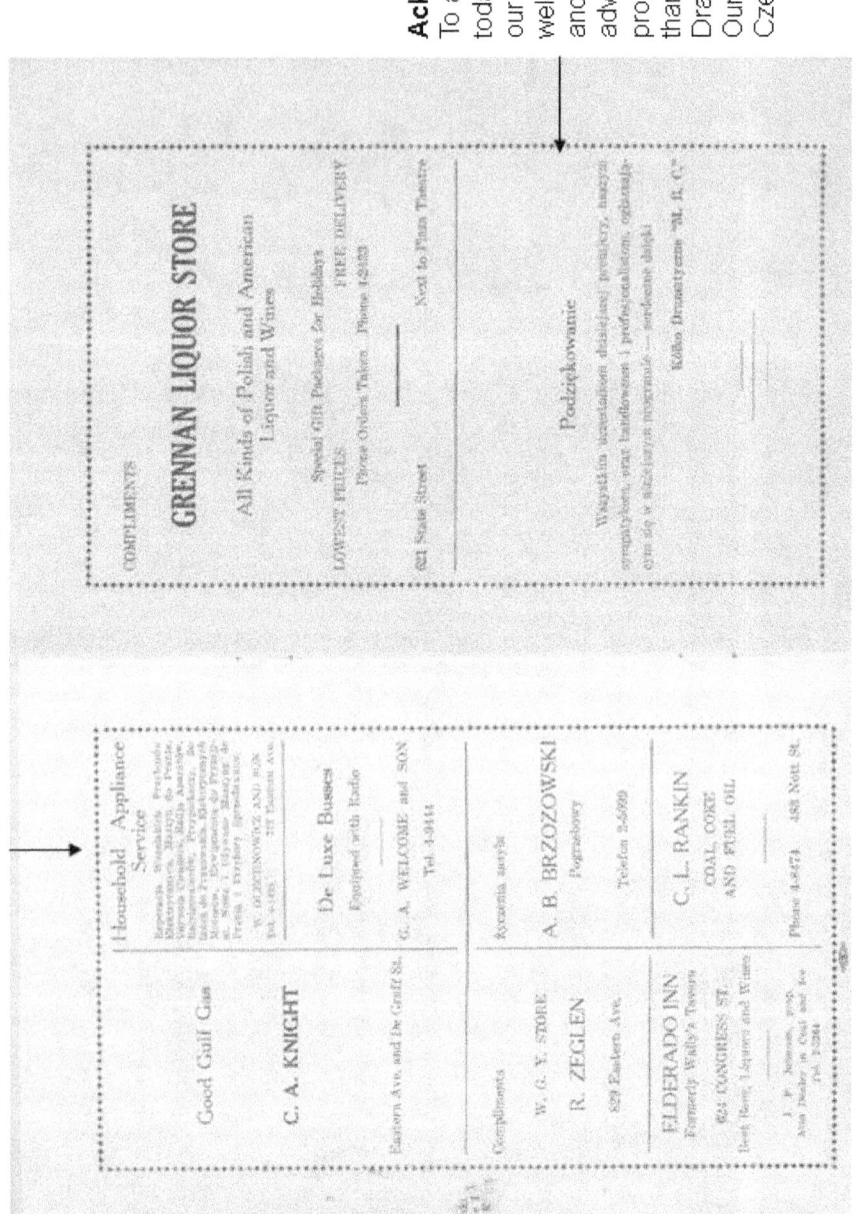

Acknowledgment
To all participants in today's premiere, our supporters, as well as merchants and professionals advertising in this program – sincere thanks. The Dramatic Circle of Our Lady of Czestochowa.

Sending Congratulations   Undertaker

1935, December 15

Dramatic Circle

MASKA

Third Presentation of the Season

1935-1936

Two Comedies

At the Polish Home

Sunday, December 15

Starting at 7:30pm

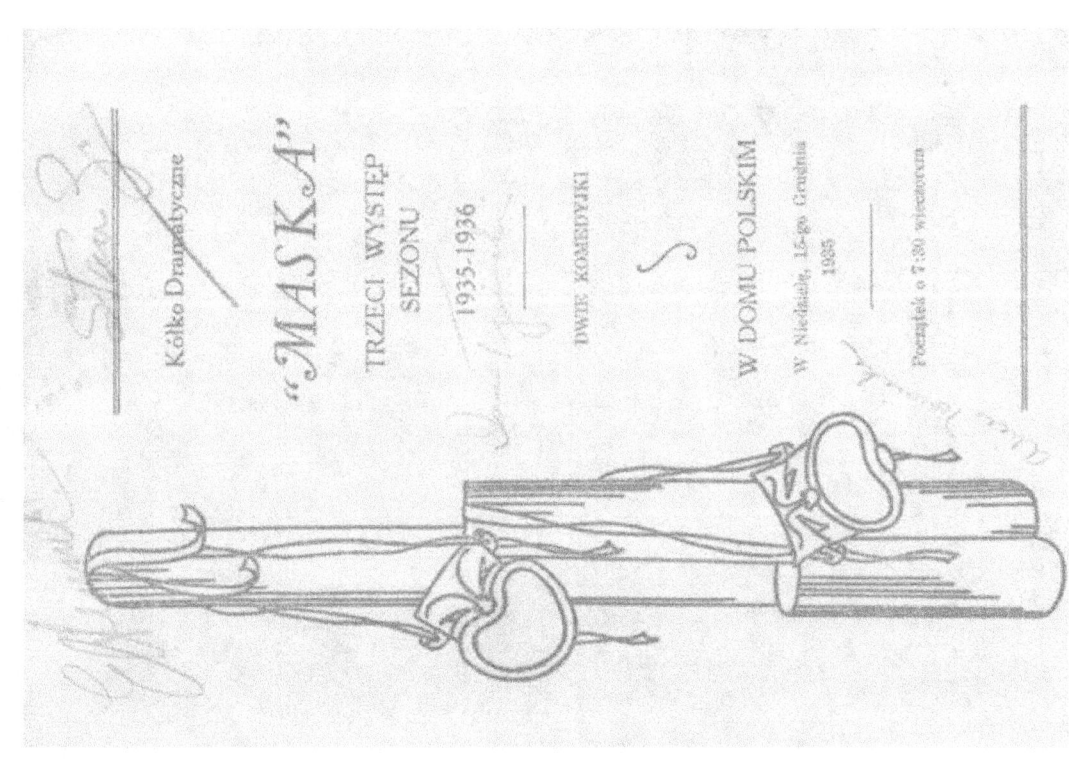

1935, December 15

Patrons and Patronesses
of the "MASKA" Dramatic Circle

My grandmother

1935, December 15

Season's Greetings

Mont Pleasant Pharmacy

Electric City Press, Inc.

Rendezvous — Stan's Tavern

Ricciardi's Flower Shop

Yale Garage Company

Clement Olszewski, Jeweler

Hub Sporting Store

Regards — Tweed's Delicatessen

Insurance — C. Wojcicki & Co.

Snyder's Tavern

Thompson's Dress Shop

Mont Pleasant Furniture House

Always Values — Englebardt's

Swięcicki Bakery

Herman Freed Liquor Store Since 1899

A. B. Brzozowski & Son

Przybyłek, Wacław D.

Peter Lewandowski & Son

Yuletide Greetings—Ben Franklin Store

N. Marcinkiewicz Confectionery

Eddie's Gas Station

Weinstein's Clothing Store

Yours Truly — Maska

Eat At George's Lunch

Auto Parts — Korkosz & Wrazen

Ray's Tavern

ZARZĄD KÓŁKA:

Prezes .... Władysław Sękowski
Wice-prezes .... Stanisław Zych
Sekretarka .... Wanda Hennel
Kasjerka .... Aniela Pitera
Marszałek .... Antoni Kopeć
Zarządcy finansowi: Józef Czechowicz i V. W. Platt
Zarządca estrady .. Mieczysław Zych
Zarządczyni scenerji .. Wanda Hennel

Zarządca własności Lucjan Sękowski
Zarządcy garderoby: Lucyna Wanik i Tadeusz Kilian
Charakteryzatorzy: Helena Kilian, Genowefa Stelmach, Zofja Chojnicka
Parlamentarka .... Joanna Pentchler
Komitet programu: Józef Czechowicz i Lucjan Sękowski

CIRCLE OFFICERS

President	Property Manager
Vice-President	Costume Managers
Secretary	Makeup
Treasurer	Parliamentarian
Marshall	Program Committee
Finance Manager	
Stage Manager	
Scenery Manager	

1935, December 15

PROFESSOR'S WIG
Antoni Jax

Antoni Jax
Young widow
Her maid
Young rogue
Professor and governor of Adolf
Hotel attendant

Kalina Choir, Mrs. A. Grabowska, Conductor

Act I-The scene takes place in a garden in Ciechocinek
Act II-The scene takes place in a room in the town hotel
Miss Agnes Pieszczoch, Director
Piano accompaniment, Miss C. Wieczynski

ROOM FOR RENT
A. Poplawski – A. Golanski

Pensioner
His wife
Piano student
Medical student
Maid
Fireman
Messenger
Boy

The action takes place in the Luzinski home in Warsaw

The judges in the "stage personality" contest are   Director

"MASKA" wishes to all participants and supporters a Merry Christmas and a Happy New Year.
The Board of Directors

The furniture for today's performance was donated by

1936, February

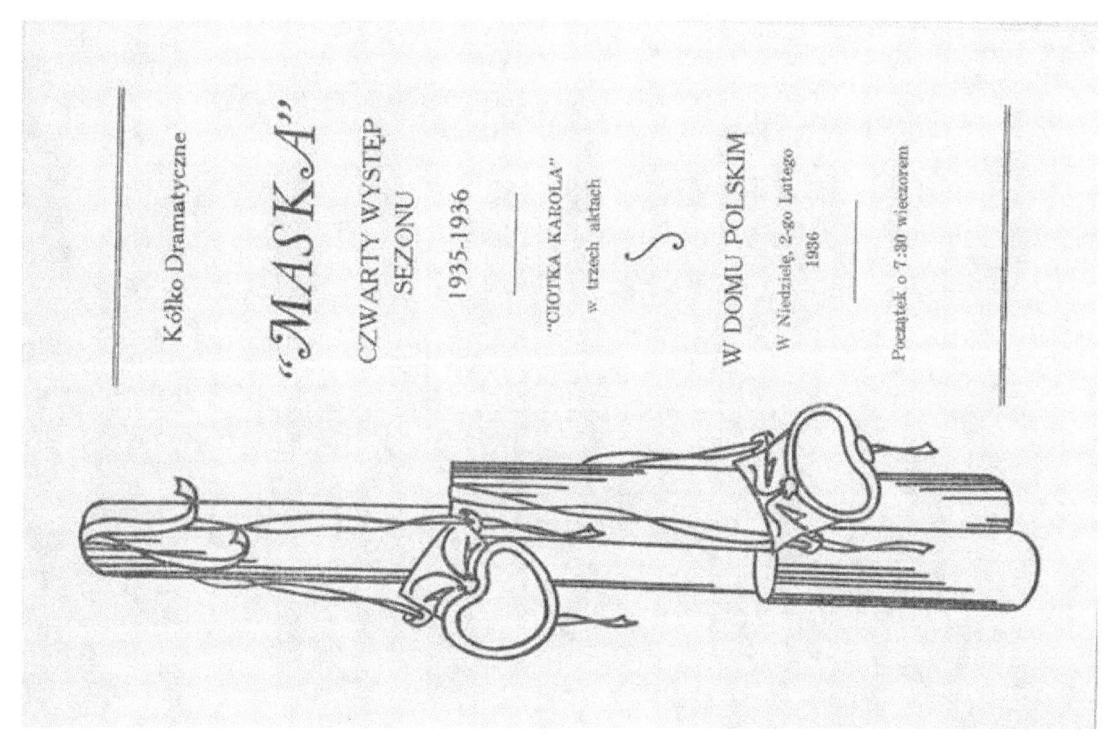

Dramatic Circle

"**MASKA**"

Fourth Offering of the Season

1935 – 1936

"CIOTKA KAROLA"
(Charlie's Aunt)
in three acts

At the Polish Home

Sunday, February 2nd, 1936

Starting at 7:30 PM

1936, February

Choice meats and vegetables

CIRCLE OFFICERS

President	Property Manager
Vice-Pres.	Costume Managers
Secretary	Makeup
Treasurer	Parliamentarian
Marshal	Program comm.
Finance Director	
Stage Director	
Corresponding Secretary	

An honorable well known Polish firm –
[Concept: Support your own]

Furniture donated by

First quality Polish bakery

LEWANDOWSKI and SON
SHOE STORE

Better Shoes For The Money You Spend

854 Crane Street   Schenectady, N.Y.

Delaney and Baker	Mohawk Valley Bakery
Wybome Mięso i Wszywa	Pierwszorzędna Polska Piekarnia
954 Crane St. Schenectady	869 Crane St. Tel. 4-9501
	A. Szwetkowski, właściciel

ZARZĄD KÓŁKA

Prezes .... Stanisław Zych
Wice prezes .... Leon Marciniuk
Sekretarka .... Wanda Bentzel
Kasjerka .... Aniela Pitera
Marszałek .... Bolesław Banaszyk
Zarządca finansów .... W. C. Sękowski
Zarządca estrady .... Mieczysław Zych
Korespondent pism .... Józef Ciechowicz

Zarządca własności ..... Jan Laskowski
Zarządcy garderoby: Stefania Lewkowicz i Jan Bełniak
Charakteryzatorka: Helena Kilian, Genowefa Steinnach, Jadwiga Godzieszka, Janina Dmgosielska
Parljamentarka .... Alicja Nowacka
Komitet programu: W. C. Sękowski, Lucjan Sękowski i Leon Marciniuk

SPRING HILL COAL CO., Inc.

Zaszczytna znana polska firma — "Swój do swego po swoje"

Edison Avenue i Erie Boulevard .... Nap. G. E. Main Entrance

Telefon 2-7044   B. Bojczuk, zarządca

CARLSON'S
PAINT AND WALL PAPER
ARTIST MATERIAL

1006 Crane Street   515 State Street

Meble dostarczone bezinteresownie przez

MONT PLEASANT FURNITURE HOUSE

722 Crane Street   Schenectady, N. Y.

1936, February

CHARLIE'S AUNT

Director
Act I – Scene takes place in the student dormitory of Oxford University
Chesney
Oxford student
Oxford student
Oxford student
Servant
London attorney
His daughter
Her relative

Union College Swordsmen
Captain; pan = Mr.; narrator

Act II – The university garden.
Characters the same as above and
Millionairess
Young Englishwoman
Act III – Scene takes place in the lawyer Spettigue's salon
The characters are the same as the other acts, and
Servant
JUDGES IN THE STAGE PERSONALITY CONTEST

SUPPORT COMMITTEE

THANK YOUS
To the Patrons of the Maska Dramatic Circle, we give a big Polish "May God Repay you" for recognizing our work and for sincere support to date. We invite the honorable Polish community to our fifth and final Program of this season which will take place on Sunday, March 29, 1936, at the Polish home.
The Maska Dramatic Circle

"CIOTKA KAROLA"
T. BRANDON

Reżyser .... Józef Czyżewski

AKT I—Scena przedstawia sypialnię studentów uniwersytetu Oxford

Lord Frank Chesney .... Józef Czyżewski
Lord Bobberley, student uniwersytetu Oxford .... Leon Marcinek
Jacob Chesney, student uniwersytetu Oxford .... Jan Łaniewski
Karol Wykham, student uniwersytetu Oxford .... Henryk Klejsmyt
Brassel, służący .... Tadeusz Kiljan
Stephen Spettigue, adwokat w Londynie .... Józef Drapała
Anna Spettigue, jego córka .... Irena Witkowska
Kasia Verdun, jej krewna .... Alicja Nowicka

FECHMISTRZE Z KOLEGJUM UNION:

Pan J. Righter, kapitan; pan E. Sheldon; pan M. Tytko, objaśniający

AKT II—Rzecz dzieje się na uniwersyteckim ogrodzie

Ci sami jak wyżej, i—
Donna Lucya D'Alvadorez, miljonerka .... Leokadja Wanik
Ella Deliahay, młoda Angliczka .... Irena Brzostowska

AKT III—Scena przedstawia salon w domu adwokata Spettigue

Ci sami co i w drugim akcie, i—
Marynia, służąca .... Aniela Pitera

Sędziami Konkursu Scenicznego "Stage Personality" Są:
Dr. M. J. Dybich, prof. S. Kosiński i prof. S. Belniak

KOMITET POMOCNICZY:

Władysław C. Sękowski, Stefanja Lewkowicz, Zofja Chojnicka, Franciszka Harasimowicz, Bolesław Bończyk i Lucjan J. Sękowski

PODZIĘKOWANIE

Patronom Kółka Dramatycznego "Maska" składamy staropolskie "Bóg zapłać" za uznanie naszej pracy i za szczere poparcie dotychczas. Zapraszamy Szan. Polonję na nasze piąte i ostatnie przedstawienie tego sezonu, które odbędzie się w niedzielę, 29-go marca, 1936 roku, w Domu Polskim

Kółko Dramatyczne "Maska"

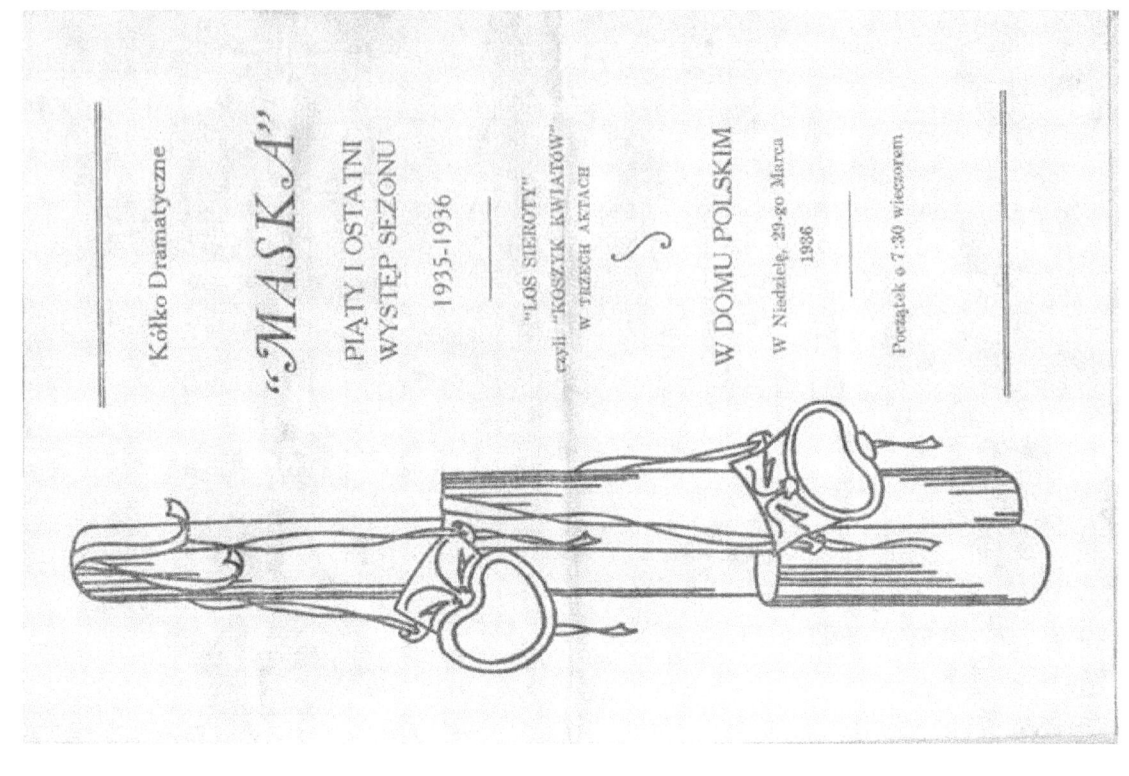

1936, March

Dramatic Circle

"MASKA"

Fifth and final offering of the season

1935 - 1936

FATE OF THE ORPHAN OR A BASKET OF FLOWERS

in Three Acts

At the Polish Home

Sunday, March 29th, 1936

Starting at 7:30 PM

1936, March

CIRCLE OFFICERS
President — Property Manager
Vice-Pres. — Costume Managers
Secretary — Makeup
Treasurer — Parliamentarian
Marshal — Program comm.
Finance Director
Scenery Director
Corresponding Secretary
Stage Manager

COMPLIMENTS OF

DR. B. C. MAZUROWSKI

813 Crane Street   Schenectady, N. Y.

Compliments of

Mont Pleasant Lunch

☆

936 Crane St., Schenectady

The Only Liquor Store in Mont Pleasant

☆

W. C. Schopman, prop.

558 Crane St.   Phone 4-5252

ZARZĄD KÓŁKA

Prezes .... Stanisław Zych
Wice-prezes .... Leon Marciniak
Sekretarka .... Wanda Hennel
Kasjerka .... Aniela Pitera
Marszałek .... Bolesław Bobczyk
Zarządca finansów .. W. C. Schowal
Dyrektorka scenerii .... W. Hennel
Korespondent pasu .. Józef Chodorecki
Zarządca estrady ... Mieczysław Zych

Zarządca własności ... Jan Lankowski
Zarządcy garderoby: Stefania Lewinowie i Jan Belluk
Charakteryzatorki: Helena Kilian, Genowefa Stelmach, Jadwiga Gębowska, Janina Darmolińska
Parliamentarka ...... Alicja Nowicka
Komisi programu: W. Ch---ałowski, Lucjan Schorski i Stan---aw Zych

---

F. Semerad and Son

Plumbing and Heating Supplies
Wholesale and Retail

913 Crane St.   Tel. 2-1599

White Eagle Bakery

POLSKA PIEKARNIA

Czesław Cieszkowski i
Władysław Szaulauski, właściciele

1138 Crane St. W pobliżu 8 Ave.
Telefon 2-7545

Meble dostarczone bezinteresownie przez

MONT PLEASANT FURNITURE HOUSE

722 Crane Street   Schenectady, N. Y.

Furniture donated by

POLISH BAKERY

Proprietors

1936, March

THE FATE OF ORPHANS OR A BASKET OF FLOWERS

According to the novels of X. Schmidt – Adapted by Jozef Chociszewski

Directors	
Gardener	
His daughter	
Judge	
Old rifleman	
His son	
Host	
Maid	
His wife	
Their son	
Jedrzej's wife	
Count	
Countess	
Their daughter	
Priest	
Two of the judge's pages	

Judges for the "Stage Personality" Contest

SUPPORT COMMITTEE

THANK YOUS

To the Patrons of the Maska Dramatic Circle, we give a big Polish "May God Repay you" for recognizing our work and for sincere support this whole season.
The Maska Dramatic Circle

THREE ACTS: Action takes place in Poland about 1858.

Scene I - Garden in front of Jakub's home

Scene II - A prison

Scene III - 4 years later. A room in Szymon's home.

Near the end of Scene III the curtain comes down, indicating that 15 minutes have passed.

Scene IV - A year later at Szymon's home.

Scene V - A room in the ducal castle

"Chopin" Men's Choir

Conductor

"Los Sieroty" czyli "Koszyk Kwiatów"

Podług powieści X. Schmidt– Opracował Józef Chociszewski

Reży-serzy —panna Agnieszka J. Pieszczoch, p. Józef Czyżewski

Jakub Kwieciński, ogrodnik	Stanisław Zych
Marynia, jego córka	Agnieszka Pieszczoch
Sędzia	Leon Marcinek
Antoni, stary strzelec	Lucjan J. Sękowski
Stanisław, jego syn	Bronisław Deptuła
Szymon, gospodarz	Henryk Klejsmyt
Joanka, pokojówka	Franciszka Harasimowicz
Katarzyna, jego żona	Aniela Pitera
Jędrzej, ich syn	Franciszek Borkowski
Brygida, żona Jędrzeja	Jadwiga Godlewska
Hrabia	Henryk Lewkowicz
Hrabina	Wanda Hennel
Zofja, ich córka	Wanda Gerut
Ksiądz	V. W. Platt
Dwóch pacholków sądowych	Tadeusz Kilian i Bolesław Bończyk

TREŚĆ SZTUKI: Rzecz dzieje się w Polsce w roku 1858

Odsłona I —Ogród przed domem Jakuba.
Odsłona II —Scena braciclawia więzienie.
Odsłona III—4 lata później. Pokój w domu Szymonostwa. Przy końcu odsłony III ściągnięte zasłony zaznaczy, że 15 minut czasu ujęto.
Odsłona IV—Rok później w domu Szymonostwa.
Odsłona V—Rzecz dzieje się w sali w zamku książęcym.

Sędziami Kontestu Scenicznego "Stage Personality" Są:
Prof. S. Kosiński, prof. S. Bełniak i Dr. M. J. Dybich

KOMITET POMOCNICZY:

Zofja Chojnicka, Agnieszka Dmochowska, Irena Nowicka, Alicja Nowicka, Velma Dombkowska, Stefanja Lewkowicz, Edward Hentel, Zygmunt Brzozowski, Władysław C. Sękowski

PODZIĘKOWANIE

Patronom Kółka Dramatycznego "Maska" składamy staropolskie "Bóg zapłać" za uznanie naszej pracy i za szczere poparcie całego sezonu.

Kółko Dramatyczne "Maska"

CHÓR MĘSKI "CHOPIN"

"Wisła"	F. Wiedeman
"The Bubble"	Rudolph Frihn
"Dumka"	St. Niedzielski

Dyrygent p. Feliks S. Woźnicki

1936, December

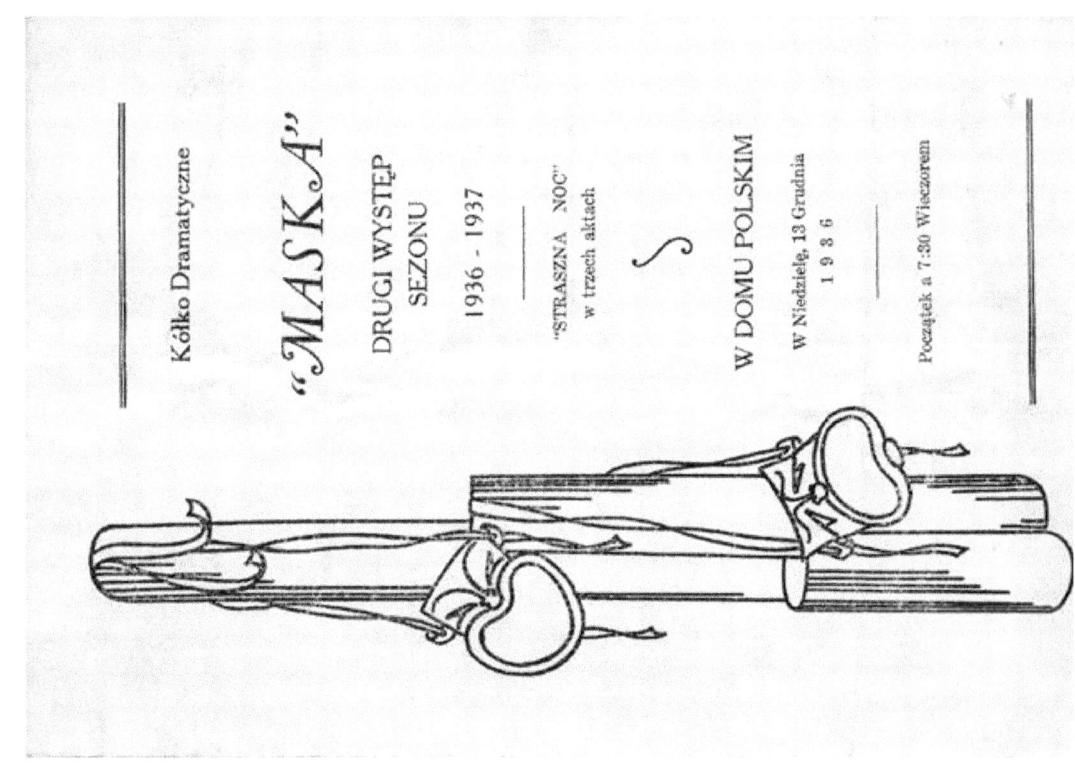

Dramatic Circle

"MASKA"

Second Offering of the Season

1936 - 1937

"TERRIBLE NIGHT"
in three acts

At the Polish Home

Sunday, December 13, 1936

Starting at 7:30 PM

1936, December, cont.

FOR—

GREEN SPOT ORANGE-ADE

MADE FROM RIPE FRUIT

—and—

STILLICI CHOCOLATE MILK

Phone 2-7853

1125 Van Cortlandt St.   Schenectady, N. Y.

Furniture donated by

Meble dostarczone bezinteresownie przez

MONT PLEASANT FURNITURE HOUSE

722 Crane Street   Schenectady, N. Y.

Support Committee

KOMITET POMOCNICY:

V. W. Platt, przewodniczący; estrada i artystyczne wykonanie, Zygmunt Kilian, Zygmunt Brzozowski; do pomocy, Irena Nowicka, Irena Witkowska, Velma Dombkowska, Marja Dziuba, Alicja Nowicka, Zofja Hojnicka, J. Łaniewski i L. Sękowski.

Best Wishes   Phone 4-4029

QUANDT BREWING COMPANY

Schenectady Branch

LAGER   ALE   STOCK   PORTER

Office and Warehouse 168-1684 Van Guysling Ave., Schenectady

George Voris, Manager

1936, December, cont.

If you want to save money on your Christmas purchases, please visit our store's shoes and boots.

TERRIBLE NIGHT

In three acts, a mysterious comedy, written by Z. A. Z.

Director

Mankiewicz's servant

Set at Mankiewicz's resort "The Swallow" in the Adirondack Mountains

ACT I – At the end of the day, December 13
ACT II – A few minutes after
ACT III – At night, the same day

JEŻELI CHCECIE ZAOSZCZĘDZIĆ NA WASZYCH ŚWIĄTECZNYCH ZAKUPNACH, ODWIEDŹCIE SKLEP OBUWIA

LEWANDOWSKI and SON

954 Crane Street   Schenectady, N. Y.

"STRASZNA NOC"

W trzech aktach, Tajemnicza Komedja—napisana przez Z. A. Z.

Jan, Karol Bogdan	Jan Laniewski
Hipollit Grzmot	Leon Marcinek
Dr. Magdalena Walczak	Frania Harasimowicz
Zosia Bejger	Agnieszka Dmochowska
Khalif, służący Mankiewicza	Tadeusz Kilian
Kapitan Bernacki	Mateusz Ozarowski
Marcin Grabicki	Stanisław Zych
Tadeusz Szymański	Henryk Klejsmyt
Paweł Mankiewicz	Józef Czyżewski
Barbara	Genowefa Stelmach

Rzecz dzieje się w letnisku "Jaskółka" Mankiewicza w górach Adirondacks

AKT I—Przy końcu dnia 13 grudnia.
AKT II—Parę minut później.
AKT III—Noc tego samego dnia.

Compliments of	Compliments of
The Only Liquor Store in Mt. Pleasant	Edward A. WEINSTEIN
WM. C. SCHOPMAN	MEN'S AND BOYS' CLOTHIER AND FURNISHER
958 Crane Street	916 Crane Street

1936, December, cont.

Patrons and Patronesses of the
"MASKA" Dramatic Circle

My grandmother,
Rozalia Rozanska Zych

ACKNOWLEDGMENT

The "MASKA" Dramatic Circle gives an old Polish
"May God Repay You" for recognizing our work
and for a sincere timely support. We
invite Esteemed Polonia to our third presentation
of this season, which will be presented on Sunday,
February 21, 1937, at the Polish Home.

The "Maska" Dramatic Circle

PATRONI I PATRONKI KÓŁKA DRAMATYCZNEGO "MASKA"

Pp. Brówka
Pp. A. R. Brzozowscy
Pp. J. Drogata
Pp. W. Gąsowscy
Pp. F. Heinzel
Pp. S. Hildebrand
Pp. B. Lewkowicz
Pp. H. Lewkowicz
Pp. D. Łoniewscy
Pp. J. Kilian
Pp. W. Klejszmyt
Pp. A. Kopeć
Pp. S. Marcinek
Ikrostwo B. C. Mazurowscy
Pp. K. S. Opalowscy
Pp. M. Penichter
Pp. F. Pieszczoch
Pp. G. Sęborscy
Pp. C. Pełczywniecy
Pp. J. Stelmach
Pp. A. Wanik
Pp. J. Zalucey
Pani M. Barczewska
Pani M. Bartosiewicz
Pani K. Bednarska
Pani P. Boaryk
Pani M. Caularnia
Pani F. Chojbłeka
Pani H. Ciezabroniewicz
Pani F. Dmochowska
Pani R. Dmochowska
Pani A. Faluszczak
Pani M. Galka
Pani Górecka
Pani M. Goszewska

Pani A. Grzywacewska
Pani R. J. Kietlińska
Pani F. Krasnowska
Pani K. Laniewska
Pani V. Laniewska
Pani Z. Majcherców
Pani M. Marchewka
Pani J. Mareinek
Pani A. Max
Pani M. Milczarek
Pani J. Mieszutowicz
Pani W. Nowicka
Pani A. Oniak
Pani S. Pawłowicz
Pani M. Pitera
Pani F. Piewencka
Pani R. Ruszczyńska
Pani J. Rutkowska
Pani R. Skamarska
Pani J. Srodońska
Pani M. Tendzigółska
Pani S. Trypaluk
Pani B. Turska
Pani S. Tyiko
Pani J. Witkowska
Pani A. Zalocka
Pani J. Życia
Pani V. Żywot
Panna A. Dreszczyńska
Panna G. Dwojakowska
Panna M. Dzluba
Panna F. Harasimowicz
Panna I. Jarvis
Panna H. Kamińska
Panna A. Kobietna

Panna M. Pieszczoch
Panna A. Rykowska
Panna J. Stelmach
Panna L. Wanik
Pan A. Aduch
Pan J. Bidlowski
Pan S. Czarter
Pan J. Czylewsi
Pan J. Depiula
Dr. M. J. Dybich
Pan E. Deluba
Pan N. Ferraro
Pan S. Hombkowski
Pan J. Jawa
Pan M. Kiędzis
Pan F. Kosiński
Pan T. Marcinkiewicz
Pan W. Okoński
Pan W. Pastorczyk
Pan A. Piali
Pan S. Piecharczyk
Pan M. Rekucki
Pan Rudicowski
Pan F. Rutkowski
Pan K. C. Sarnowski
Pan A. Sarnowski
Pan Z. M. Sawaniewski
Pan F. E. Stafford
Pan F. Surowiec
Pan T. E. Święcicki
Pan C. Urbański
Pan Z. Wiśniewski
Pan Wołoszniewicz
Pan A. Zwolski
Pan R. Dmochowski
Tow. "Prawda i Praca"

PODZIĘKOWANIE

Patronom Kółka Dramatycznego "Maska" składamy staro
polskie "Bóg zapłać za uznanie naszej pracy i za szczere
dotychczasowe poparcie. Zapraszamy Szan. Polonję na nasze
trzecie przedstawienie tego sezonu, które odbędzie się w niedzielę, 21 lutego, 1937 roku, w Domu Polskim.

Kółko Dramatyczne "Maska"

1937, February 21, cont.

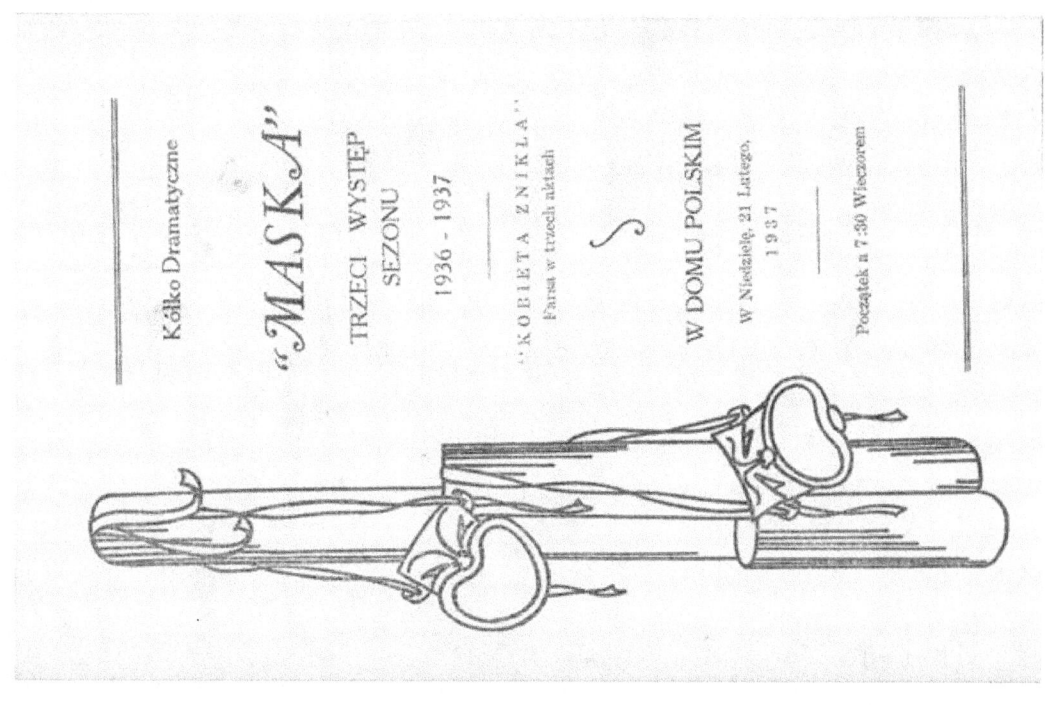

A WOMAN DISAPPEARS
A farce in three acts

At the Polish Home
Sunday, February 21, 1937

Starting at 7:30 pm

1937, February 21, cont.

—FOR—

GREEN SPOT ORANGE-ADE

MADE FROM RIPE FRUIT JUICES

—and—

CHOCOLATE MILK

PLEASANT VALLEY DAIRY

Phone 2-7853

1125 Van Cortlandt St. Schenectady, N. Y.

Furniture provided courtesy of

Meble dostarczone bezinteresownie przez

MONT PLEASANT FURNITURE HOUSE

722 Crane Street Schenectady, N. Y.

COMMITTEE

KOMITET:

Chairman — V. W. Platt, przewodniczący; H. Klejsmit, Z. Brzozowski, Z. Kilian,
Stage and Artistic performances — estrada i artystyczne wykonanie; panny Zofja Chojnicka i Agnieszka Pleszczoch,
Helpers — oraz Leon Marcinek, do pomocy;
Press — Bernard Deptuła, prasa.

Shoes and boots of the best quality at the lowest prices.

OBUWIE NAJLEPSZEJ JAKOŚCI PO NAJNIŻSZYCH CENACH

LEWANDOWSKI and SON

854 Crane Street Schenectady, N. Y.

1937, February 21, cont.

A WOMAN DISAPPEARS
A farce in three acts – written by J.C.

The boarding house owner
Police inspector
Mrs. Domagalski's maid
Grant's window decorator
Young woman
Young Serbian
Novel writer
Man from Georgia
Who wants to become "Mae West"
Policeman
Who brought a package
A woman dressed in black, a mysterious figure
Mrs. Domagalski's kitten

The play takes place in the evening in Mrs. Domagalski's room. Everything takes place in the parlor. The house is located in a large city in the eastern United States. Present time.
Act I - At eight in the evening in fall
Act II - A little later
Act III - Five minutes later

F. L. LESZCZYNSKI
FUNERAL DIRECTOR

Chapels at 778 Eastern Ave., and at 716 Crane Street
Phone 4-3200

"KOBIETA ZNIKŁA"
Farsa w trzech aktach.—Napisał J. C.

Urszula Domagalska, właścicielka domu dla stołowników. Marj. Driuba
Konstanty S. Piernik, inspektor policyjny .... Stanisław Zych
Dorota Pokraka, służąca pani Domagalskiej .... Zofja Korycińska
Adrjan Pyszny, dekorator okien w Grant's .... Bronisław Deptuła
Zuzanna Gołombek, młoda panienka .... Genowefa Stelmach
Teodor Gregorievich Petruszka, młody Serbjanin .... Józef Czyżewski
Stefanja Samida, pisarka noweli .... Helena Kilian
Pułkownik Eugenjusz Bonaparte Bogaś, pan z Georgia . M. Ozarowski
Marta Połyczek, która pragnie zostać "Mae West" .... Jadwiga Woltner
Marcin Ostrembak, policjant .... Lucjan Sękowski
Marcela Dzwonek, która przyniosła pakunek .... Alicja Nowicka
Kobieta na czarno ubrana, tajemnicza figura .... Marja Zborowska
Oleś, kotek pani Domagalskiej .... Toby

Reżyser sztuki, Józef Czyżewski

Sztuka przedstawia wieczór w pokoju pani Domagalskiej. Wszystko dzieje się w ławiahnym pokoju. Dom znajduje się w wielkiem mieście na wschodzie Stanów Zjednoczonych. Czas dzisiejszy.

AKT I—O ósmej wieczorem w jesieni.
AKT II—Trochę później.
AKT III—Pięć minut później.

ADVANCED BAKERY
T. E. Święcki, właściciel

NAJPIERWSZA POLSKA PIEKARNIA W MIEŚCIE
Wszelkiego rodzaju pieczywo dla detalicznej sprzedaży

719 Windsor Terrace   Tel. 4-4064

The first [i.e., best] Polish bakery in town.
All types of baked goods for sale

1938, October 9 — Dramatic Circle

LEGIONNAIRE ON THE FIELD OF HONOR

Director

CAST
Count and captain
His son, lieutenant
Soldier from 1863
Old teacher
His wife
Their daughter
Young teacher
Countess
Her trustee
Russian spy
Grave digger
Trumpeter

SCENES
Act I - Room in Count Anzelm's palace
Act II - Garden at Zytnicki's home
Act III - Garden
Act IV-A room in Zytnicki's home
Act V - Cemetery
Act VI - Ending and Tableau

The scenery was prepared by Patrons and Patronesses

First presentation of the Season

Sunday, October 9, 1938
at the Polish Home

Legionnaire on the Field of Honor
A drama in 6 acts

Appendix 4 — Page 170 — Maska Programs

1938,
October 9
continued

Kółka Dramatycznego

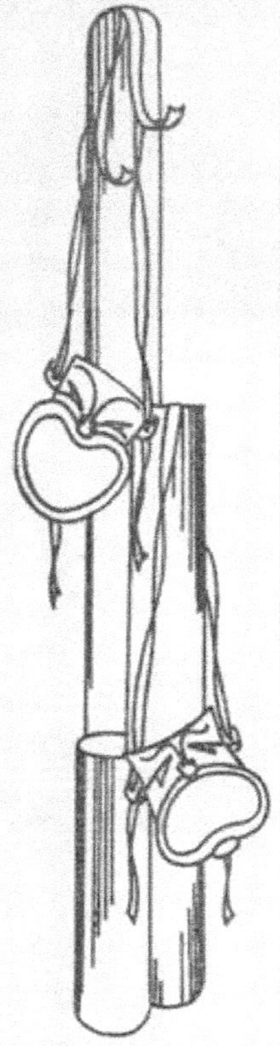

'MASKA'

Pierwszy Występ
Sezonu
1938-1939

Niedziela, 9 Października, 1938
W Domu Polskim
"Legjonista na Polu Chwały"
Dramat w trzech aktach

PROGRAM

"LEGJONISTA NA POLU CHWAŁY"

Reżyser .... Stanisław Zych ← My Father

OSOBY:

ANZELM ZAPOLSKI, hrabia i rotmistrz .... Mieczysław Ozarowski
KAROL, syn jego, porucznik .... Władysław Zborowski
WĄSAŁA, żołnierz z roku 1863 .... Józef Czyżewski
ŻYTNICKI, stary nauczyciel .... Henryk Klejsmyt
MARTA, jego żona .... Wanda Korycińska ← My Mother's Sister
WANDA, ich córka .... Genowefa Stelmach
SOSNOWSKI, młody nauczyciel .... Władysław Żołądź
AURORA MISENKO, hrabina .... Zofja Korycińska ← My Mother
SŁOMKA, jej powiernik .... Stanisław Bachleda
MOSIEK PINKELES, szpieg rosyjski .... Henryk Ausfeld
GRABARZ .... ??
TRĘBACZ .... Stefan Gorzyński

SCENY:

AKT I—Pokój w pałacu hrabiego Anzelma.
AKT II—Ogród. Dom Żytnickiego.
AKT III—Ogród.
AKT IV—Pokój w domu Żytnickiego.
AKT V—Cmentarz.
AKT VI—Zakończenie i żywy Obraz.

Rzecz dzieje się w Polsce podczas wojny światowej w roku 1916

Przygotowania sceniczne wykonane przez p. Zygmunta Brzozowskiego, pannę M. Zborowską i pannę Z. Korycińską. ← My Mother

PATRONI I PATRONKI KÓŁKA DRAMATYCZNEGO "MASKA"

Pp. W. Ausfeld
Pp. A. B. Brzozowscy
Pp. W. Klejsmyt
Pp. S. Korkosz
Pp. P. Korycińscy
Pp. B. Lastowscy
Pp. G. Sękowscy
Pp. S. Tytko
Pani A. Kostek
Pani M. Pajerska
Pani R. Zych
Pani J. Pentkowska
Pani J. Przybylska
Pani S. Ciesiel
Pani K. Dziuba
Pani M. Woje
Pani B. Turska
Pani J. Dziuba
Pani E. Bartoszewicz
Pani A. Wiśniewska
Pani N. Chlewińska
Pani A. Czyżewska

Pani J. Ambrozek
Pani T. Bartoszewicz
Pani T. Jaroszewska
Pani V. Żywot
Pani E. Wyszomierska
Pani M. Stelmach
Pani A. Chodzka
Pani S. Piecharczyk
Pani S. Piecharczyk
Pani Borowska
Pani W. Ogurewska
Pani M. Milczarek
Pani M. Petera
Pani M. Malinowska
Pani R. Glender
Pani H. Lewkowicz
Panna S. Kostek
Panna M. Krampa
Panna E. A. Rogowicz
Panna J. Stelmach
Panna S. Dwojakowska

Pan A. Nosal
Pan J. Zborowski
Pan J. Nowakielski
Pan E. Morawski
Pan J. Gryzka
Pan K. Szalewski
Pan J. Drycola
Pan J. Saminiec
Pan W. D. Przybyłek
Pan A. Szpak
Pan A. Marcinkiewicz
Pan K. S. Ogurewski
Dr. B. C. Mazurowski
Pan F. Kosiński
Pan J. Lastowski
Pan M. Rekucki
Pan K. C. Baranowski
Pan Z. Szwankowski
Pan F. Surowica
Pan D. Zmysłowski
Pan A. Zwolski
Pan B. Lewkowicz

Jedyna Polska Firma Futernicza w okolicy ← The only Polish furrier in the area

Skład Najnowszego Fasonu Futer i Pracownia. Zupełna gwarancja. Za gotówkę lub na spłaty.

PRZERÓBKI I REPERACJE PO NISKICH CENACH

SKŁAD I PRACOWNIA
931-933 FRANCIS AVE.
FILJA—10 ERIE BLVD.
E. Lewkowicz, właściciel
Telefon 8-XXXX

BEST WISHES

Walter Daniel Przybylek, Ph. G.

MYERS DRUG STORE
COR. CRANE STREET AND FRANCIS AVE.
PHONE 6-8774

The action takes place in Poland during the World War in 1916.

STAN'S TAVERN
NEW LOCATION AT
917 CRANE STREET
Old Location, 113 Crane St.
Best Beer, Wines and Liquors
Zarazem smaczne przekąski
S. Szczepański, właściciel

Crane St. Liquor Store
William C. Schopman, prop.
ALL KINDS OF DOMESTIC AND IMPORTED LIQUORS AND WINES
Orders Promptly Delivered
959 Crane St. Phone 4-6262

SNYDER'S TAVERN
BEER, WINE, LIQUORS
740 Crane St., Opp. P. N. A.

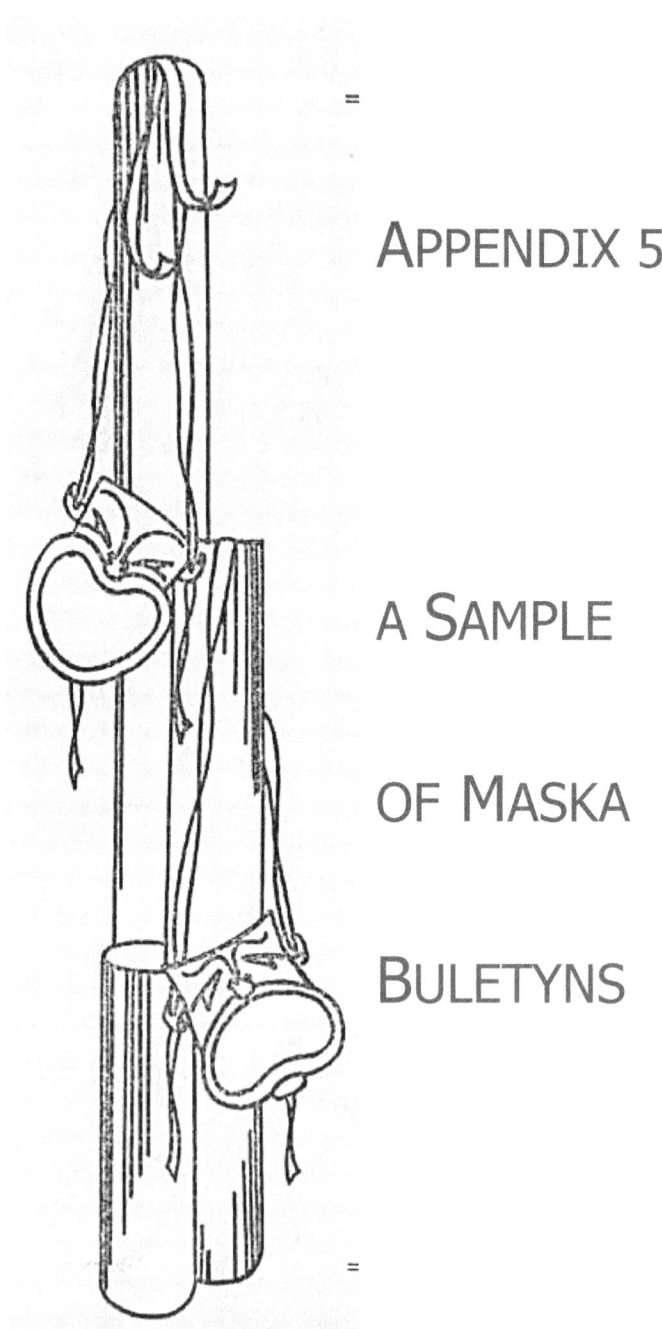

Appendix 5

A Sample of Maska Buletyns

1938, December

1938, December

Tailor
Performing all work
Clothing on commission

Beer – Liquor and Polish refreshments   Proprietor

MASKA
Dramatic Circle
Second Presentation
of the 1938-1939 Season

Sunday Dec. 4, 1938

QUICK WORK –
A Comedy in 3 Acts
Directed by Jozef Czyzewski

Mom's Sister

Mom

Promote one of our younger generation who are rendering our hill more pleasant With good liquors, beer and a Polish kitchen...

Owner

CAST: Mr. & Mrs. Potocki's maid; Mr. Smietanka's butler; President of the firm; "Smietanka's Pickels Inc.; Smietanka's clever lawyer; First class detective; Writer, author of the novel "The Cheated Goat;" Smietanka's aunt from Holyoke; Her daughter; A young woman from Chicopee.

Time-Today-a spring morning between seven and nine. The scene takes place in the lounge of the Smietanki's home in Brooklyn. Scenery by Z. Brzozowksi-Z. Kilian

1938, December

MASKA BULETYN

Num. 1 Grudzien '38

(Ten artykul jest pierwszy rzadu ktory bedzie wychodzic w kazdy miesiac z innem czlonkim kolka)

LUCJAN J. SEKOWSKI

Szosty sezon "MASKA", kolka dramatycznego, jest teraz celebrowany przez praktycznie kazdego jednego z nas z serdecznymi zyczeniami dla dalszych dokonam szczescia i pomyslnosci. Celem zalozenia tego kolka jest dla promocyji dramat, sztuk teatralnych, i ksztalczenia w Polskim jezyku czlonkow na polach konkurencyji w rozmaitych ksztaltach rozwebelajacych czynnosci przez nasza POLSKA mlodziez. My ten cel dobrze utrzymali i dozyli do terazniejszego czasu i spodziewami ze dalej bedziem prowadzic ta dobra prace. Wowczas spolecznie wieksza harmonijna, jednozgodna i tej samej natury postawa jest takze wybitna pomiedzy naszemi towarzysz czlonkami.

W tych latach ktore przeszli wiele zmian przysli dokola z nowemi ideami i nowe czlonki, wiec, my mysleli ze to by byl stosowny giest w tym czasie przez przedstawienie MASKA BULETYN, z spolpracowaniem kazdego czlonka, aby zaczac zaznajomic do was czynnosci i wykonania o tem i tamtem towarzysz czlonku, i w jakiej role on lub ona wypelnili swoja czesc w przyprowadzenia szczescia i pomyslnosci kolka.

Zaznajomienie naszego pierwszego, front nakrycia, czlonka jest praktycznie niepotrzebnie. Dobrzy wygladajacy czlonka jak nakrycia fotografja twarzy wynosi, jest naczelnym "MASKA" Kolka Dramatycznego w terazniejszym czasie, i my mozemy powiedzic ze jego dowodztwo jest polegajacego kaliberu.

Lucjan Sekowski byl przedstawiony do naszej organizacji w roku 1933, jakie trzy lub cztery miesiace po organizacji "MASKA" K. D. W tem czasie on przypomina nie bylo zadnych poczatkowych w prowadzen tak znanych po Angelsku, initiations. Produkt miejscowego bociana Lucjan moze powiedzic wam bardzo malo o swoich kolebki kornecie przypadkach, ale to jest nic o czem sie dziwic bo my wszyscy gak byli male mieli krotka pamiec.

Urodzony czwierc wieku temu w Schenectady, N. Y. Wazy sto szescdziesiat piec funty i powiada nam ze nie pamieta zeby kiedy byl chorym, ze zawsze jemu zdrowie sprzyjalo, to jest ze byl i jeszcze teraz jest w dobrym zdrowiu. Ksztalcil sie w szkole Sw. Wojciecha, i nalezy do tej parafji. W zial udzial w przedstawieniu ktore bylo pokazane przez

2

1938, December

ta szkole. Jest dobrym Polakiem, Katolikiem. Takze ksztalcil sie w Mc Kinley i w Schenectady Wyszej Szkole. Pozni przemochowali sie do Rotterdam sekcyji, i dalej sie tam uczyl w Draper W. Szkole, wlasciwie z powodu niemieszkajacy w miejscu swego urzadowego pobytu sciesnien. Gdy byl w tej szkole gral w pilke co sie rzuca do kosza i w pilke co sie uderza palka, czyli basket ball i baseball. Przemochowali sie nazat do Mont Pleasant powiatu, i w tem powiatu ukonczyl Mont Pleasant High Szkole.

Harcerstwo organizowane w Polskim Domu w roku 1935. On byl jeden z nauczycieli przez dwa lata. Takze czlonkiem "Konrad Naukowego Spoleczenstwa" w ktorym on jest vice prezes. On jest czlonkiem towarzystwa, "Zgoda", Z. N. P.

Gdy byl w wyszej szkole zainteresowany byl w dramat, sztuki teatralne, ale nie mogl w ziasc udzial w nich z powodu drugich dzialalnosci. Kiedy ukonczyl wysza szkole jego marzenie sie sprawdzilo. W stapil do "MASKA" K. D. ktore w tem czasie bylo w poczatkowym stanie. Podczas tego czasu co nalezal do tego Kolka on sie zajmowal wlasnosciami, ciezko pracowal przy dostawaniu ogloszen, byl pomocnikiem przy ustawianiu scen teatralnych, oglosicielemprzedstawien, pomagajacym dyrektorym, glownym dyrektorym sztuki co nam jak najlepiej sie udala "Trudy i Troski" Sluzyl razem z Helena Kilian na Komitecie zabaw i na barzarzo mojowym. Oglosili go na vice prezesa "Maska" K. D. 1936 do 1937. Szyzyt towarzystwa ufnosci byl powierzony na niego z prezestwem urzadem w roku 1937. Podczas jego terminu jako prezesa "Maska" celebrowala piata rocznice swojego istnienia. Tak wrazeniem sprawdzone byli skutki jego pierwszego terminu ze towarzystwo jednomyslnie powtornie wybrali naszego weterana jako prezesa, i znowu przedstawili i dali jemu mlot drewnianny., ktorego sie uzywa podczas posiedzenia. Jego w czesne wywiczenie tak dobrze usposobilo i uzdolnilo jego ze w krotce "Maska" K. D. gwarzylo z czynem Towarzystwa duch rozszerzyl sie tak jak ogien. Nie tylko my z skorzystali przez jego przewodnictwo ale takze przez jego wykonania w sztukach teatralnych i Kolka czynnosciach.

Lucyan Sekowski bral udzial w nastepujacych sztukach; Stryj Przyjechal; Gruby Skandal; Tatus Pozwolil; Malzenstwo Na Probe; Wet za Wet; Generalna Proba; Szpital Warjatow; Peruka Profesora, Koszyk Kwiatow; Niewinnosc Zwycieza; Kobieta Znikla; Chwalibieda; Djabel Z Monoklem; Szmieszna Glupota; Trudy i Troski.

W ruchomych obrazkach Lucjan dostaje najlepsze zadowolenie gdy widzi jak Frederic March, Amerykanski aktor odgrywa. Dla niego on jest najlepszym aktorym ten zdatny kochanek i milosnik Amerykanski. Lucjan uczeszcza na przedstawienia w parafji Sw. Wojciecha, Matki Boskiej Czestochowskiej na Eastern Ave, w Polskim Domu i u slowiakow. Woli odgrywac w roli charaktera zamiast jako zakochany; a role co nie sa za latwe podobaja sie mu. Jego ulubione rozrywki sa grac w pilke z palantem "Tennis", w pilke co sie rzuca w kosz, basket ball, i w kregle, bowling. Ulubione zatrudnienie, zeby zbierac pieniadze czyli praktykowac oszczednosc. Bo "Oszczednoscia i praca; ludzie sie bogaca" a dobrze jest byc przygotowany na deszczowy dzien, jak to mowia.

Lucjan Sekowski jest obyczajny, grzeczny, ciche mowiacy, sprawuje

1938. December

jak się należy i nie jest predki do gubienia swego usposobienia, to
jest ze jest łagodny i powolny w okazaniu i w czynnosci. Zdaje sie
byc czlowiekem wykształconym, dobrze wychowanem, miłym, ktory zawsze
myśli o drugich. Jest dobrym słuchaczem, dając innemu więcej niż
równa sposobnosc do rozmawiania. Nie proboje sprawic wrazen na innych
z jego własną waznoscią.

30-go azdziernika dzwiek organa mu i narzeczonej brzmiał -
uszach, znaczy mowiąc ze sie ozenił. Lucjan Sekowski ozenił sie z
Panna Janina Dwojakowska. Nie pali papierosy lub pije trunek. Mozna
sie spodziewac ze bedzie dobrym mazem z niego.

ZYCZY CI DOBREGO SZCZESCIA

Zygmond Kilian sacrificed much of his valuable time to make
a masterpiece drawing for the title sheet of this bulletin. Do we
appreciate it? We say we do.

We are glad to hear that Walter Zołądz, an active member of
our club, is progressing as manager of the Empire Market on Union St.
Here's to greater success andmay he keep his feet on the ground.

Walter Sekowski, attending Alliance College in Cambridge
Springs, Pa., has the highest scholastic standing in his class. He
is very active in the school social circles being chairman and speaker
on several occasions.

Hank Ausfeld was the person beneath that Jewish make up
which and who paraded around Polish Centers to advertise the play
"Predka Robota". Nice job---Hank---Tho---The whiskers itched.

23-rd of April is the date of our last performance of the
present season, this gives us time to formulate a grand show. So
expect, but fret over not, the coming smash hit.

ZYCZENIA OD
TOW. "Jedność"
GRUPA 2417   **Wishes from the "Jednosc" Society**

SERDECZ E ZYCZENIA ZASYŁA

Władysław Daniel Przybyłek PH.G.
Sending Sincere Wishes

MYERS Drug STORE

FRANCIS I GRANT ULICY   TELEFON 6-3774

1938, December

Patrons and Patronesses of the Maska Dramatic Circle

Pp. – Mr. & Mrs.
Pani – Mrs.
Panna – Miss
Pan – Mr.

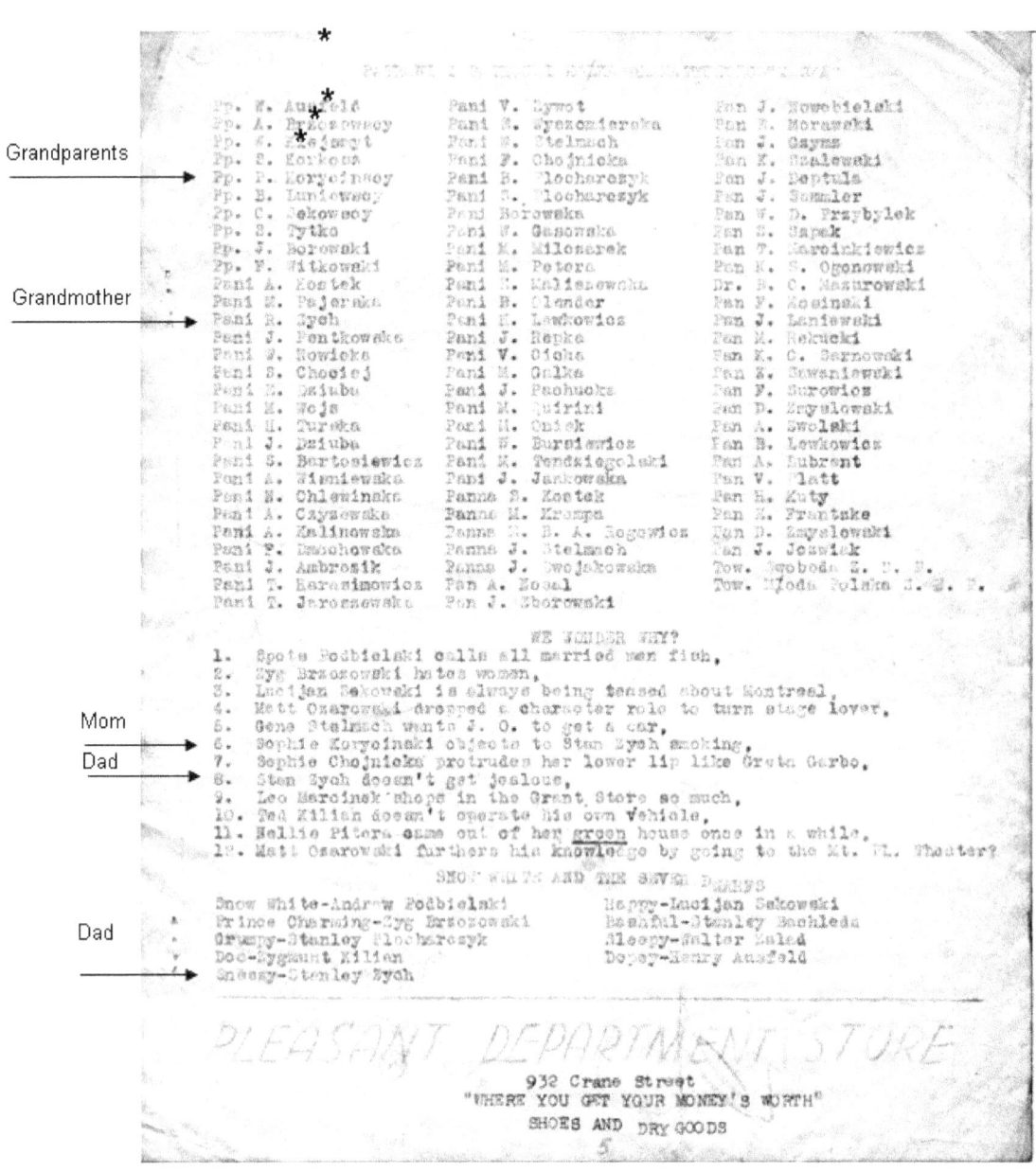

* Names with asterisks are the plural form of a name ending with "ski;"
my Grandparents, Mr. & Mrs. P. Korycinski, are Pp. P. Korycinscy.

1938, December - Translation

[Translator's Note: This article is the first in a series, appearing each month and presenting a different member of the circle]

LUCJAN J. SEKOWSKI

The sixth season of "MASKA," a dramatic circle, is now celebrated by everyone of us with sincere wishes for further accomplishments, happiness and success. The whole foundation of this circle is for the promotion of drama, theater arts, and education in the Polish language, training our youthful Polish members in a variety of related fields. This goal has been well maintained and has survived to the present time and we hope we will continue to provide this good work. At this time, this attitude which was harmonious, unanimous and of this same nature, is also outstanding between our friend - members.

Over the past few years, many changes have taken place with new ideas and new members, thus, we think that this was a suitable time to introduce the "MASKA BULETYN," with the collaboration of every member, to begin to acquaint you with the activities and performances of various members, in what role he or she fulfills their part in furthering the happiness and success of the Circle.

Introduction of the person on our first cover is practically unnecessary. The opening photograph is of handsome Lucjan Jan Sekowski, the leader of "MASKA" at this time, and we can say that his leadership is of the highest caliber.

Lucjan Sekowski was introduced to our organization in 1933, 3 or 4 months after organization of the "MASKA" D. C. (Dramatic Circle). At that time, he remembers, there were not any initial directions or, as it is called in English, initiations. A product of the local stork, Lucjan can tell you very little about his cradle accidents, that is nothing about which to be surprised because we all had short memories when we were young.

He was born a quarter century ago in Schenectady, N. Y. He weighs 165 pounds and tells us that he cannot remember when he was sick, good health has always favored him, that is he was and is currently in good health. He was educated at Saint Adalbert School and belongs to that parish. He participated in presentations given at that school. He is a good Pole, Catholic. He also went to McKinley and to Schenectady High School. Later they moved to the Rotterdam section, and later he studied at Draper High School, their stay was limited because they were not living there officially. When he was in that school, he played with a ball that you throw in a basket and with a ball that you hit with a bat, or basketball and baseball. They returned to the Mont Pleasant section, and there he finished Mont Pleasant High School.

The Polish Boy Scouts (Harcestwo) were organized in the Polish Home in 1935. He was one of the teachers for two years. He is a member of the "Conrad" Literary Society, in which he is vice-president. He is a member of "Zgoda" Z. N. P.

1938, December - Translation

When he was in high school, he became interested in dramatics, theater arts, but he could not take part in these because of other activities. When he finished high school, his dreams came true in joining the "MASKA" D. C. which at that time was in its beginning stages. During that time he belonged to that Circle but was busy with properties, worked hard on getting advertising, helped with scenery, advertising, presentations, helping with directing, and was director of our favorite play, the successful "Cares & Worries." He served together with Helen Kilian on the play committee, on the May playoffs committee. He was voted vice-president of "Maska" D. C. from 1936 to 1937. The society's highest trust was placed in him when he was elected president in 1937. During his term as president "Maska" celebrated five years since its inception. So impressive were the results of his first term that the society unanimously again selected our veteran as president, and gave him a wooden mallet to use during meetings. At the same time, the society's spirit has expanded like a fire. Not only have we benefited during his presidency but also during his performances in the plays and the Circle's activities.

Lucjan Sekowski performed in the following plays: "Uncle Arrived;" "Great Scandal"; "Papa Permits;" "Trial Marriage [aka Marriage on Trial];" "An Eye for An Eye;" "Dress Rehearsal;" "Hospital for the Insane;" "Professor's Wig;" "A Basket of Flowers;" "Innocence Conquers;" "A Woman Disappears;" "In Praise of Poverty;" "Comical Goofiness;" "Devil With a Monocle;" "Cares & Worries."

In the moving pictures Lucjan gets the most enjoyment when Frederic March, the American actor, is playing. For him (LS), he (FM) is the best actor, this fit lover and romantic American. Lucjan took part in presentations in the parishes of Saint Adalbert and Our Lady of Czestochowa (St. Mary's) on Eastern Avenue, at the Polish Home and the Slovaks. He prefers to play a role as a character instead of a lover; he prefers more difficult roles. His favorite entertainments are playing ball with a "tennis" racket, playing with a ball that is thrown into a basket, basketball and with pins, bowling. His favorite paid employment or money-saving practice. Because "Through thrift and work; people are simply rich," and it is good to be prepared for a rainy day, as they say.

Lucjan Sekowski is decent, kind, soft spoken, how one should be and is not quick to lose his temper, that is that he is mild and deliberate in his actions. It seems that he is an educated man, well-brought up, agreeable, who always thinks of others. He is a good listener, giving others more rather than an equal opportunity to speak. He does not try to impress others with his importance.

On October 30 to the sound of the organ he and his fiancee – with bells ringing in their ears, were married. Lucjan Sekowski married Miss Janina Dwojakowska. He does not smoke or drink liquor. One can speculate that he will be a good husband.

WE WISH YOU GOOD LUCK

1938, December

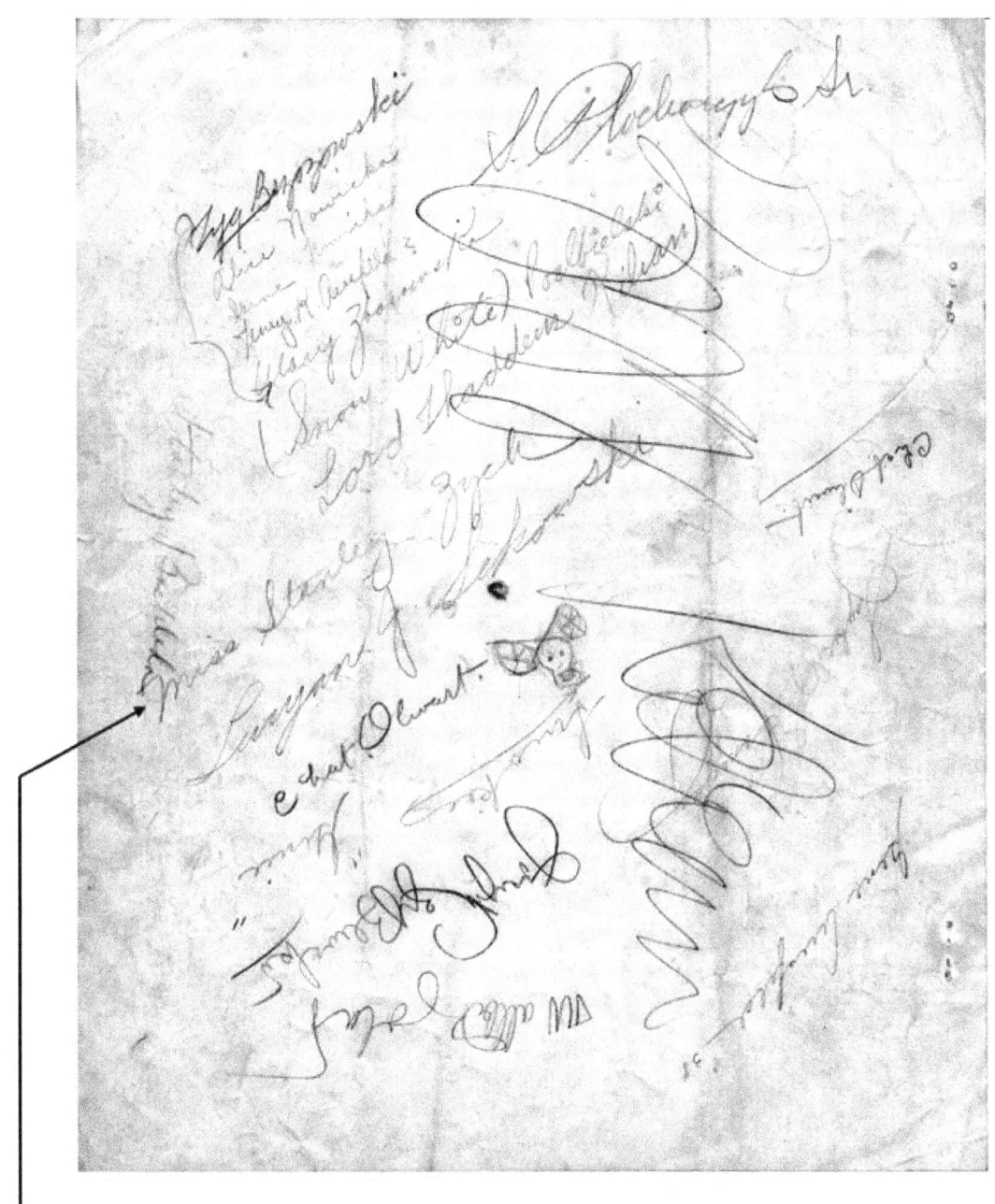

Mom's signature, playing with her future name.

1939, February

1939, February

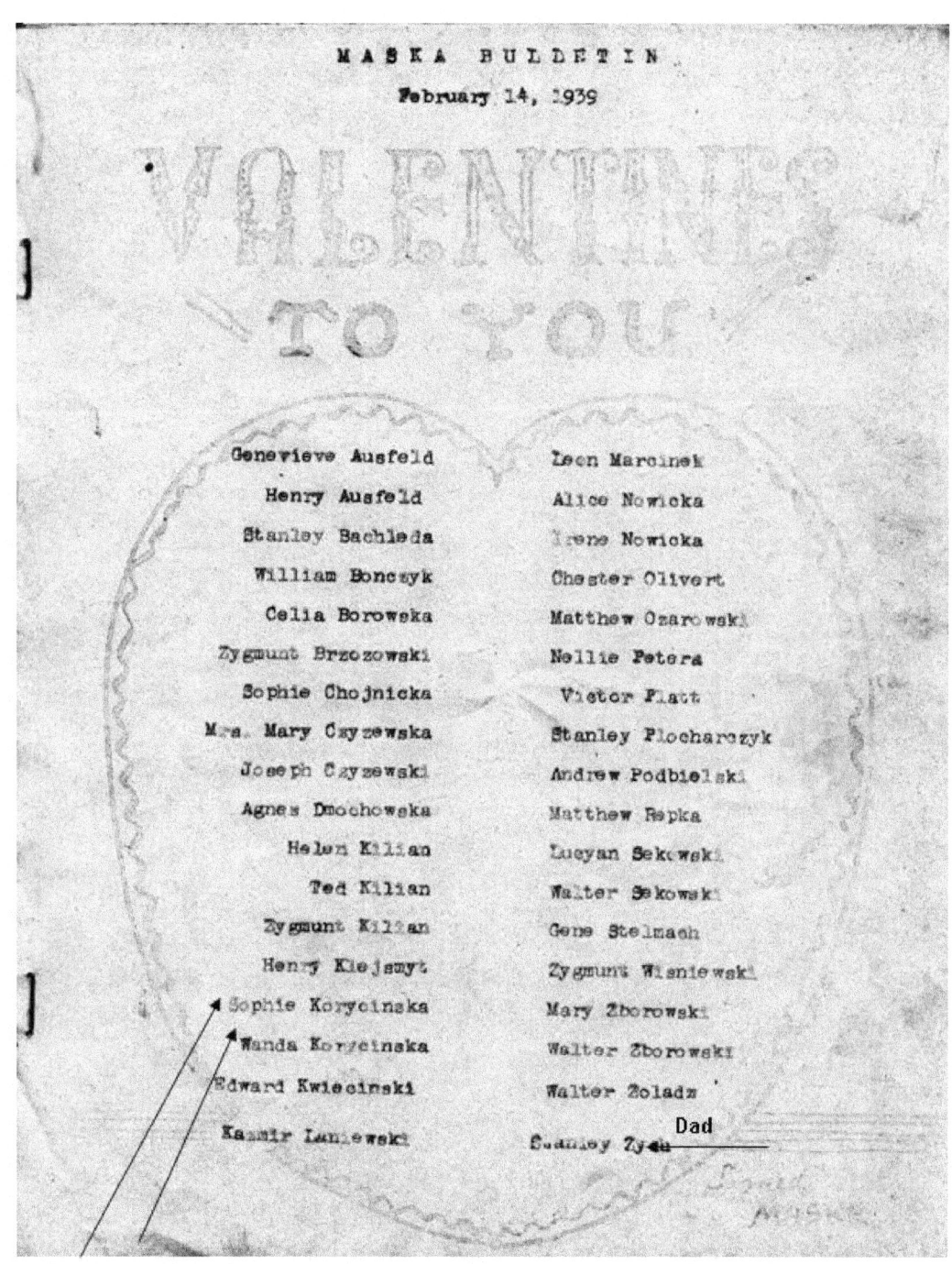

Mom   My Aunt

1939, February

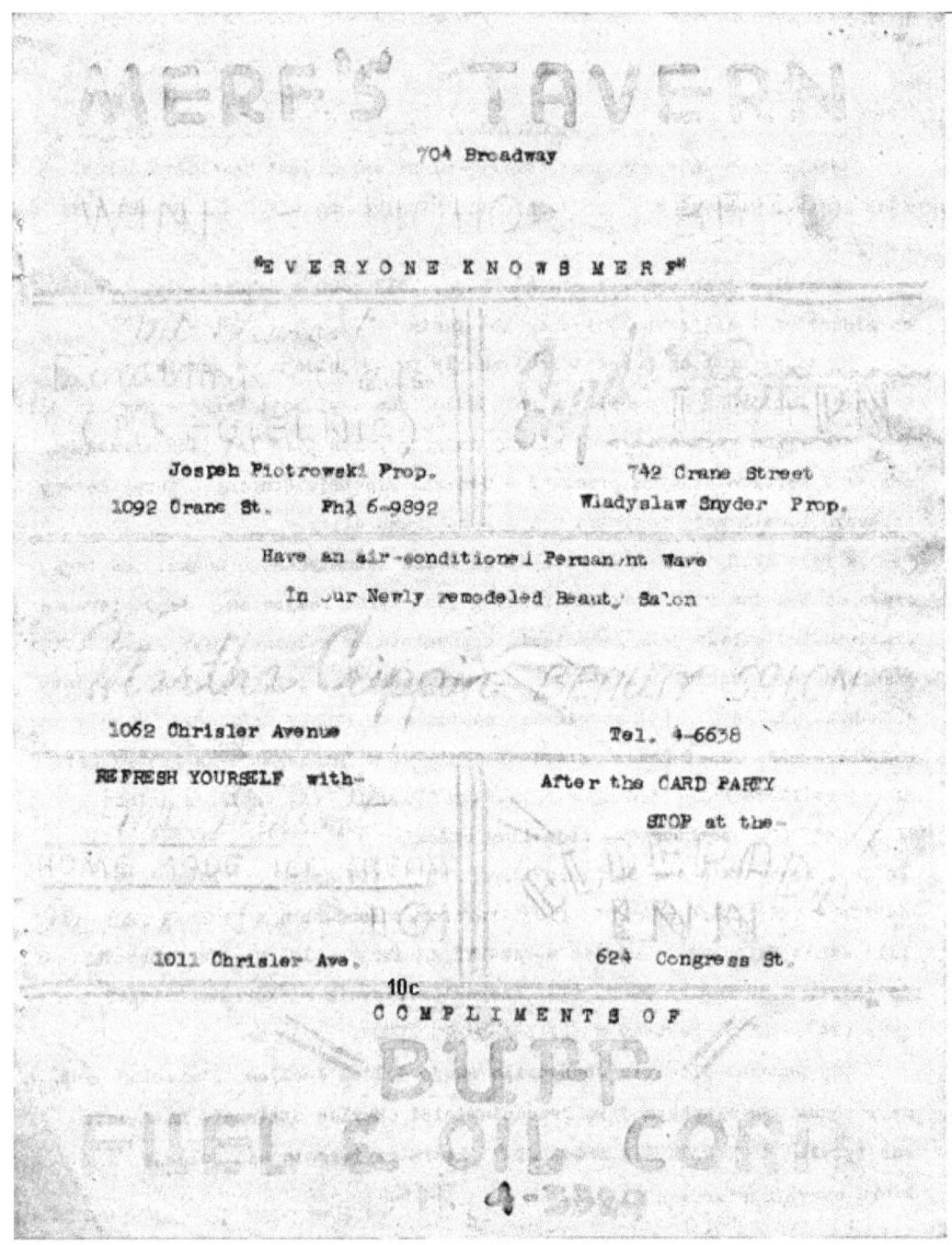

Second Row from the top, Left: Mt. Pleasant Bowling Alleys, Right: Snyders' Tavern.
Below across: Martha Crippin Beauty Salon. Second Row from the bottom, Left: Mt. Pleasant Home Made Ice Cream; Right: Elderado Inn. Bottom across: Buff Fuel & Oil Corp.

1939, February

See below for translation.

STANISŁAW J. ZYCH

Wesoły, dobrze wystrojony, skory, młodzieniec jest Stanisław Jakob Zych którego portret się znajduje w tem miesiącu na przodku MASKA BULETYN nakrycia.

Stanisław Zych urodził się 2go Maja, 1913 roku w Schenectady. Jest on pięc stóp 7 cali wysoki i waży 154 funty.

On uczeszczał do parafijalnej szkoły Sw. Wojciecha, a później do McKinley Junior High School. W roku 1930, ukonczył Nott Terrace High School.

Stanisław prowadził swoj własny interes przez pare lat jako sprzedawca owoców i warzywa a potem pracował w General Electric Company. Teraz możemy zobaczyć Stasia przy regystru w A & P na Crane ulicy.

W roku 1933, Stanisław wstąpił do Kółka Dramatycznego Maska. Od tego czasu on był dwa razy prezesem Kółka i jest teraz reżyserem. Jego pierwsze przedstawienie było jako Kwaśnicki, byznesista, w sztuce "ŻYWY NIEBOSZCZYK" Stanisław brał udział w nastepujących sztukach: (1) jako Zdzisław, bałamut w "RADCY PANA RADCY, (2) Grubiński, ojciec w "PRZYGODY MAŁŻEŃSKIE W PODROŻY POŚLUBNEJ, (3) Jozef Bandl, sierzant ogniowy, w "MAŁżeństwo na Próbę" (4) Policjant i Żyd Fulgeldesang w "STRASZNA CIOTUNIA, (5) Profesor Inicki w "KALOSZE", (6) Osetkiewicz, zająkliwy człowiek w "GENERALNA PRÓBA", (7) Wojtek, kochanek w "NA BEZRYBIU I RAK RYBĄ", (9) Hydrogen, głupowaty doktor w "SZPITAL WARJATÓW", (10) Profesor Safandurski w "PERUKA PROFESORA" (11) Jakób Kwieciński, ojciec w "KOSZYK KWIATÓW", (12) Marcin Grabicki, detektyw, w "STRASZNA NOC", (13) Inspektor Piernik w "KOBIETA ZNIKŁA" i jako (14) Stanko, garbaty w "DJABEŁ Z MONOKLEM".

Gdy General Electric obchodziła swoje Golden Jubilee, Stanisław Zych miał honor być wybranym jako Przedstawiciel Charles Steinmetz na flocie pod tytułem "ICH OSTATNIE SPOTKANIE", która reprezentowała Polonje, i która wygrała pierwszą nagrodę.

1939, February

— 2 —

Oprócz odgrywania, Stanisław lubi na łizbach jeździć, iść na przechadcki i rybować. Wallace Beery i Myrna Loy są jego ulubione aktorzy.

Za jego udział w Harcerstwie przy Gminie #53 Stanisław był wynagrodzony wycieczką do Polski, gdzie spędził lato roku 1936go.

Stanisław Zych był dyrektorym artystycznego przedstawienia, "LEGJONISTA NA POLU CHWAŁY." Te przedstawienie było pierwszy Maska K. D. tryumf 1938go roku. On także będzie dyrektorym następnego przedstawienia ktore będzie pokazane 23 Kwietnia, w Polskiem Domu.

Serdecznie życzymy ci dalszych dokonań, szczęścia i pomyślności.

ZARZĄD REDAKCYJNY

I-Joseph Czyzewski
II-Maryanna Czyzewska
III-Helena Kilian
IV-Zofja Korycińska
V-Mieczysław Ożarowski
VI-Lucjan Sękowski
VII-Stanisław Zych

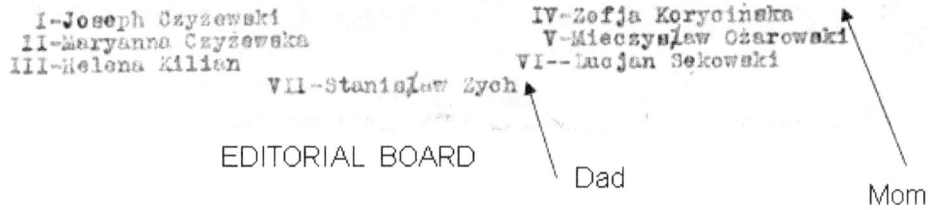

EDITORIAL BOARD — Dad — Mom

1939, February - Translation

Stanley Jacob Zych is a happy, well dressed young man whose picture is found on the "Maska Buletyn" cover.

Stanley Zych was born on May 2, 1913 in Schenectady. He is 5 foot 7 and weights 154 pounds. He attended Saint Adalbert School and later McKinley Junior High School. He finished Nott Terrace High School in 1930.

Stanley had his own business for a few years selling fruits and vegetables and then worked in the General Electric Company. These days we can see Stas near the register of the A&P Company on Crane Street.

In 1933, Stanley joined the Maska Dramatic Circle. From that time he was president twice and is currently the stage manager. His first performance was as Krasnicki, a businessman, in the play "The Live Ghost." Stanley had parts in the following plays: (1) as Zdzislaw, the philanderer in "Counselor of Mr. Councilman," (2) as the father Grubinski in "Adventures on Honeymoon," (3) Jozef Bandl, a fire sergeant in "Marriage on Trial," (4) Policeman and Jew Fulgedesang in "The Terrible Aunt," (5) Professor Inicki in "Galoshes," (6) Ocetkiewicza, a stuttering man, in "Dress Reheearsal," (7) Wojtek the lover in "Catching Fish without Fishing," (8) Hydrogen, the crazy doctor in "Hospital for the Insane," (9) Professor Safandurski in "The Professor's Wig," (10) Jacob Kwiecinski, the father, in "A Basket of Flowers (Fate of the Orphan)" (11) Marcin Grabicki in "Terrible Night," (12) Inspector Piernik in "Woman Disappears," and (13) Stanko the hunchback in "Devil with a Monocle."

When General Electric had its Gold Jubilee, Stanley Zych had the honor of playing the inventor Charles Steinmetz on the float under the title "Their Last Meeting," which represented Polonia, and which won first prize. In addition to acting, Stanley likes to skate, go for walks, and fish. Wallace Beery and Myrna Loy are his favorite actors.

For his participation in (PNA) Council 53's Scouts, Stanley was awarded a trip to Poland where he spent the summer of 1936.

Stanley Zych was the artistic director of the play, "Legionnaire on the Field of Honor." That play was the first Maska K. D. triumph of 1938. He will also be the director of the next play which will be given on April 23rd at the Polish Home.

We sincerely wish him further accomplishment, luck and prosperity.

1939, February

Thank Yous

> PODZIĘKOWANIE
>
> Niech Pan Bóg pobłogosławi szczególniejszym błogosławieństwem wszystkich naszych Dobrodziejów.
>
> HISTORYA KÓŁKA MASKA
> (ciąg dalszy)
>
> Maski pierwszy program, czyli "Gra Karciana," w Kwietniu 1933 roku miał wielkie powodzenie, i sala Szczepańskiego była przepełniona. Dwa szkice były wystawione przez Maskę. Odgrywali w nich Aniela Pitera, Stanisława Zabłocka, Rajmond Golembiowski i Józef Czyzewski.
>
> Maski pierwsze przedstawienie było wystawione w Niedzielę, 1go Listopada w Polskiem Domu. Program się składał z "ZNAWCA KOBIET", komedyjka w jednem akcie i "SŁOWICZEK" operetka jedno-aktowa. Program wykazał że Maska nietylko miała talent ale i dobre głosy. W "SŁOWICZKU" zaśpiewali ładnie Panna Zabłocka jako soprano; Klemens Olszewski, jako tenor i Michał Tytko jako basso. A przy tem to bardzo ładnie się popisali doskonale jako aktorzy Sabina Gutowska, Helena Kamińska, Czesław Rudowski, Władysław Sekowski i inni. A co do sceneryi to Kółko Polart, (które się później przyłączyło do Maski) wspaniale zbudowało. Aniela Pitera to przyniesła prawie całą swoja kwiaciarnie na scene dla "SŁOWICZKA. Zygmunt Kilian, Zygmunt Brzozowski, Genowefa Szatkowska, Wanda Hennel i Marya Zborowska pracowali szczerze aby uzyskać piękną scenerye.

Let God bless with particular blessing all our Benefactors.

Maska Circle History (continued)

Maska's first program, or "Gra Karciana," in April 1933 had great success, and Szczepanski's hall was full. Two skits were presesnted by Maska. Actors were Aniela Pitera, Stanislawa Zablocka, Rajmond Golembiowski and Josef Czyzewski.

Maska's first performance was given on Sunday, November 1st at the Polish Home. The program was "Connoisseur of Women," a one act operetta. The program showed that Maska not only has talent but also good voices. In "Nightingale," good singers were Miss Zablocka, soprano; Klemens Olszewski, tenor and Michal Tytko base. And in addition, the very accomplished actors included Sabina Gutowska, Helena Kaminska, Czeslaw Rudowski, Wladyslaw Sekowski and others. Polart did the scenery (which later were joined with Maska's excellent construction). Aniela Pitera brought nearly her entire flower shop for "Nightingale's" scenery. Zygmunt Kilian, Zygmunt Brzozowski, Genewefa Szatkowski, Wanda Hennel and Marya Zborowski worked hard to make the beautiful scenery.

1939, February

Na ten pierwszy program to sala w Polskiem Domu była przepełniona a amatorzy się doskonale popisali a to trzeba dać dużo uznania Danielowi Budnikowi za jego pracę jako reżyser.

Drugi program był wystawiony 10tego Grudnia. Składał on się z trzech jedno-aktowek. CACUSIA PRELUDJUM SZOPENA i STRYJ PRZYJECHAŁ. Ten drugi program odkrył dużo talentu Maski. Władysława Moros jako Cacusia odegrała rolę ślicznie. Także wspaniale odegrali Ryszard Olkowski, Franciszek Borkowski i Aniela Pitera w tej sztuce CACUSIA. A co do PRELUDJUM SZOPENA to po raz pierwszy Maska użyła głos ładny Bronisława Deptuły. Także doskonale odegrali role Wanda Hennel, Regina Giniecka i Henry Lewkowicz. W STRYJ PRZYJECHAŁ, Maryanna Dziuba i Florcia Beleusz znakomicie się popisali i także nieśmiały Karol Szymański.

Polart także przyczyniło się szczerze do pracy nad scenerya. Do tych trzech sztuk D. Budnik poprosił Agnieszkę Pieszczoch i Jozefa Czyzewskiego aby mu pomogli w reżyserstwie sztuk i także ich poduczał. Orkiestra C. Zemana przygrywała w tym programie tak samo jak i na pierwszym. Stanisław Pitera członek Maski ulepszył muzykę do sztuki CACUSIA. Tak Maska skończyła rok 1933. (Ciąg dalszy nastąpi)

Prześliczna Godzina "Carnation Contented Hour". Amerykanie nauczyli się Polskiego programu na Radio.

For the first program the hall of the Polish Home was full and the amateurs performed perfectly and we must give a lot of recognition to Daniel Budnik for his work as Director.

The second program was given on December 10th. It was in three one act skits, "Plaything," "Chopin's Prelude in C Minor" and "Uncle Arrived." This second program showed Maska's great talent. Władyslawa Moros as Cacusia played the role beautifully. Also excellent were Ryszard Olkowski, Franciszek Borkowski and Aniela Pitera in the skit "Cacusia." And in "Chopin's Prelude," for the first time Maska used the beautiful voice of Bronislawa Deptula. Also excellent in roles were Wanda Hennel, Regina Giniecka and Henry Lewkowicz. In "Uncle Arrived," Maryanna Dziuba and Florcia Beleusz performed admirably and also the shy Karol Szymanski.

Polart also made an excellent contribution in its work on the scenery. For these three plays D. Budnik asked Agnieska Pieszczoch and Jozef Czyzewski to help him with directing the plays and he mentored them. C. Zeman's orchestra played in that program as it did for the first one. Stanislaw Pitera, a Maska member, provided the music for the play "Cacusia." That is how Maska ended the year 1933. (To Be Continued)

A beautiful hour "Carnation Contented Hour". Americans learned of the Polish program on the radio.

1939, February

ZACHĘTA
Do Krzewienia Znajomości Piśmiennictwa Polskiego.

Słusznie my, Polacy, chlubić się możemy, że posiadamy bogate i wspaniałe piśmiennictwo, tak iż w rzędzie europejskich literatur i Polska niepoślednie zajmuje miejsce. Arcydzieła naszych znakomitych pisarzy tłumaczone są na różne języki, jak n. p. pisma Mickiewicza na dziewięć obcych przełozono języków, a Sienkiewicza, nieomal na wszystkie języki narodów cywilizowanych. Ale niestety! wszystkie te piękności i bogactwa są dla niższych i średnich warstw naszego narodu jakoby zaklęta kraina. Na palcach zliczylibyśmy tych z ludu wiejskiego i z rzemieślników, co by nam mogli choć nieco opowiedzieć o Kochanowskim, Skardze, Krasickim, Mickiewiczu, Słowackim, Krasińskim, Zaleskim, Polu i innych pisarzych polskich, ojczystych chlubach naszych, których dzieła na obce przełożone języki, zachwycają dalekie narody, a lud Polski, dla którego ci mistrze słowa złote prawdy nucili i pisali, nawet nie wie o ich istnieniu! Smutna to i bolesna rzecz, ale niestety! aż nadto prawdziwa.

Znajomość, choćby tylko pobieżna, piśmiennictwa ojczystego jest koniecznie potrzebna i niższym klasom narodu, a mianowicie młodzieży. Uczmy się piśmiennictwa ojczystego. Znajomość ta budzi dzielnie poczucie i godność narodową, rozpala święte iskry miłości Ojczyzny, i jest jednym z węgielnych kamieni oświaty ogólnej. Stąd ze wszech sił starać się należy o jak największe zaszczepienie znajomości piśmiennictwa polskiego między naszym ludem, a mianowicie między młodzieżą.

DO CZŁONKÓW:
Weźmy się do pracy z całym zapałem i poświęceniem. Rozszerzajcie

TO MEMBERS: Let us get to work with enthusiasm and dedication. Spread the word

ENCOURAGEMENT
To Promote Familiarity with Polish Literature

We rightly, we Poles, can rejoice, that we sit on a rich and excellent literature, so that in a list of European literature Poland is not inferior. Masterpieces of our excellent writers have been translated into various languages, as for example the writings of Mickiewicz have been translated into nine other languages, and Sienkiewicz, into almost all the languages of civilized nations. But unfortunately all that beauty and richness are for lower and middle layers of our nations of that enchanted land. We can count on our fingers those peasants and craftspeople who know something about Kochanowski, Skarga, Krasicki, Mickiewicz, Slowacki, Krasinski, Zaleski, Pola and other Polish writers, the pride of our fathers, who worked in both superior languages, enchanting distant lands, and the Polish people, for whom these masters of golden words sang the truth and wrote, do not even know of their existence. It is a sad and sore thing, but unfortunately it is true. Knowledge, even if superficial, with the writings of their home is certainly needed among the lower classes of the nation, and namely the young people. Let us learn the literature of the home land. Familiarity raises the courage and sense of national dignity, a spark ignites love for their homeland and is one of the cornerstones of a general education. From this all should derive strength about how to immunize our people with familiarity with Polish literature, especially the young people.

1939, February

MASKA BULLETIN. Please encourage and win over as many readers as possible through the acquisition of new members.

A bilingual poem followed by jokes: *My Dear / What can I do? I cannot sleep / The whole night thru, / It seems to me / That I love you.*

MASKA BULETYN. Zjednywajcie mu jak najwięcej czytelników przez zdobywanie nowych członków.

    Moja Kochanko   The whole night thru,
    What can I do?   Mnie się zdaje
    I cannot spać   That I love you.

HUMOR

CO KWADRANS
Wiktor Platt zachorował, zawołał doktora który po zbadaniu mówi:
—Lekarstwo to zazywać Pan będzie co kwadrans.
—A brandy pic mogę?—zapytuje Platt. Najwięcej szklanczkę—odpowiada doktor.
—Czy także co kwadrans?—pyta Platt.

DLA PAMIĘCI
Marya D. do męża: —Wiesz co mężu, powinieneś bezwarunkowo kazać się fotografować.
—Poco, dla kogo?—Pyta się maż.
—Dla mnie mój kochany. Jesteś u Maski często a w domu to tak rzadko, iż zapomnę jak wygladasz.

W CZASIE OŚWIADCZYN
ZOSIA CHOJNICKA: —Ostatecznie decyduję się zostać twoją żoną!
C. OLWERT:—Ostrzegam cię jednak ze ja gotować nie umiem.

OPTYMISTA
Po przedstawieniu Maski, S. Płócharczyk szuka coś na podłodze—
TYTKO:—Czego ty szukasz po podłodze?
S. PŁÓCHARCZYK:—Dwadzieścia dolarów.
TYTKO: Bój się Boga, zgubiłeś tyle?

TĘGI MYŚLIWI
ZYGMUNT KILIAN do ZYGMUNTA BRZOZOWSKIEGO:—Na ostatniem polowaniu od jednego wystrzału zabiłem zająca i dwie kaczki—
—Ja tak nie potrafię—mówi Zygmund Brzozowski.
—Strzelać?—Pyta Kilian.
—Nie—kłamać! odpowiada Brzozowski.

W ARMYI WUJA SAMA
Kapitan: Andrzej Podbielski, ten pan skarży się, że nakłułeś bagnetem jego psa na śmierć!
PODBIELSKI: Tak jest Panie kapitanie ale pies ugryzł mnie kiedy stałem na warcie.
Kapitan: To czemu kolbą go nie odpędziłeś?
PODBIELSKI: A czemu on mnie ogonem nie ugryzł?

LUCIAN S.: —No, gdybym ja umarł, słodkie serce, będziesz o mnie pamiętać?
ZONA:—Ależ naturalnie Aniołku!—zawsze cię będę stawiała drugiemu mężowi za przykład.

S. PŁÓCHARCZYK: Nie ale może znajdę aby Panu za sale zapłacić.

For all we recommend reading Maska's newest young men and women's news copy—MASKA BULETYN. So here it is—and it is with considerable pride that we distribute this publication on this special occasion, MASKA CARD PARTY, without the slightest obligation or cost.

The MASKA BULETYN is edited by young men and women—For young men, women, and Maska Patrons. It is adult, sophisticated, clean and informative. Its chief function is to represent young MASKA COMERS and MEMBERS, like ourselves, in a true, unaffected light. It accomplishes this in a manner never before achieved.

1939, February – Translation

TRANSLATOR'S NOTE: Text of jokes printed above]

EVERY 15 MINUTES
Victor Platt became ill and called the Doctor who, after examining Victor, said,
Take this medicine every 15 minutes.
Can I drink brandy? asked Victor
At most a small glass, answered the Doctor.
Every 15 minutes? Asked Victor

FOR REMEMBRANCE
Marya D. said to her husband, Know what, husband, you should definitely get a photograph taken.
Why? For whom? asked the husband.
For me, my dear. You are at Maska so often but rarely at home, that I forget what you look like.

AT THE TIME OF DECLARATION
ZOSIA CHOJNICKA: I've finally decided to become your wife.
C.OLWERT: I'm warning you that I don't know how to cook.
OPTIMISM

After a Maska play, S. Plocharczyk was looking for something on the floor.
TYTKO: What are you looking for on the floor?
S. PLOCHARCZYK: Twenty dollars.
TYTKO: Dear God, did you lose that much?
S. PLOCHARCZYK: No, but I might find some so that I can pay you for the hall.

TAG HUNTERS
ZYGMUNT KILIAN TO ZYGMUNT BRZOZOWSKI: On my last hunt, I killed a rabbit and 2 ducks with a single shot.
I don't understand how to do that, said Zygmunt Brzozowski.
You don't know how to shoot? asked Kilian
No, how to lie, answered Brzozowski

THE ARMY EXPLAINS ITSELF
Captain: Andrzej Podbielski, that man complains that you stabbed his dog to death with a bayonet.
PODBIELSKI: It is so Mr. Captain, but the dog bit me when I was on guard.
Captain: Why didn't you hit him with the butt of your gun?
PODBIELSKI: Why didn't the dog bite me with its tail?

LUCIAN S. So, when I die, dear heart, will you remember me?
WIFE: Of course, my Angel! You will be my second husband, for example.

1939, February

Some of the best brains of the Maska Dramatic Club are associated with its editorial staff: Big names in Dramatics, Directors, Actors, Artists, Playwrights, Club Officers, Typists and many others--each tops in his field.

We know you will like the MASKA BULETYN, its wide and interesting array of features, and are depending on Members, also on interested Readers to help us constantly improve it. Ask your friends too, if they would like to receive a copy of the MASKA BULETYN monthly.

SOCIAL GOSSIP

The Maska Club is delighted to hear of the engagement of Alice Nowicka and Bill Bonczyk. Congratulations.

Nellie Pitera is the proud possessor of a new 1939 Chevrolet.

Chester Olivert has been introduced into the Maska Club.

Lucyan Sekowski has been advanced to the position of Eastern New York State distributor of the Polish Daily (Dziennik Dla Wszystkich) Good for you.

We have noticed that Helen Kilian has improved a great deal in her ice-skating. Keep it up Helen.

Who's the little honey F. D. has been seen with quite often? Perhaps it is a certain lassie from Forest Road?

Zyg Wiśniewski has afforded for himself a new Dodge sedan.

When Matthew Ozarowski was told to "make yourself at home" he modestly asked for a bed.

Zygmunt Brzozowski was seated as an auditor of the executive staff of Gmina 53, Central body of the Polish National Alliance at a ceremony in P. N. A. Hall Sunday, February 11.

A gay foursome seen recently ice-skating at Central Park included Sophie Hojnicka, Chet Olivert, Sophie Korycinska and Stanley Zych. ← Mom & Dad

What would a certain bowling league do without Walt Zborowski?

Ted Kilian has a hard choice between basketball and roller-skating. Not to mention ping-pong.

A Chinese Laundry has a certain significance in Stanley Płocharczyk's life. Junior couldn't be the cause of it, could he, Stan?

What does "Snow White" find on Fourth Avenue that he doesn't find on other streets.

Our "Birthday Girl" for the month is Mary Zborowska. We extend our heartiest wishes to you, Mary.

JUST AMONG US GIRLS:
On a joyride you may have to <u>choke</u> the car to get it started, and CHOKE the boy friend to make him STOP!

1939, February

- 6 -

If you are interested in having your hair well-groomed, Gene Ausfeld will gladly take care of you. That means you too, fellas.

# # #

What have the other side-of-town girls got that the Mont Pleasant girls haven't got? Ask Zyg Brzozowski.

Gee, that's a lovely picture of you (Agnes D) on his dresser. How about letting us in on the secret?

# # #

Celia Borowska has acquired her scholastic achievement and has been rewarded a high school diploma.

# # #

Thanks to Henry Ausfeld, chairman, and his committee of Mary Zborowska, Sophie Hojnicka, Sophie Korycinska, Zyg Kilian, and Zyg Brzozowski for the success of our Card Party. ⟵ *Mom*

TO HONOR PULASKI

Several ways of honoring Casimir Pulaski Revolutionary war hero, are proposed in numerous bills that have been introduced in the Seventy-sixth Congress.

There are nine proposals to name October 11 of this year as General Pulaski Memorial Day. The general was killed in action at Savannah on October 11, 1779.

DRAMA AND THE STAGE
POLAND

Polish drama is of late growth. Through the first centuries of Polish literature it appeared merely in sporadic or exotic forms, Kochanowski's Dismissal of the Greek Envoys (1758) being its sole masterpiece until the end of the 18th century. At that date the Polish theatre rose under King Stanislaus Augustus' patronage. Founded on French models, it rapidly developed on national lines. After the partition of Poland, it reached high artistic beauty during the years of the nation's bondage, frequently serving as a patriotic stimulus. Fredro (1783-1876) remains the master of Polish comedy. His Maidens' Vows, Revenge, etc/, sparkle with wit and national colour.

Slowacki (1809-49) gave Poland her finest tragedies in his dramas on Polish history and legend (Mazeppa, Balladyna, Lilla Weneda) Two of the greatest masterpieces of Polish literature were written at the same period in dramatic form:--Mickiewicz's national lamentation, The Ancestors (1832) and Krasinski's forecast of social revolution? The Undivine Comedy (1835). The brilliant symbolical S. Wyspinski (1869-1907) created the plays, notably The Wedding, created an epoch in Polish drama. Although no subsequent work has equalled those already mentioned the Polish output has continued. Among contemporary dramatists Rostworowski (Caligula; Charitas) merits special mention.

MASKA'S FUTURE LIES IN ITS YOUTH.

1939, February

- 7 -

GOOD SPEECH

Nothing is more disagreeable than slip-shod speech and annoying enunciation coming from the mouth of a person who obviously, spent a great deal of time on grooming routines and prides himself on always looking his best, but has done practically nothing to improve his speech.

Here are a few helpful rules to improve your speech:
1. Avoid slang.
2. Speak clearly and distinctly.
3. Use good pronunciation.
4. Read aloud, (20 Minutes a day
5. Consult a dictionary.
6. Refer to books on Public Speaking.

#####

STRICTLY PERSONAL
(check yourself)

1. Are you fond of playing practical jokes?
2. Do you try to make a joke of some little accident that has occurred?
3. Do you hold a grudge longer than a day?
4. Do you make an answer with a wisecrack when you are complimented?
5. Are you a grouch in the home before breakfast?
6. Does even your family (at times) find you funny and laugh at your jokes?
7. Have you ever burst out laughing when you yourself took a tumble just as you were trying to put on a "dignity act"?

YOUR STORY TECHNIQUE

1. Do you start out by saying "I can't tell a story the way he does, but it's terribly funny"? Ha-Ha.
2. Do you use sweeping gestures to emphasize a funny story?
3. Do you go into great detail before you get to the point?
4. Can you keep a straight face (or a Poker Pan) while telling a joke?
5. When you're describing an ordinary event (such as, getting a haircut or shopping in a store) do folks laugh?
6. Can you take it if the joke is on you?

IN COMPANY

1. Can you pass an embarrassing moment with a jest?
2. If a new game makes you look slightly ridiculous, are you among the first to try it anyway?
3. Do you wisecrack your way from Entrance to Exit?
4. Do you like to laugh uproariously in night-clubs and restaurants to show people what a good time you're having?
5. Do you like to amuse people?
6. Do folks frequently laugh at your remarks?

After reading the above questions which one of these are you?
1. A four-bell riot?
2. A good humorist in the making?
3. A funny-bone definitely fractured?

1939, February

THANK US

"The Lord prefers common-looking people that is why He made so many of them."—Abraham Lincoln

"Let us have faith that right makes might, and in that faith let us to the end, dare to do our duty as we understand it."—Lincoln

"Speak little, do much"—St. John Berchmans

"If you want to be big, find some good in your enemy."

"I say try; if we never try, we shall never succeed."—Lincoln

MY IDEAL FOR THE MONTH
TO ADMIT MY MISTAKES

It is so easy to place blame on someone else to excuse one's own mistakes but that is a weak and cowardly thing to do. If the mistake really was your own, be brave and honest enough to say, "I'm sorry," instead of "It wasn't my fault." Do not imagine that it makes you seem small and mean to admit that you were in the wrong. On the contrary, such an admission shows that you are honest, courageous, and humble. It is a sign of sturdy character.

This month I shall take care to admit my mistakes and not to place the blame for them on others.

ST. VALENTINE'S DAY

Many legends are told of St. Valentine's Day and its origin. One of them runs as follows:

In February 278, A. D., a Bishop in Rome was imprisoned. His caretaker had a daughter who was blind. The Bishop was very good to the blind girl and finally restored her sight, which of course made her and her father extremely happy.

While this Bishop was in prison, he had no reading matter, so he spent his time in writing verses and decorating parchment. One day an order came that the Bishop was to be executed and on the day this was to happen, February 14, he wrote a poem to the girl he had befriended and who also had been so kind to him and signed it "Your Valentine."

Claims are made that this was the first Valentine, whether or not we do not know, but we do know it is a day thoroughly enjoyed by the young folks and often times by the older ones.

HUMOR

Perhaps many of you are too young to remember this old gag. Just so long as it is good, we don't care how old it is... At any rate this one deals with the full-blooded Cherokee Indian who came to New York and needed some cash... He told one bank that he needed $200 for two months... "What security can you offer?" he was asked... "Me got 200 horses," replied the Indian... The bank agreed to the loan... A short time afterward, the Indian came into the bank with $2,000, paid off the note and started to leave with the rest of his bankroll... "Why not let us take care of that money for you?" queried the banker... The Indian looked the banker straight in the eye and solemnly asked: "How many horses you got?"

A WORD OF THANKS

The MASKA DRAMATIC CLUB desires to express its appreciation to its advertisers in the MASKA BULETYN and to everyone who in anyway contributed to the success of this CARD PARTY and souvenir bulletin.

1939, May

Mom

1939, May

See the translation on the next page.

ZOFJA WIKTORYJA KORYCIŃSKA

Zofja Korycińska urodziła się w Schenectady w okolicy Avenue B, 2-go Pazdziernika w roku 1918. Pierwszy początek jej nauki był w Yates School. Gdy Zosia miała siedem lat, jej rodzice przenieslej się na Forest Road, gdzie oni obecnie mieszkają. Wty okolicy, Zosia poszła do szkoły parafjalnej, gdzie ona zasłużyła na nagrodę za dobrą naukę. Potem, ona poszła do Pleasant Valley School, McKinley Junior High School, i Mount Pleasant High School, gdzie on skonczyła naukę w roku 1936.

Zosia z stapiła do Kółka Dramatycznego "Maska" w roku 1936 i brała udział w paru sztukach, rowniez jako (1) Dorota Pokraka, służąca, w sztuce "Kobieta Znikła" (2) Basia Niedoszyta, 12-to letia dziewczynka, w sztuce "Trudy i Troski" (3) Aurora Misenko, hrabina, w sztuce "Legjoniste Na Polu Chwały" (4) Izabela Zielonka, farmerka w sztuce "Predka Robota" i takze (5) Klara Makowka, w sztuce "Pazura". Ona była sekretarką Kółka podczas sezonu 1938-39 i teraz jest jedna w przewodni ozących "Maska Bulletin" i takze jest agentka prasy Kółko.

Zosia bardzo lubi lyzwowac, łowić ryby, jest zakochana w recznych robotch, w muzyce i w pisaniu w roznych artykułów. Zosia obecnie robi w Berkeley-Smith Dress Shop.

1939, May - Translation

Sophie Korycinska was born in Schenectady in the area of Avenue B, on October 2, 1918. She started her education at Yates Elementary School. When Sophie was seven years old, her parents moved to Forest Road, where they live now. From this location, Sophie went to the parish school (Saint Adalbert's), where she received an award for good scholarship. Then she went to Pleasant Valley School, McKinley Junior High School, and Mont Pleasant High, where she graduated in 1936.

Sophie joined the Maska Dramatic Circle in 1936 and had parts in several plays, including (1) the servant, Crazy Dorothy, in "Woman Disappears," (2) Basia Niedoszyta, a 12 year old girl, in "Cares and Worries," (3) Aurora Misenki, a countess, in "Legionnaires on the Field of Honor," (4) Izabela Zielonka, a farmer, in "Speedy Work," and also (5) Klara Makowaka, in "Trapped." She was the secretary of the Circle during the 1938 - 1939 season and is also the Circle's press agent.

Sophie likes to ice skate, fish, and loves handwork, music and writing articles. Sophie currently works at the Berkeley-Smith Dress Shop.

1939, May

HISTOR A KOLKA MASKA

(Ciąg dalszy)

W Styczniu 1934 r. obrano nowy zarząd. Daniel Budnik powiedział ze nie moze spelniac dwa obowiazki jako Prezes i Rezyszer. Nastepny zarzad byl obrany:- Jozef Czyzewski, Prezes; Agnieszka Pieszczoch, Vice-Prezeska; Wanda Hennel, Sekretarka; Aniela Petera, Skarbniczka; Karol Szymanski, Marszalek; Daniel Budnik, Generalny Reżyser; Czeslaw Rudowski, Dekorator Scenerji; Jan Zielanis, Zarzadca Wlasnosci; i Jozef Czechowicz, Zarzadca dochodu.

Pierwszy program roku 1934 byl nadany 14-go Stycznia. Byl to program wodowilowi na ktore artisci WGM odgrywali tak zwani, "Skip Step and Happy Anna." Po programie wodowilowem to byl taniec z orkiestra Pana Zemana.

Pierwsze przedstawienie w 1934 bylo 4-go Marca. Sztuka byla "Gruby Skandal" komedya w trzech aktach. Ryszard Olkowski i Helena Kilian bardzo ladnie sie podpisali. Po raz pierwszy dwuch starszych amatorów wystapilo na desce Maski a ci byli Stanislaw Petera i Julja Szymanowska ktorzy dobrze swe role odegrali.

Ostatnie przedstawienie sezonu 1933-34 bylo Kontestowe. Kolko Literackie z Albany, New York; Kolko Amatorskie z Amsterdam, New York, Maska urzadzili Kontest jedno-aktowy. W kazdem miescie byl ten sam program odegrany. Maska przedstawila Zygmunta Przybylskiego ladna sztuke "Pierwszy Bal". Kolko Literackie przedstawilo spasmowa komedye, "O.S.S." czyli Malzenska Wyprawa, a Amatorskie Kolko z Amsterdam wybralo sliczna wiejska komedyjke, "Kokusia Podlotkiem" napisana przez pobratymsa

(Ciag dalszy nastapi)

BULLETIN STAFF

Co-Chairmen: Sophie Korycinski   Helen Kilian
              Lu Sepkowski   Stanley Zych
              Mary Czyzewski   Joseph Czyzewski

1939, May

HISTORY OF THE MASKA CIRCLE

(Continued)

New officers were elected in January 1934. Daniel Budnik said that he could no longer perform his duties as president and director. The next set of officers was selected: Joseph Czyzewski, President; Agnes Pieszczoch, Vice-President; Wanda Hennel, Secretary; Nellie Petera, Treasurer. Karol Szymanski, Marshal; Daniel Budnik, General Director; Chester Rudowski, Scenery Decorator; Jan Zielanis, Property Governor; Joseph Czechowicz, Income Governor.

The first program of the year was given on January 14th. It was a vaudeville program during which the WGY actors called "Skip Step and Anna" played. After the vaudeville program there was a dance with Mr. Zeman's orchestra.

The first presentation of the year was given on March 4th. The play was "Great Scandal," a comedy in three acts. Richard Olkowski and Helen Kilian performed very nicely. For the first time, two older amateurs came on board, and they were Stanley Petera and Julia Szymanowska, who played their roles very well.

The last programs of the 1933 – 1934 season were contests. The Literary Circle from Albany, New York; the Amateur Circle, from Amsterdam, New York; and Maska organized a one-act contest. The same program was given in each city. Maska presented Zygmunt Przybylski's "The First Ball." The Literary Circle presented the convulsive comedy, "O.S.S., or The Marriage Portion," and the Amateur Circle of Amsterdam selected "Fledgling" (Boarding School Miss) written by Pobratym.

(To Be Continued)

1939, May

WANTED !!

A girl on the typed of Brenda Frazier to satisfy a certain Maska member's taste.

A recipe of "Spots" Podbielski's upside down cake and berry pies.

A coat rack for Kaz Laniewski! to hang all the coats he had to hold at a certain social affair. That's what you get for doing one person a favor.

A life-sized doll for Joseph Grzyzewski.

A brand of perfumed cigars for Vic Platt.

A private table for Zyg Brzozowski to sit on.

An unchangeable mind for Gene Ausfeld.

More leisure time for our too, too busy treasurer.

!! JOKES !!

VANITY

Mrs. Jean S.: (learning to drive) Lucyan, that little mirror up there isn't right.

Lucyan: Isn't it?

Mrs. S.: No, I can't see anything, but the car behind.

Men who spread much baloney,
Often end in matrimony.

Nellie P.: I made a screen test this afternoon.

Sophie K.: For the movies?

Nellie P.: My goodness, no, for mosquitoes.

Doctor: I will examine you for five dollars.

Ted K.: Swell, go ahead. If you find them I'll give you half.

Sophie C.: (Day after marriage) You're an awful dumb-bell!!!

Chet O.: Well, dumb-bells always go in pairs.

EMERGENCY

Stanley P.: I have to perform an operation on a nose.

Joseph C.: Oh, are you a surgeon?

Stanley P.: But no, I'm the father of a small boy who never has a handkerchief.

Kas L.: (at the GREASY SPOON) Give me a piece of that huckleberry pie

Counterman: That ain't huckleberry pie — It's custard — Shoo! Shoo!

Zyg K.: (at the Farms): Say have you any wild roast duck today?

Waiter: No, Sir, but we can take a tame one and irritate him for you.

Doctor: Are you taking good care of your cold?

Joseph C.: You bet I am. I've had it for six weeks and it's as good as new.

Doc: You cough more easily this morning.

Andy P: Well, I ought to. I've been practicing all night.

1939, May

MASKA GOSSIP

July birth day greetings to: Lucyan Sękowski, Andrew Podbielski, Gene Stelmach, William Bonczyk and Regina Cha tnicka.

How come Mr. L. G. let lovely Mrs. S out of his sight to spend a week in Buffalo?

Glad to hear that Nellie P's brother is recovering after his illness.

Our former member, John Laniewski, has taken his marriage vows at St. Adalbert's Church. Our felicitations to you, John, and your little "Aniolek!"

Agnes Mack made a very sweet and demure bridesmaid at her uncle's recent wedding.

Gene Ausfeld celebrated her birthday recently by entertaining a group of her friends at her home. Maska congratulates you!

We are to have Walter Sękowski with us for the short time that it will be.

Maska Club enjoyed having Ted Podkiel, a school friend of Walter Sękowski's, at our special meeting. We hope he'll visit us again real soon.

Matthew Popka was doing some fancy diving at Rudd's Beach.

The next time you go riding, pepare yourself for a walk to where he parks his car, Regina C.

The Kilian boys have left their dramatic talents and have turned to the field of house painting.

It is my joy to find, At every turning of the road.
The strong arm of a comrade to help me onward with my load.
And since I have no gold to give and love alone must make amends,
My only prayer is while I love,
"God make me worthy of my friends."

1939, May

Mom's art work

1939, May

GOSSIP ABOUT THE SEMI-FORMAL

I----A group of twenty-five made "Whoopee" at the annual "Maska Semi-Formal" held June 25, 1938 at the Bohemian Tavern, on Troy Road.

   Don't forget "Maska Jamboree" July 27, 1939.

II---It was new to see Miss Regina Chatnicka and Company having a good time.

   Don't forget "Maska Jamboree" July 27, 1939.

III--Can you believe it! During the exchange of partners in the Grand March it so happened that Mrs. Olivert was paired with Lu Sekowski and Mrs. Sekowski with Chet Olivert. Was it an accident?

   Don't forget "Maska Jamboree" July 27, 1939.

IV---After making his first official public address to the gathering Mr. Henry Ausfeld, our Vice President, Chairman of the Board of Directors and Chairman of the July Jamboree was so exhausted that he could only spend the remaining part of the evening cooing his lovey. Of course you know Mary Z.

   Don't forget "Maska Jamboree" July 27, 1939.

V----The "Maska Semi-Formal" was too much for Stanley Zych, so he decided to rest up by taking a trip to Ohio. We're pretty sure it isn't your fault Sophie K.   ← Mom & Dad

   Don't forget "Maska Jamboree" July 27, 1939.

VI---Leo Marcinek certainly enjoyed himself at the dinner.

   Don't forget "Maska Jamboree" July 27, 1939.

VII--It's about time Andrew "Tarzan" Podbielski showed off his lady-love. She's pretty nice at that.

   Don't forget "Maska Jamboree" July 27, 1939

THE "FLASH" OF THE MONTH

VIII-Zygmunt Brzozowski actually danced. Was it the atmosphere or Miss A. M.

   Don't forget "Maska Jamboree" July 27, 1939.

IX---Gene Stelmach and John Olivert were really going to town to the "Beer Barrel Polka"

   Don't forget the "Maska Jamboree" July 27, 1939.

1939 May

(continued)

X----Who said Maska members couldn't sing? You should have heard the chorus of that certain popular polka.

Don't forget "Maska Jamboree" July 27, 1939.

XI---There were two married couples present at this Semi-Formal namely, Mr. and Mrs. Lucyan Sekowski, and Mr. and Mrs. Chester Olivert. We wonder how many more there will be next year.

Don't forget "Maska Jamboree" July 27, 1939.

XII--Bene Ausfeld is quite a dressmaker. Yes sir, her gown was made by her own dainty fingers.

Don't forget "Maska Jamboree" July 27, 1939.

XIII-The first couple to leave the party at quarter to twelve----?

Don't forget "Maska Jamboree" July 27, 1939.

XIV--The last couples to leave the party were Mr. and Mrs. Sekowski Miss Ann Magelinska and Zygmund Brzozowski and Walter Sekowski.

Don't forget "Maska Jamboree" July 27, 1939.

XV---Someo of the "Nite Spots" visited by the members were as follows: "Circle Inn", "Murray's Inn", "Shaker-Ridge", "Rudds Nite Club", "Swing Inn", "Town Tavern", "Rays Tavern", and last but not least the "Pal's Tavern".

Don't forget "Maska Jamboree" July 27, 1939.

XVI--Someone has "Breathed" a word that the "hots" with onions were delicious. Is th right, Miss A. M. and W. S.?

Don't forget about the July Jamboree. Show your "Maska Spirit".

That's all until next year!

1939, May

JULY JAMBOREE: July 27 PNA Enclosed Fairgrounds

1939, December

1939, December

Seventh Season - "MASKA" DRAMATIC CIRCLE
First performance in the 1939 – 1949 season

ON OUR SOIL
Melodrama in two acts at the Polish Home - Sunday, December 10, 1939
Directed by Helen Kilian

CAST
Settler
His wife
Their daughter
Settler
His wife
Their daughter
Settler
Innkeeper
Girls & Farmhands
From the settlement

[Mom's younger brother]

Miss Korycinska will play the piano

ACT I
In front of Settler Wojciech Osadnik's cottage

ACT II
Action takes place in the Prussian Kingdom

SIODMY SEZON
KÓŁKA DRAMATYCZNEGO
"MASKA"

Pierwszy występ sezonu 1939 – 1940

"NA NASZEJ GLEBIE"

Melodramat w dwuch Aktach

W Domu Polskim

W Niedzielę, 10-go Grudnia 1939

Reżyserka Helena Kilian

OSOBY :

Michał (osadnik)	Edward Repka
Barbara (jego żona)	Kazimiera Gorska
Franusia (ich córka)	Helena Kilian
Piotr (osadnik)	Lucjan Sekowski
Magda (jego żona)	Stefanja Chylinska
Antosia (ich córka)	Genowefa Ausfeld
Wojciech (osadnik)	Artur Brukowski
Bartos	Stanisław Bachleda
Stach	Stanisław Plocharczyk
Jan Myler (karczmarz)	Henryk Ausefeld
	Mary Zborowska
Dziewczęta i Paroboy z osady	Mary Kilian
	Alexander Korycinski
	Patricia Lake

Panna Korycinska przygrywa na fortepjanie

AKT I
Przed Chatą Wojciecha Osadnika

AKT II
Rzecz Dzieje Sie w Prusach Krolewskich

SERDECZNE ZYCZENIA !
Powodzenia Zasyła

Pani Aniela Boychuk
SPRING HILL COAL CO.

EDISON AVE & ERIE BLV'D   PHONE 6-7044

Heartfelt wishes! Sending good luck - Mrs. Aniela Boychuk

1939, December

SENDING HEARTFELT WISHES!

SERDECZNE ZYCZENIA

Zasyła

Wacław Daniel Przybyłek

MYERS DRUG STORE

FRANCIS i CRANE Ulicy   Tel. 6-3774

HELENA KILIAN

    Gwiazdor zawitał rychle u Państwa Kilian gdy zostawił pakunek 9-go Grudnia zawierający naszą Helenę. Ktoby myślał ze ona będzie kiedyś dyrektowała sztuki amatorskie.

    Panna Kilian jest jedną z pierwszych członkiń tego Kółka, wstępując w krótce po założeniu takowego i gorliwie pracowała dotychczas.

    Trudniła się ona z początku garderobą, później charakteryzatorstwem, a teraz jest reżyserką pierwszej sztuki tego sezonu.

    Jak wam jest wiadomo brała udział w wielu sztukach dlatego że kocha się w tem i znajduje to jedną z jej ulubionych rozrywek.

    Na estradzie można było ją widywać w następujących sztukach: "Żywy Nieboszczyk", "Pierwszy Bal", "Kobieta Znikła", "Straszna Ciotunia", "Djabeł z Monoklem", "Straszna Noc", "Generalna Próba" i "Pazura."

    Ona także była współ-przewodnicząca Bulletynu miesięcznego i przewodnicząca zabaw.

    Panna Kilian obecnie pracuje w zakładach General Electric.

COMPLIMENTS   FROM

Nerf's Tavern

804 BROADWAY

1939, December - Translation

HELEN KILIAN

A star was welcomed at the home of Mr. and Mrs. Kilian and on December 9th left a Package containing our Helen. Who would think that she would become a director Of amateur plays.

Miss Kilian was one of the first Maska members, joining shortly after its formation and has eagerly worked to the present.

Initially she was the wardrobe mistress, next makeup and currently she is the Director for the first play of this season.

As you know, she has taken part in many plays because that's what she loves And it is one of her favorite past-times.

On the stage you could have seen her in the following plays: "The Live Ghost," "The First Ball," "A Woman Disappears," "The Terrible Aunt." "Devil with a Monocle." "Terrible Night," "Dress Rehearsal" and "The Claw."

1939, December

Sending wishes from the makers of soda water

BOARD OF
THE MASKA
CIRCLE
President
Vice President
Secretary
Treasurer
Finance manager
Directors
Scenery manager
Property manager
Parliamentarians
Makeup

SCENERY
COMMITTEE
President

BOARD OF
THE BULETYN
Chairwoman
[Mom]
[Dad]

Greetings from PODBIELSKI'S HOTEL - Polish foods, wines and liquors

1939, December

Sending heartfelt wishes – White Star Delicatessen -Proprietor

SERDECZNE ZYCZENIA ZASYŁA

White Star DELICATESSEN

Tadeusz Kostyniak --- Właśc.

865 Crane St.

SOCIAL GOSSIP

December birthday greetings are in store for Helen Kilian.

Mary Budka is sporting a new short haircut which gives her a charming appearance.

Did you ever watch Regina C. make cookies and fill eclairs at Federals' window? (Not an ad) That's a subtle clue that she is quite a capable cook.

Incidentally, both Regina C. and Mary B. are generally seen entertaining themselves at the P. N. A. Home on Saturday nites.

That new uniform Kaz Laniewski has is very becoming. We still insist that a uniform does something to a man. (Editor's Note) So does the right woman.)

Chester Olivert was honored at a surprise birthday party last month given by Mrs. Chester Olivert. Among guests present were: Miss Julia Olivert, Miss Sophie Korycinski, Edward Semerad, Stanley Zych, Mr. & Mrs. Edward Rybicki, and Mr. and Mrs. John Olivert.

Because of our secretary's temporary leave of absence a new secretary has been appointed and she is Gene Ausfeld.

Behind the candy counter at the Metropolitan Co. (Darn it, no ad) we spotted Henrietta Jozefowicz.

Sophie Korycinska and Stanley Zych had the thrill of speaking by shortwave from station WaKUD to WyAOL in Atalnta, Georgia, to Sophie's brother.

With the Christmas holidays coming on, both Walter Sekowski and Matthew Repka are expected to spend them with their parents.

This play "Na Naszej Glebie" has some new Maska players who are making their stage debut. Included are Kazmera Goraka, Stephanie Chylinska, Edward Repka and Arthur Bankowski. We're hoping they are our future stars.

By helping out at rehearsals, Zyg Brzozowski has played the part of the hero, the villain, and he also, sang. (Believe it or not) (Editor's note: "I don't.")

Sorry to hear about Zyg Kilian's Paint Store burning down. (Editor's note: or is the word, "up?")

We heard that Edward Repka has joined the St. Adalbert's choir and he is thier one and only baritone. You'll be an opera star yet, Ed.

Best wishes to Stanley Zych who has been fortunate enough to get a job with the General Electric Co. (Editor's note: Or should we congratulate the G.E.?)

That's that until the next time, so meanwhile a Merry Christmas and a Happy New Year to all! (Editor's note: That goes for me too.)

1939, December

Sending heartfelt wishes

SERDECZNE ZYCZENIA
ZASYŁA

Advanced BAKERY

7 1 9 / 6   Windsor Terrace   Tad. Święcicki --- Właśc.

(P.S) J O K E S

Stan Plocharczyk: That's a queer pair of socks you have on, Art -- one red and the other green.

Art Bankowski: Yes and I've got another pair like it at home.

Hank Ausfeld: How did you break your leg, Ed?

Ed Rapka: I threw a cigarette into a man-hole and stepped on it.

Zyg Kilian: What's worse than being a bachelor?

Zyg Brzozowski: Being a bachelor's son.

The captain of an Atlantic liner approached a young woman leaning on the rail.
"Waiting for the moon to come up?" He asked.
"Oh, ye Gods," she groaned, "Has that got to come up, too?"

Some girls are like cigarettes; they come in packs, get lit, hang on your lips, make you puff, go out unexpectedly, leave a bad taste in your mouth, but still they satisfy.

A hotel was on fire and the guests, gathering out in front, were watching the flames. "Nothing to get excited about," one traveling man was boasting. "I took my time about dressing. Lighted a cigarette. Didn't like the knot in my tie and retied it. That's how cool I was."
"Fine," remarked a bystander, "but why didn't you put your pants on?"

"The hospital called and said I have another mouth to feed."
"Boy or Girl?"
"Neither, the wife's got a tapeworm."

Doctor: I'd like to have a quart of blood for a transfusion, can you give it?
Stan Zych: I can only give you a pint. I gotta shave tomorrow.

1939, December

Mrs. C. Olivert: We're going to give the bride a shower.

C. Olivert: Count me in. I'll bring the soap.

Ted. K: Do you owe any back house rent?

Andrew P: We haven't got any back house. We've got modern plumbing.

P O E T R Y -
(Only for those Maska members poetically inclined.)

THE BRIDEGLOOM:-

Will you take this woman
    For your lawful wedded wife?
Will you honor and obey her
    Throughout your natural life?
Will you let her have her way
    And fulfill her each desire;
Start the breakfast every morning,
    Chop the wood and build the fire?
Will you let her drive your car?
    Will you give her all your money,
Go to parties every night?
    Will you always call her "honey?"
Will you support her mother,
    Father and her brothers,
Uncles, aunts, cousins,
    And a half dozen others?
He gazed queerly at the parson,
    Then he gave his head a tilt,
And hopelessly he raised his eyes,
    And weakly said, "I wilt."

Mary had a little swing,
    It isn't hard to find,
And everywhere that Mary goes
    The swing is just behind.

The girl I left behind me
    I think of night and day,
If ever she should find me,
    There would be heck to pay.

KÓŁKO DRAMATYCZNE "Maska" ZASYŁA
SERDECZNE ŻYCZENIA WESOŁYCH ŚWIĄT
BOŻEGO NARODZENIA I SZCZĘŚLIWEGO NOWEGO ROKU

The "Maska" Dramatic Circle sends sincere wishes for a Merry Christmas
And a Happy New Year

1939, December

MASKA PATRONS

Mr. W. Dziegielewski	Mr. & Mrs. Borowski	
Mr. F. Quirini	Mr. & Mrs. G. Sekowski	Young Poles Society
Mr. J. Rekucki	Mrs. S. Gasowska	Harmony Society
Mr. A. Kielowski	Tow. Mloda Polska	Truth & Work Society
Mr. W. Gbara	Tow. Zgoda	Freedom Society
	Tow. Prawda i Praca	
Dr. Bednarkiewicz	Tow. Swoboda	
Mr. M. Roach	Mr. & Mrs. J. Kilian	
Mrs. J. Lkaszewicz	Mrs. C. Marcinkiewicz	
Mr. B. Lewkowicz	Mrs. A. Kostek	
Mr. R. Szczepanski	Mr. J. Zborowski	
Dr. M. Dybich	Mr. & Mrs. Felix Ropka	
Mr. J. Piotrowski	Mrs. R. Zych	My grandmother
Dr. Mazurowski	Mrs. N. Jankowski	
Mrs. Sendlewski	Mr. J. Novobielski	
Mr. & Mrs. Pokrzywnicki	Mr. & Mrs. P. Korycinski	My grandparents
Mr. C. Wojcicki	Mr. S. Krosnowski	
Mr. John Wicks	Mr. J. Gzyms	My great uncle
Mr. John Ogrodnik	Mr. L. Okonsky	
Mr. F. Lesczyhski	Mrs. Prewencka	
Mrs. V. Bursiewicz	Mrs. A. Kowakska	
Miss G. Bursiewicz	Mrs. A. Kalinowski	
Mrs. M. Pitera	Mrs. C. Obremski	
Mrs. Marchewka	Mrs. E. Kulczyk	
Mr. F. Smith	Mr. & Mrs. W. Ausfeld	
Mr. & Mrs. Luniewski	Mrs. A. Kostek	
Mr. K. C. Sarnowski	Mrs. E. Dziuba	
Mr. W. Wieletinski	Mrs. F. Wierzbowski	
	Miss G. Chylinski	

1939, December

PATRONS CONT.

Mr. & Mrs. F. Kosinski
Mr. A Swetkowski
Mr. A. Zwolski
Mr. & Mrs. T. Witkowski
Mr. W. Malicki
Mr. B. Jakubowski

Mr. & Mrs. A. B. Brzozowski
Mr. W. D. Przybyłek
Mr. G. T. Zurn
Mr. J. Deptola
Mrs. P Wisniewska
Mrs. J. Rowna

1940, May

Mom's art work

Appendix 5   Maska Buletyns

1940, May

MAY 1940

SOCIAL GOSSIP

Today, May 2, we extend our heartiest birthday greetings to Stanley Zych. On May 20, a few years back, Celia Borowska made herself known in this world. Nevertheless, we wish you two all the success and happiness possible.

Maska Club has welcomed into its membership Helen Lemanska, Joseph Roranowski, Frank Baranowski, Chester Baranowski and Steven Kwiecinski.

Many thanks are offered to our guests, members, and the committee, which made our annual card party a huge social success.

Fingers that are developing callouses are the property of Casmera Gorska, which she uses to play the bass fiddle. Incidentally, Cas has joined the Royal Rhythmette Orchestra. Good work, Cas!

George Mosojko made a terrible mistake the night of the last play--not on the stage, but by accidentally walking into the girls' room, instead of the make-up room.

Speaking of mistakes, we reminded ourselves of a mistake we (the staff) made in the last month's bulleting. Arthur Benkowski's height was six feet four and a half inches and he grew to be now six feet five inches tall.

Chester Baranowski has joined the St. Adalbert's Choir. Maybe he wants to practice up on the art of serenading some fair young lady.

Have you notices that new diamond ring which Zyg Brzozowski has been wearing? And it's on the engagement finger, too.

[Mom, Dad, Mom's brother →] Casmira Gorska, Sophie Korycinska, Stanley Zych and Alexander Korycinski have been initiated last Tuesday into the St. Adalbert's Choir.

$$$$$$

This week, dear members, we want to give you the latest fashion styles that were seen at a recent highly social affair.

While I was in the lounge, who should swagger in but that old hussy Lucyanne Sekowska. I'll bet she thought she was the "stuff," but her bustle was out of line. She was a revolting sight with that new hair-do. I just laughed myself silly. In the midst of my hilarity, in walked Sandra Zych, as stunning and petite as ever. She was wearing one of those new backless, sideless, topless, bottomless, frontless, evening gowns with a long pleated skirt and a train of handsome men. It must be

1940, May

- 2 -

awful to be so pretty and have all those men following you about with their tongues lolling out.

Practically on Sandra's heels were those look alike, act alike, dress alike girls,, Arlene Bankowska and Zenia Kilian. They were all wrapped up in their legs when they tripped fantastically into the salon. They were wearing divine creations direct from Joisey. The cerise material of the bodice and the shimmering velvet of the skirt were bunched at the waist. They said they were trying to create a new Leap Year fashion.

You should have seen Brenda Brzozowska. She looked lovely--for a change. It must have been that new corset she has been bragging about. The new Maidan Forms work wonders with the figures. I'd never have recognised her but for her face--the big show-off.

Susan Plocharcsyk, Shirley Bachleda, and Wendy Sekowska, were more beautiful than you could ever imagine. Wendy wore a long lace frock from under which peeked the frilled edges of her new, linen pantalettes. Susan's bare arms were hanging out of an elbow length sleeve, padded at the joint. Shirley Bachleda's striped stockings were fastened to her skin by gold-pleated safety pins speckled with rhinestones. Such marvelous originality.

The sensation of the ball was Henrietta Ausfeld in her own creation, a hipper-dipper double zipper affair. The back was cut away to her ankles, and the front came up to the bags under her eyes.

And what did Josephine Czysewska wear? A beautiful white, three-quarter length dress, with slits on the sides. It was loose fitting and made of the new canseethru satin.

Well, next year is another year, with it's new styles and new faces. Toodle-doodle!

(Ed.'s note: Am I forgiven, fellas?)

ODE TO RED FLANNELS

All of spring's historic annals
Show no case where two-legged mammals
Had the sense to wear their flannels
Right up into May!
March and April's arctic breezes
Fan the coed's purple kneeses,
Start a hundred million sneezes
By the bare display.
Weather-trusting college Joses
Go beer-busting, get red noses,
More from shirtless, shortless clothes,
Than from filthy brew.

1940, May

- 3 -

Gals too early hide their snuggies,
Woolen skirts, and red fox chubbies,
Hatless ride in horseless buggies,
Then come down with flu.
People are such crazy creatures!
Spring's not all golf-course and bleachers,
Blanket parties can be freezers
In an April rain!
Worse than pitching woo off-season
Is the darned fool stripped of reason
Who goes swimming with ice freezing
Round his balmy brain!
When you Jillies catch pneumonia,
Just remember that I told you,
Summer's undies that enfold you,
Won't keep cold away!
Go on! Rush the spring, you Ghandies!
Wear your ankle-sox and scanties!
But I'll keep my woolen panties
Scratching me 'till May!

WHY I HATE MEN
I hate men because----------

1. They all object to nail polish but they don't know why.
2. They always, always ask you where you want to go when you set out on a date, but you always go where they want to.
3. They talk all the time about how wonderful they are and never give you a chance to tell them how wonderful you are.
4. They laughed at the idea of girls being friends, and if they are, they'll flirt with both of them to see what will happen.
5. They think you aren't a lady if you can't hold your liquor, and if you can, they still think you aren't.
6. Never in God's world have they been known to use an ash tray if there's a rug handy.
7. If they take anything to eat out of the refrigerator, they put the dirty dishes back in.
8. They object to hearing a woman swear, but not to swearing at her.
9. They are all too thin before they're 30 then all at once they become too fat.
10. They laugh at women's interest in clothes, but they will tell you in minute detail how they happened to buy their new top-coat.
11. They only tell you that you look nice when there's a lull in the conversation.
12. After making love to you all evening, they suddenly get up and stretch and say that they are hungry.

1940, September

1940, September

Wrzesien, 1940   September, 1940

STEFANIA CHYLINSKA

Było to w roku 1918-ym, jeden dzień po Świętach Bożego Narodzenia kiedy Santa Claus zwiedził dom Pp. A. Chylinskich, zostawiając im w podarunku 6-cio funtową córeczkę. Była ona umieszczona na ten czas we wielkim białem domu przy 65 Vernon ulicy, Worcester, Mass. Ochszczono ja Cecilia Stefania. "Cecilia" z racji patrona muzyki a "Stefania" by uczcić pamięć dnia Św. Stefana.

Uczęszczała do Ward St. Elementary School w Worcester, Mass. Podczas pobytu w Worcester, była członkinią "Worcester Girls Club" i czynną w dramatach i "Glee Club."

W Sierpniu, roku 1931, familja przeniosła rezydencję do Schenectady, do miasta w którym matka zamieszkiwała wiele lat wstecz. Tu jej ojciec otrzymał posadę organisty przy parafji Św. Wojciecha, a Stefania uczęszczała do McKinley Jr. High School i Mont Pleasant High School, z której uczelni graduowała w klasie styczniowej roku 1937. Obecnie jest zatrudniona w H. S. Barney CO.

Przystąpiła do grona Choru Św. Wojciecha zwanego "Junior Choir" w roku 1931 a trzy lata poźniej była przyjętą do St. Adelbert's Choral Society. Przez ostatnie dwa lata piastowała urząd Sekretarki finansowej przy tem stowarzyszeniu.

Po wielu namowień, Stefania zapisała się do Kółka Dramatycznego "Maska" w jesieni roku, 1939. Od tego czasu była bardzo energiczną i czynną członkinią. Służyła na wielu komitetach oraz i z okazji tak zwanego "Card Party" i "July Jamboree." Jest ona także jedną z naszych charakteryzorek do przedstawień na przyszły sezon.

Panna Stefania Chylinska do tych czas odgrywała w trzech sztukach: "Na Naszej Glebie", "Końska Kuracja", i "Pozycz Mi Swej Zony."

############

ZARZĄD BULETYNU

Zofja Zych---Przewodnicząca

Assystenci:

Stefanja Chylinska
Marya Czyzewska
Stanisław Bachleda
Czesław Baranowski

The Buletyn Board Sophie Zych – President, Assistants

1940, September - Translation

Stephanie Chylinska

It was the day after Christmas in 1918 when Santa Claus visited the home of Mr. & Mrs. Professor Chylinski, leaving them a gift of a 6 pound daughter. She was placed at that time in a big white house at 68 Vernon Place in Worcester, Mass. She was Baptized Cecilia Stefania. "Cecilia" after the patron saint of music and "Stefania" to celebrate the remembrance of Saint Stephen's Day [December 26].

She attended the Ward St. Elementary School in Worcester, Mass. and was a member of Worcester Girls' Club and was active in drama and the "Glee Club."

In August 1931 the family moved to Schenectady where the mother had lived previously. Here her father became the organist for St. Adalbert's Church. Stephanie attended McKinley Junior High and Mont Pleasant High School, from which she graduated in the class of January 1937. Curently she is employed by the H.S. Barney Co.

She joined the Junior Choir of St. Adalbert's and three years later she was accepted into the St. Adalbert's Choral Society. For the past two years she has been finance secretary for that organization.

After many encouragements, Stephanie joined Maska in the fall of 1939. Since that time she has been a very energetic and active member. She has served on many committees, for example the "Card Party" and the "July Jamboree." She is also one of the makeup artists for this past season.

To date, Miss Stefania Chylinska has had parts in three plays: On Our Soil, The Horse Cure and Lend Me Your Wife.

1940, September

Wrzesień, 1940   - 2 -   September 1940

SOCIAL GOSSIP

Birthday greetings for September are extended to Joseph Czyzewski and Chester Baranowski.

Congratulations to Henry and Mary Ausfeld, who were married August 25 at the St. Adalbert's Church. Maska certainly has taken to walking up that church aisle.

Another wedding in sight is that of Regina Chantnicka and Edward Prusak, which will take place September 15. Our best wishes are offered to you.

Celia Borowska has been busy bookkeeping at the D'Jimas Bros. Fur Shop, which us girls think would be an ideal place to work in. Air-conditioned and everything.

Is that really Chet behind that so-called "mustache?"

[Mom's brother] Alex Korycinski, Walter Sekowski, Jean Dziuba, Henry Klejewyt have been some of the many guests of the World's Fair and New York.

Henrietta Jozefowicz has been lucky enough to get a job at the G. E. Co. Is that why you've been wearing those glasses, Henrietta?

If you want to see some beautiful flowers, be sure to visit Pearl and Louis Okonski at their home. Their place is a Garden of Eden in the summertime. Ask Mary and Joseph.

Stanley Plocharczyk has been vacationing at Connecticut, his birthplace.

Arthur Bankowski and Zyg Kilian have both been suffering from sore ankles. Maybe it's good to be short after all.

We are very glad to have among our happy faces, the face of a new member, in the person of Victor Deptola.

Helen Dziuba has been located in a downtown five and ten cent store.

Joseph Czyzewski has gone to Brockport, N. Y. to attend The Summer Institute on Forums and Public Affairs. He attended this conference from August 26 through August 31. To hear him speak of it, we wonder if he went there for business or PLEASURE.

Stephanie Chylinska has spent her vacation at Atlantic City and came home with a cold.

The Baranowski brothers, Chet and Frank, are always seen working at a grocery store in Mont Pleasant.

1940, September

- 3 -

Marion Plocharczyk has been spotted jitterbugging at the Riverside Park Casino. And can she jitterbug!!!

When Joseph and Mary Czysewski attended a recent picnic, they were found occupied as Chairman and Kitchen aide, respectively.

Now let's speak of Honeymoons. What couple enjoyed itself so much on its honeymoon that it hated to come back home. Even though one of the party suffered a fall in a puddle of beer, it didn't dampen her spirits. The beer they had served to them wasn't a very good thirst quencher because there wasn't enough beer left in the bottle after it was opened. It went to the ceiling instead of their throats.

Marion Plocharczyk is very anxious to act in our plays. That's the type of members we like to have in our Club.

Many of the male members are asking about what happened to the idea of the dancing instructions to be given by the female members of the Club after the meeting. Yes, how about it?

A very lively debate or shall I call it trying to convince a person that he is wrong, was held after the last meeting of the Club in Zyg Z.'s car between "Debater at the drop of a hat" Joseph Czyzewski, "I don't say much, but when I do say it it's worthwhile listening to" Zyg Brzozowski and "If I only had the time, I'd do this" Zyg Kilian on the affirmative side and a former member of "Maska" on the negative. It's hard to say whether the affirmative side succeeded in convincing the negative side, that he was wrong. He is quite a stubborn person to be convinced.

PERIODIC LITERATURE

Magazine	Member
"The Vogue"	Stephanie Chylinska
"American Boy"	Stanley Bachleda
"Modern Priscilla"	Pearl Okonska
"Popular Mechanics"	Chester Baranowski
"Physical Culture"	Ted Kilian
"True Romance"	These Newlyweds of Maska
"Country Gentleman"	Louis Okonski
"Esquire"	Zyg Brzozowski
"Woman's Home Companion"	Joseph Czyzewski
"Life"	Arthur Bankowski
"Look"	Daniel Klimas
"Judge"	Zyg Kilian
"Review of Reviews"	Stanley Plocharczyk
"Good Housekeeping"	Sophie Zych
"Glamour"	Jeanne Dziuba — Mom
"Pathfinder"	Stanley Zych
"Home Arts"	Mary Badka
"Lure"	Helen Dziuba
"Action Stories"	Henry Ausfeld — Dad
"Vanity Fair"	Celia Borowska
"Bride's Magazine"	Regina Chantnicka
"Field and Stream"	Alex Korycinski
"War Atlas"	Joseph Czyzewski
"The Shadow"	Frank Baranowski — Mom's brother

1940, September

- 4 -

"Love Story"	Marion Plocharczyk
"Opportunity"	Helen Wisniewska
"Boy's Life"	Victor Deptola
"Outdoor's Man"	Joseph Godlewski
"Your Beauty"	Regina Godlewska
"Fur Fish Game"	Zygmunt Wisniewski
"Your Future"	Lucyan Sekowski
"Variety"	Mary Czyzewska

JOKES

"It's the little things that tell," she said, as she dragged her little brother from under the davenport.

"Wait a minute officer, I want to get my hat."
"Trying to give me the slip are ye? You stay here, I'll get the hat."

"Looks like rain today," said the milkman as he poured the milk from the can.

"It always does," replied the housewife.

Pearls come from oysters, but some girls get diamonds from nuts.

It is better to have loved a short guy and lost than never to have loved a tall.

Telegram to friend: "Washout on line, cannot come."
Reply: "Come any way, borrow a shirt."

If all the Pullman cars in the United States were placed in a line on a single rail, it would be foolish.

Tim—"How are you getting along at home while your wife's away?"
Jim—"Fine. I've reached the height of efficiency. I can put my socks on now from either end.

Perpetual Motion
Doors are made out of trees, trees grow out of doors.

"My razor doesn't cut at all."
"Come, Come," replied the wife. "Your beard is no tougher than the linoleum I cut with it yesterday."

Will the members please give us material which will make this bulletin more interesting. We are making an effort to please you, but we do need your cooperation. By the way, this is no joke, even though it may be under the heading "JOKES."

1940, December

1940, December

Eighth Season "Maska" Dramatic Season First program of the 1940 – 1941 season

CATHERINE GOES TO COURT
Comedy in Three Acts

At the Polish Home
Sunday, December 1, 1940

CAST

Lawyer

Judge

Policeman

OSMY SEZON

KOŁKA DRAMATYCZNEGO

"MASKA"

Pierwszy występ sezonu 1940 – 1941

KATARZYNA W SĄDZIE

Komedja w Trzech Aktach

W Domu Polskim

W Niedzielę, 1go Grudnia, 1940

OSOBY:

Katarzyna Rzodkiewka	Mary Czyzewska
Jozef Rzodkiewka	Stanislaw Zych
Adwokat	Jozef Czyzewski
Kazimierz Kochliwski	Stanislaw Plocharczyk
Marta Kochliwska	Helen Dziuba
Sędzia	Lucyan Sekowski
Edward	Daniel Klimas
Zosia	Marion Plocharczyk
Mosiek Kugielszpic	Jozef Godlewski
Policjant	Eugeniusz Kopec
Frank Pietruszka	Artur Bankowski

AKT PIERWSZY -- W mieszkaniu adwokata

AKT DRUGI -- W mieszkaniu adwokata

AKT TRZECI -- W sali sądowej

Rzecz dzieje sie podczas prohibicji.

FIRST ACT – Lawyer's home   SECOND ACT – Lawyer's home   THIRD ACT – In the courtroom.
Action takes place during Prohibition.

1940, December

Sending wishes

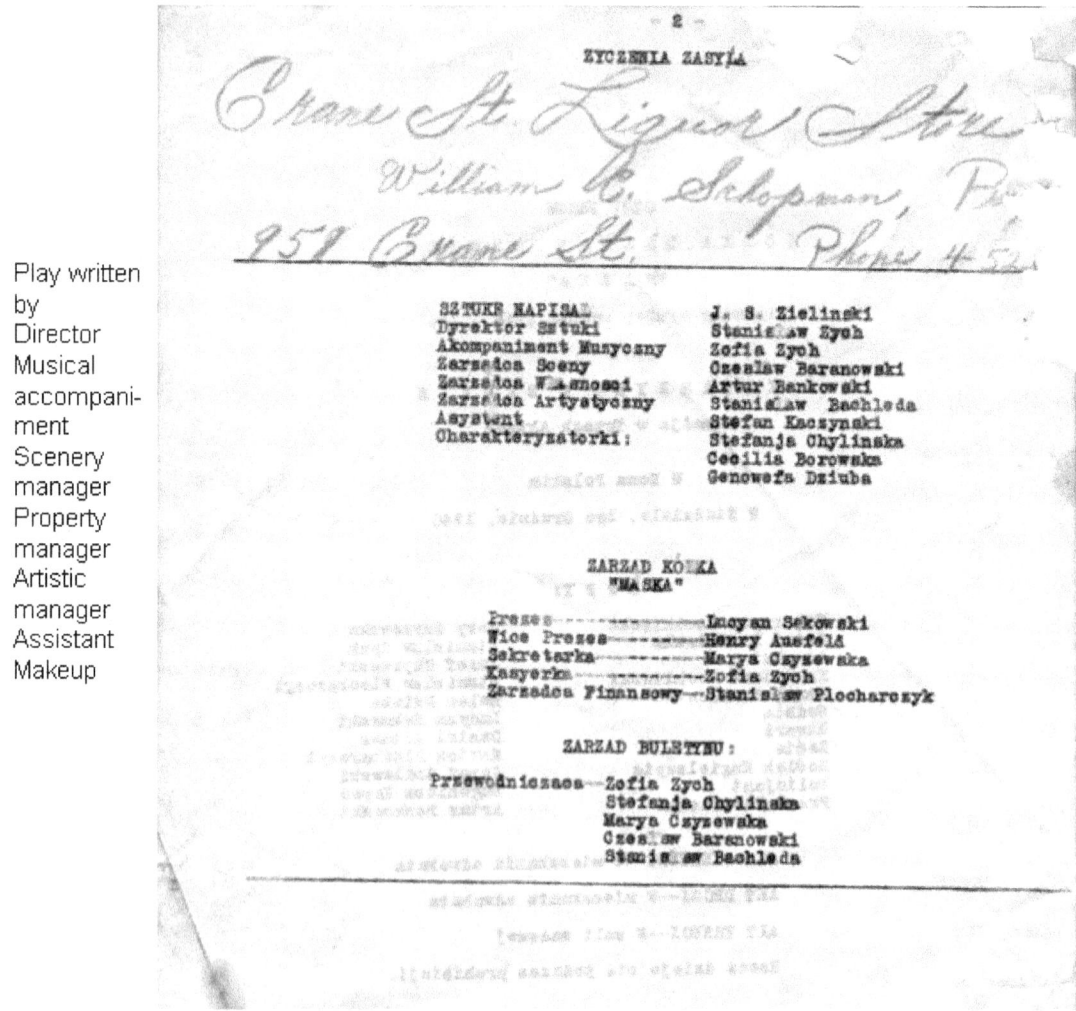

Play written by
Director
Musical accompaniment
Scenery manager
Property manager
Artistic manager
Assistant
Makeup

MASKA OFFICERS: President – Vice President – Secretary – Treasurer – Finance manager

BOARD OF THE BULETYN: Chairwoman

1940, December

HENRYKA JOZEFOWICZ

Henryka Jozefowicz urodziła się 15go Lipca w roku 1921. Uczęszczała przez osm lat do naszej parafjalnej szkoły, Sw. Wojciecha. Jest także graduantka Mont Pleasant High School w Czerwcu, 1939.

Henryka wstąpiła do Kolka Dramatycznego "Maska" pare lat temu. Brała także udział w sztuce tak zwanej "KANDYDATURA SOLIWODY."

W tym czasie jest zatrudniona w Central Electric Company.

HUMOR

KORZYSC Z MAŁZENSTWA

"Odkąd ożeniłeś się, już nie chodzisz z poobrywanymi guzikami jak dawniej."

"To prawda. Zaraz po ślubie zona nauczyła mnie przyszywać guziki."

"Mamusiu, nasza guwernantka ma takie dobre oczy, ze widzi nawet w ciemnosciach," rzekła córeczka.

"A skąd ty to wiesz?" zdziwiła się matka.

"Słyszałam, jak w nocy powiedziała do tatusia: "Pan się chyba dzisiaj nie golił."

POJETNY PACJENT

"Pigulki te zażywać pan będzie na wodzie."

"Niemożliwe, panie doktorze."

"Dlaczego niemożliwe?"

"Ja nie umiem pływać."

ZNAŁ GO DOBRZE

"Ach, jak to dobrze, ze drogi przyjacielu, cie spotykam. Zostawiłem w domu portfel i jestem teraz w wielkim kłopocie. Pożycz mi do jutra pięć dolarów.

"Wolę ci pożyczyć pięć centów na subway i jedź do domu po swój portfel."

NOWA SŁUZACA

Pelagia, która niedawno przybyła ze wsi do miasta, jest jeszcze mało rozgarnięta. Pewnego dnia chlebodawczyni wręcza jej ścierecke do ścierania kurzu z mebli i powiada:

"Niech Pelasia szybko wytrze kurze."

Pelasia rozgląda się po pokoju, wreszcie zapytuje: "A gdzie jest ta kura, proszę pani?"

WSROD MLODYCH ARTYSTOW

A: "Cos jadł dzis na obiad?"
B: "Nic. Nie miałem za co kupić i odgrzeje obiad na kolację."

HENRIETTA JOZEFOWICZ

Henrietta Jozefowicz was born on July 1st 1921. She attended our parish school St. Adalberts's for eight years. She also graduated from Mont Pleasant High School in June 1939.

Henrietta joined the "Maska" Dramatic Circle a few years ago. She took part in in the play called Soliwoda Runs for Alderman.

She currently works at the General Electric Company.

HUMOR

BENEFITS OF MARRIAGE
"Since you got married, you no longer walk around with missing buttons."

"That's true. Right after the wedding my wife taught me to sew on buttons."

"Mother, our governess has such good eye sight that she can see in the dark," said a daughter.
"How do you know this?" Asked the mother in surprise.
"One night I heard her say to daddy: I don't think you shaved today."

A TEACHABLE PATIENT
"These pills should be taken in water."
"I cannot, doctor."
"Why can't you?"
"I don't know how to swim."

KNEW HIM WELL
Oh, this is so good, dear friend, that I met you. I left my wallet at home and I am now in big trouble.
Lend me five dollars until tomorrow.
"I would rather lend you five cents for the subway and you can go home and get your wallet.

A NEW MAID
Pelagia, who not long ago arrived in the city from the country, is still a little confused. One day, her patron handed her a dust cloth for the furniture and said:
Pelagia, quickly dust the furniture.
Pelagia looked around the room and finally asked: "And where is the hen, please madam?"
Comment: This is a play on Polish words: kurzu is dust; kura is hen.

AMONG YOUNG ARTISTS
A: "What did you eat for lunch?"
B: "Nothing. I didn't have any money so I reheated dinner for lunch."

1940, December

- 4 -

SOCIAL GOSSIP

DECEMBER

Mary and Joseph Czyzewski were recently tripping the light fantastic in formal attire at the Phi Gamma Delta Fraternity House and Silliman's Hall at the Union College.

Dad Jean Dziuba has been seen dancing at the Firemen's Ball and also skating at the Palace Roller Rink.

Stan Zych claims that the other person was carried out when asked about the cut on his forehead.

Evidently Helen Dziuba lived through that Thanksgiving Dinner at her boyfriend's house. Maybe we all should have been in evidence there, after hearing her favorable comments on it.

Stan Plocharczyk and Lu Sekowski were two very busy people before the elections and all for Maska, too. They can sit peacefully now.

Congratulations to Lu Okonski who has been recently employed by the General Electric Company.

The Christmas rush is getting the best of our salesgirl members, including Celia Borowska, Pearl Okonska, Helen Dziuba, Reggie Godlewski, Stephanie Chylinska and Sophie Zych. By the way, Reggie Godlewski is that cute little girl who waits on the fountain in Liggett's Drug store on State St.

Among the new members making their debut in this performance we find: Marion Plocharczyk, Helen Dziuba, Daniel Klimas, Eugene Kopec and Joseph Godlewski.

Junior: Daddy, if you give me ten cents, I'll tell you what the iceman said to Mama.

Stan Plocharczyk (all excited): O. K. son, here's your dime.

Junior: He said,"Do you want any ice, today, lady?"

"Why does an engine always stand and never sit on a track?"
"Because it has a tender, behind."

1940, December

Susan: "Yes'm, I'se getting everything ready for my wedding. Is I happy? Why ma'am, could anyone be happier than a bride preparing her torso?"

Zyg B: "Say, aren't your socks inside out?"
Zyg K: "Yes, my feet were hot so I turned the hose on them."

Seems as though a little girl was talking to her mother:
"Oh, mama, I saw the nicest man today."
"Who was he, dear?"
"He was the garbage man, mama."
"And why was he so nice?"
"Well, he was carrying a can of garbage over his head to the wagon; and while he had it over his head the bottom came out and the garbage fell all over him, and he stood there and talked to God."

Celia: This shoe pinches my joint.
Clerk: Well, Miss, there are very very few joints that don't get pinched these days.

Seen in Some Restaurant:
"The world is coming to an end. Pay when served, so we won't have to look all over hell for you."

Ben: I like psychology when it isn't over my head.
Frosh: "That's the way I feel about pigeons."

Lady—Now, professor, I suppose that this is one of those horrible portraits you call art?
Prof:—No, madam, that is a mirror.

ZYCZENIA ZASYLA

Sending Wishes

1940, December

Patrons and Patronesses of the Maska Circle

- 6 -

PATRONKI I PATRONI KOŁKA MASKA

Pp. Antoni J. Cichy
Pp. Robert Cox
Pp. Alexander Godlewski
Pp. Władysław Klejmyt
Dr. i Pani August Korkoss
Pp. Piotr Korycinski
Pp. Bernard Luniewski
Pp. Władysław Okonski
Pp. Henry Przybylek
Pp. Gustaw Sokowski
Pp. Antoni Wroblewski

Pani Antonia Bartkowska
Pani Władysława Borowska
Pani Antonia Chylinska
Pani Agnieszka Dziengielewska
Pani Ewa Dziuba
Pani Julia Dziuba
Pani Stanisława Gąsowska
Pani Marya Jankowska
Pani Josefa Jerozalska
Pani Marya Jozefowicz
Pani Benjamin Kassubska
Pani Antonia Kopec
Pani Anna Klimas
Pani Katarzyna Palaszewska
Pani Marya Pajerska
Pani Jozefa Rutkowska
Pani Antonia Saniewska
Pani Jozefa Stelmach
Pani Helena Szargiewicz
Pani Antonia Szatkowska
Pani Zofia Wajda
Pani Adam Wisniewska
Pani Marya Woja

Panna Irena Borowska
Panna Zofia Grzywna
Panna Wanda Mankiewicz
Panna Berta Marcinkiewicz
Panna Władysława Justin

Pan Władysław Andrzejewski
Pan Wallace Armour
Dr. Ignacy Bednarkiewicz
Pan Jozef Bietka
Pan Charles A. Brundage
Pan Paul Christian
Pan Jan Cieplinski
Pan Morris Marshall Cohn
Pan David Cohn
Dr. Edmund Colby
Pan Jozef Dassewski

Pan Lewis B. Dewk
Pan Jozef A. Dick
Pan Joseph A. D'Jimas
Dr. Myron J. Dybich
Pan Władysław Dziengilewski
Pan Leon Florkiewicz
Pan Jan Falkowski
Pan Jozef A. Gallup
Pan Władysław Galkiewicz
Pan Jan Golembiowski
Pan Carroll A. Gardiner
Pan Władysław Gnara
Pan Stanisław Grabicki
Pan George A. Graves
Pan Jozef Gzyms
Pan Carl Heisler
Pan Jozef Holland
Pan William Jackson
Pan Benjamin Jakubowski
Pan Bronislaw Kazyaka
Pan Adam Klimowicz
Pan Frank Kosinski
Pan Antoni Kozlowski
Pan Tadeusz Kostyniak
Pan Kazimierz Krasucki
Pan Stanislaw Krosnowski
Pan Benjamin Kucsynski
Pan Frank Leszczynski
Pan Roman Lesniewski
Pan Richard Levy
Pan Blazej Lewkowicz
Pan Henry Lewkowicz
Pan Piotr Lewandowski
Pan Charles Lynch
Pan James C. MacDonald
Pan Edward Malik
Pan Władysław Malicki
Pan Andrzej Makowski
Pan John Matson
Pan Czeslaw Marcinkiewicz
Pan Edward Murawski
Pan Joseph Nusbaum
Pan Franciszek Odass
Pan Adam Ogonowski
Pan Tadeusz Ogonowski
Pan Adolf Pachucki
Pan Walter Patton
Pan Paweł Perkowski
Pan Matthias P. Poersch
Pan Stanisław Pokrzywnicki
Pan Benjamin Predal
Pan Ralph J. Ury
Pan John Sauls

1941, June

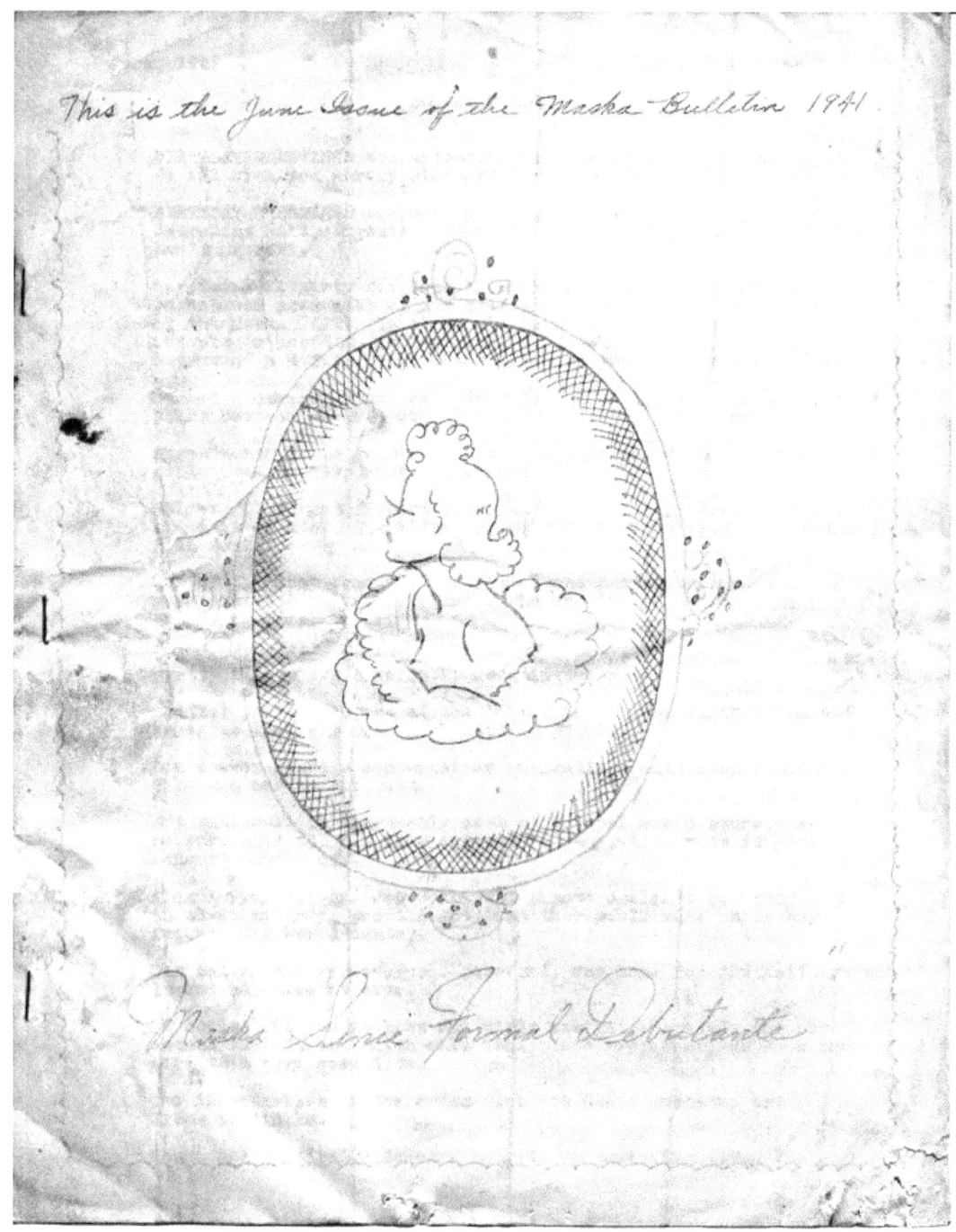

My mother's art work

1941, June

June, 1941   Czerwiec, 1941

SOCIAL GOSSIP

BIRTHDAY GREETINGS are extended for this month to Stanley Zych. We all wish you a very pleasant birthday, Stan. May Greetings.

BIRTHDAY GREETINGS are also extended for the month of June to Josephine Fall, Eugenia Kilian, Victor Deptola, Helen Dziuba, and Louis Okonski.

Our farewell party for Joseph Czyzewski was quite a success. Joseph was presented with a military case from all his friends of the Maska Club. To those who have not heard, Joseph has accepted a position in Newburgh, N.Y. where he will be in charge of a N.Y.A. Center. We all wish you lots of luck, Joseph.

Marian Plocharczyk and John Wojtulewicz do quite a bit of holding hands between scenes, etc.

Zyg Brzozowski is getting to be a regular dancer now, but us girls have to keep right after him.

Believe it or not, Robert Bankowski has actually paid that month old debt of his. The witnesses at the occasion were Sophie and Stan Zych. [Mom & Dad]

One of the most beautiful scenes at the Easter parade, was our very pretty Stephanie Chylinska who was the object of many approving eyes.

Zyg Kilian seems to think the married girls of the Maska Club are pretty nice. Zyg Brzozowski seconds the motion.

Another pretty picture at the Easter parade was Julie Cygan and we agree that she does look good in purple.

Don't ever start a conversation on families with Stan Plocharczyk. That man has us all beat.

Art Bankowski is frequently seen at a local music store where he purchases all his drum equipment. Say, Art, when is your concert coming off?

Alex Korycinski and Joe Godlewski almost couldn't get away from an admiring lady, who thought that they would make nice boy-friends for her daughter.

Our collegiate member, Walt Sekowski, was home for the holidays and looked handsome as ever.

Of course all you fellows and girls are getting ready for our annual semi-formal which will take place very soon, so look forward to a very good time.

Two inseperables of the Maska Club are Celia Borowska and Irene Zielinska.

Maska has acquired a dancing spirit, or something, even Vic

1941, June

– 2 –

Deptola danced at the party.

We were told, Josephine, to tell you to watch your step as far as men are concerned.

Our Pearl Okonska has been another fortunate one to land a job at the General Electric.

Two male inseperables are Danny Klimas and Eugene Kopec.

Celia Borowska made a very pretty bridesmaid at that wedding in Ballston Spa.

"Maska's" first Hot Dog roast of the summer season was a huge success. The Roast was held at Indian Ladder and all that attended had a swell time hiding, climbing, exploring the trail and last but not least our annual soft ball game which ended by the score of 39-40 in our favor. The members are still puffing from running the bases.

Most amusing was the Roast where everyone took a hand in it. One could see the Dogs roasted on sticks, forks, wires, fish poles and what not.

We are looking forward to see the same bunch as well as new faces and we're bound to have a swell time at our next affair. The following were present at the Outing: Pearl Okonska, Gene Kilian, Celia Borowska, Irene Zielinska, Sophie Zych, Josephine Pell, Marian Plocharczyk, Sophie Grzywna, Jean Sekowski and Adele Mniaski, also, Louis Ikonski, Karol Gursenski, Zygmunt Brzozowski, Stan Zych, Arthur Bankowski, Robert Bankowski, Victor Deptola, Gene Kopec, Lucyan Sekowski, Val Plocharczyk, John Wojtulewicz, Dan Klimas, Alex Korycinski, John Marcinek, Zygmunt Kilian, Joe Godlewski and Steve Kaczynski.

Don't forget the "MASKA" semi-formal, which will be held real soon now. What do you say, let's all go and have the time of our lives. The Committee headed by Stephanie Chylinska are making various arrangements for our annual event which always spells success.

JOKES

A man in a restaurant finally had to give it up on his steak. It was too tough to cut. He called the waiter over, and demanded that he take it back and get a new one. The waiter shook his head. "Sorry, but I can't take it back now. You've bent it."

"Really, Bill, your argument with your wife was most amusing."

"Wasn't it, though? When she threw the axe at me, I thought I'd split."

Danny Klimas—"What are you doing with my raincoat on?"
Eugene Kopec—"Keeping your suit dry."

1941, June

- 3 -

An infant was awakened from a peaceful slumber in a hospital. Looking down at his raimant he yelled over to the occupant of the next crib. "Did you spill water on my diapers?"
"Naw," was the answer.
The first speaker looked puzzled for a moment and then said, "Hmmm, must have been an inside job."

Proud father: "My boy ran ninety yards in one game."

Coach: It seems he forgot to tell you he didn't catch the guy in front of him.

Visitor (to prisoner): Why are you here?

Prisoner: For the simple reason I cannot get out.

"So you desire to become my son-in-law?"

"No, I don't but if I marry your daughter, I don't see how I can get out of it."

"You've read that passage wrong Miss Adams--it's 'all men are created equal'--not 'all men are made the same way'!"

"Mama, what becomes of a car when it gets too old to run?"

"Somebody sells it to your father."

Mistress: Mary, we have breakfast promptly at 8 o'clock.

New maid: All right, ma'am, if I ain't down don't you wait."

If she looks young she's old; if she looks old she's young; if she looks back, follow her.

APPENDIX 6

SAMPLE PAGES FROM MASKA PLAYS

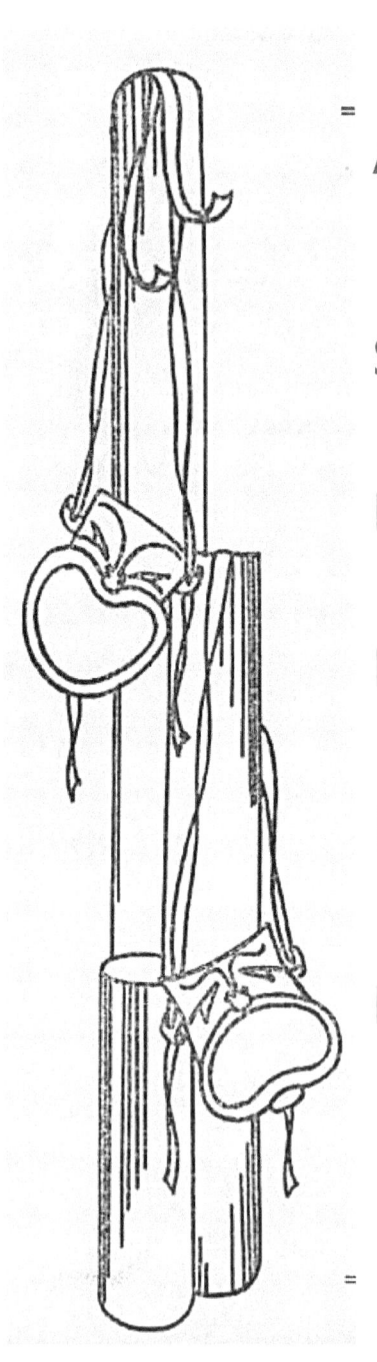

Smieszna Glupota – [Comical Goofiness]
Act I Page 1

March 6, 1938

Setting: The bedroom of Mr. Zdzislaw Biedoklepski
in a beautiful home near Milwaukee Ave. in Chicago

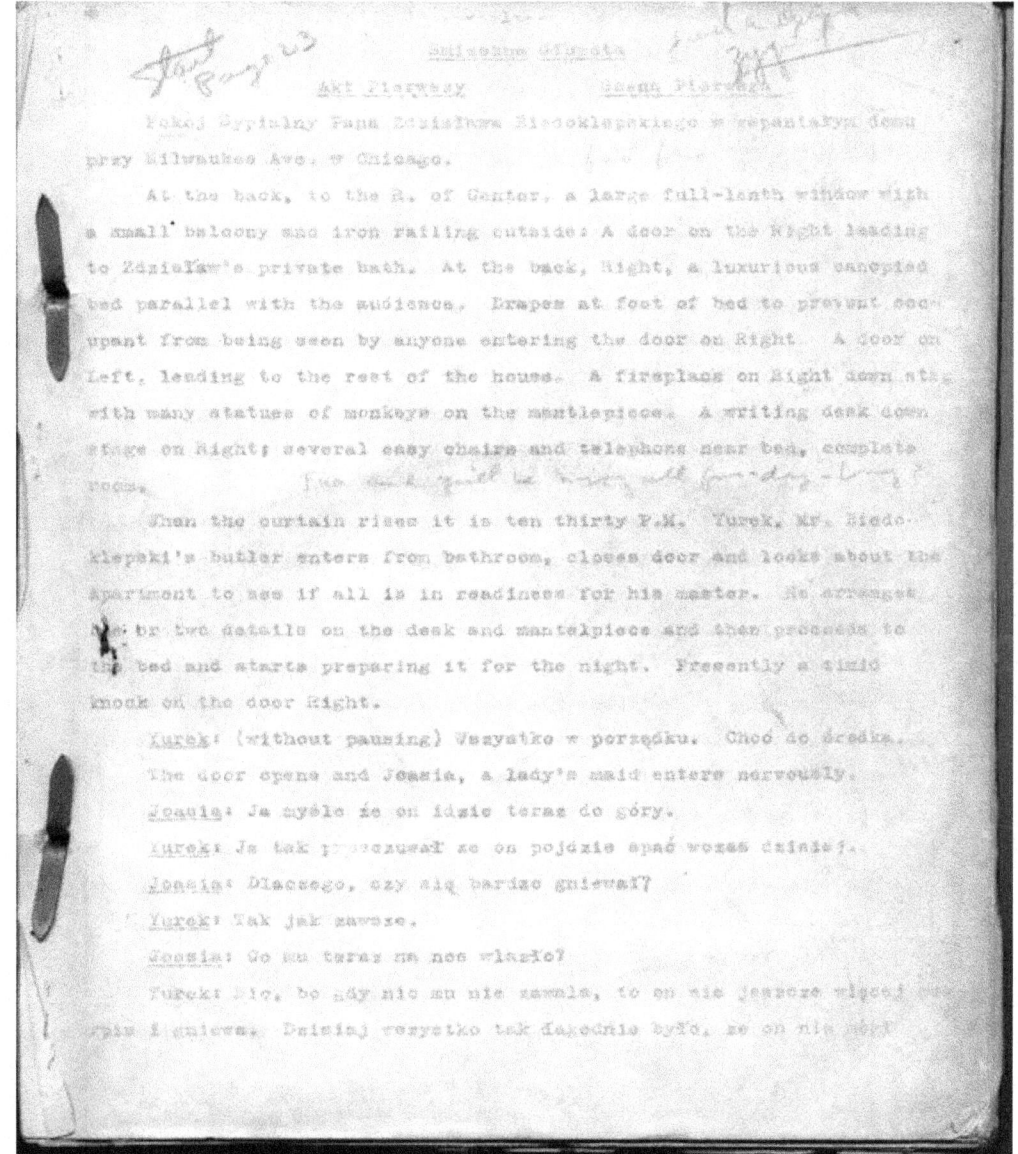

The program was supplemented with musical selections by Miss Sophie Korycinski, pianist. Miss Wanda Korycinski on general committee.
Cast includes Stanley Zych.

LEGIONNAIRE ON THE FIELD OF HONOR AND THE BRIDE'S DEATH – A Tragedy in Five Acts
By Antoni Jax   October 9 1938
Directors Joseph Czyzewski and Stanley Zych

A patriotic tragedy with songs based on the action of the Polish Legions on the Eastern Front in 1916. The play was chosen by Maska in commemoration of the 29th anniversary of the Declaration of Polish Independence by the Warsaw Committee.

Legionnaire - Continued

Czyzewski, Director

Legionnaire - Continued

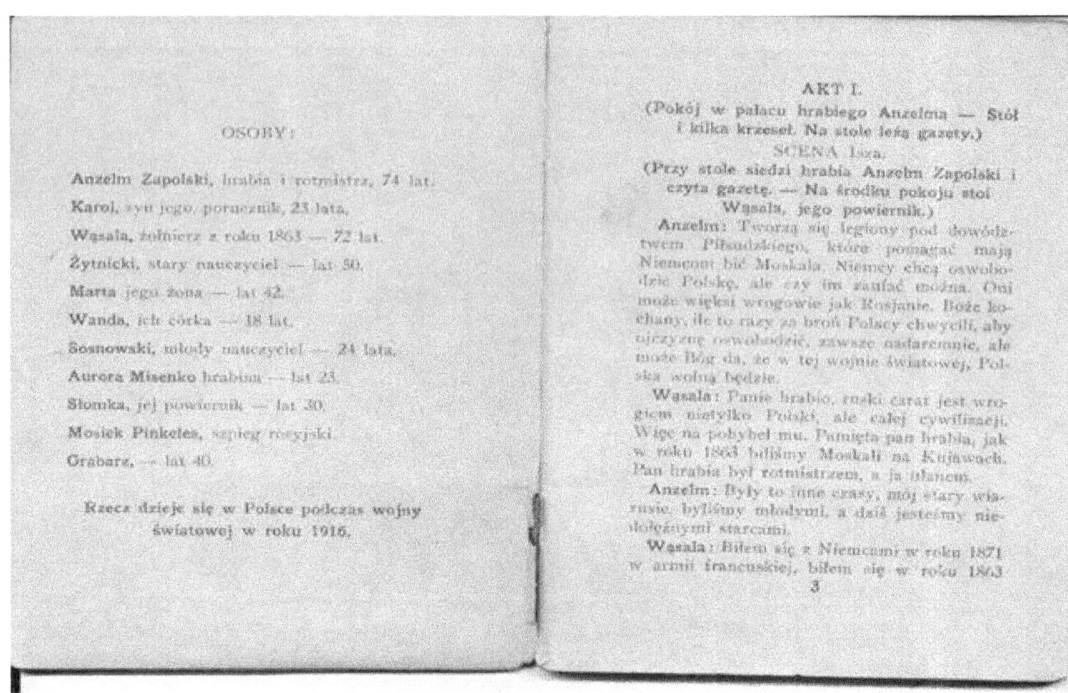

CAST

Count and captain, age 74
His son, lieutenant, age 23
A soldier since 1863, age 72
Old teacher, age 50
His wife, age 42   Wanda Korycinski – Mom's sister
Their daughter, age 18
Young teacher, age 24
Countess, age 23   Sophie Korycinski - Mom
Her confidant, age 30
Russian Spy
Gravedigger, age 40
Takes place in Poland during the world war in 1916.

Legionnaire – Conclusion and Living Tableau

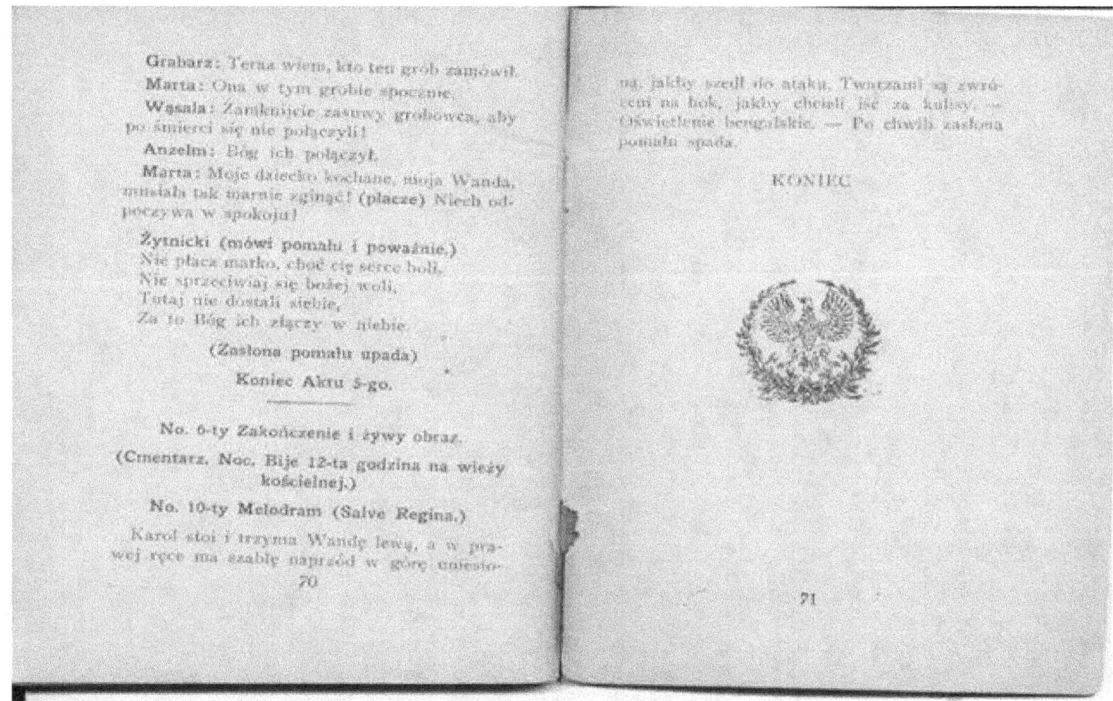

(Cemetery. Night. The Church tower rings the 12th hour.)

Karol stands and holds Wanda left, and in his right hand has a sword held on high, as if he were going to attack. The faces are turned aside as if they wanted to go behind the scenery. – the Bengal lighting [bright blue flare].
After a while, the curtain falls slowly.

THE END

PAZURA – THE CLAW
by Zygmont Antoni (Zygmunt Brzozowski) Maska Member
Act I Page 1

May 14, 1939

SCENE – Library in a rich home
TIME – 11:30 in the evening

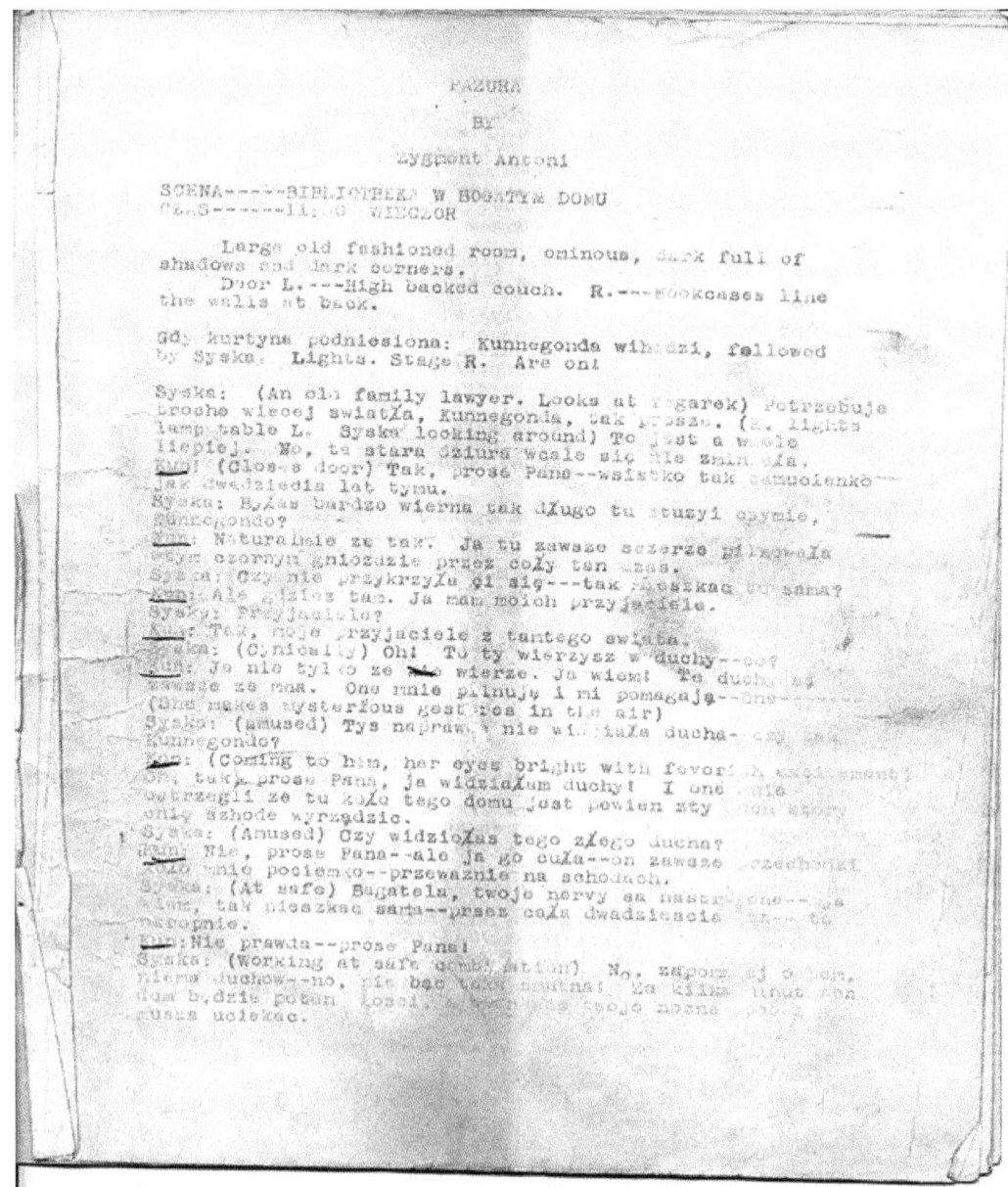

Sophie Korycinski as Klara. Stanley Zych as Marek Syaka

Pazura – The Claw
Act II Page 1

Scene: Bedroom near the library
Time: A few minutes later

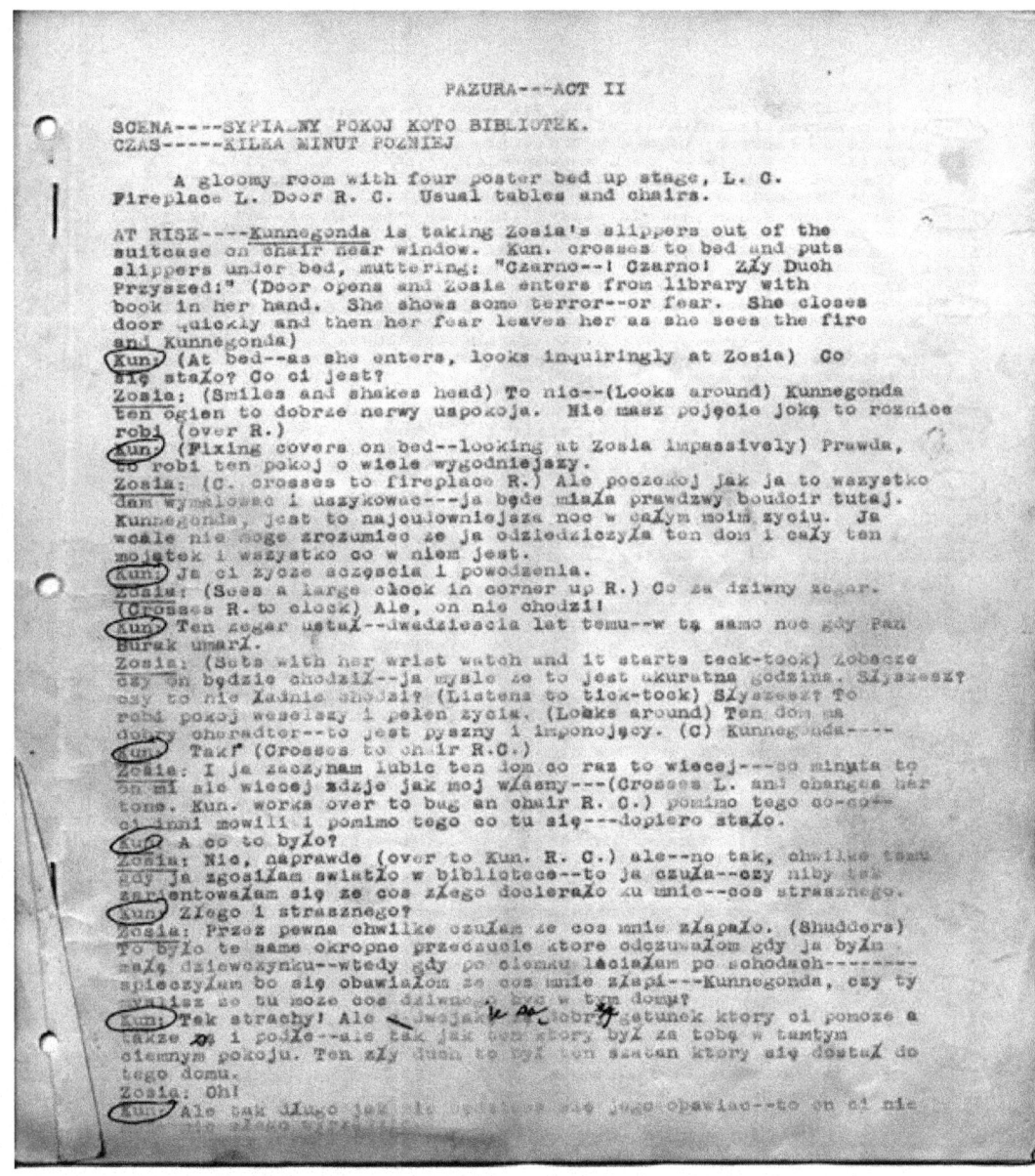

Pazura – The Claw
Act III Page 1

PAZURA--ACT III

SCENE---Same as Act I
TIME----A few minutes later.

ON STAGE: Kunnegonda opening door, allowing Stas to enter, carrying Zosia who has fainted again. Then Kunnegonda goes down to table L. and turns on lamp. Clara, Paweł, Broncia, and Tomek follow. Tomek closes door. Clara goes to table R. and turns lamp on. Paweł, at table L. pours out liquor, Broncia sits R. of table L. Tomek at door looking off L.

Stas: (Puts Zosia on couch and motions to Paweł on knees in front of sofa) Podaj mnie to--tam jest. (Clara offers him smelling salts. Points at bottle of whiskey on small table. Paweł comes over with glass of whiskey which Stas refuses. Clara takes glass and puts it on table L. All act in quiet manner. Mammy (Kunnegonda) alone is impassive. She is like a sphink. Tomek walks up and down the room. Broncia is almost out. she is sunk.)

Clara: (Back of sofa) Oh, czy to nie jest okropne; biedny Pan Syska--(Stas takes salts from Clara)

Tomek: (Silences her with a gesture. At door. Kunnegonda above table L.) Tak--tak------

Paweł: (Goes to Stas) Czy już przyszładо siebie?

Stas: (Shakes his head) Jeszcze nie.

Paweł: Boże!-----Co ona już przeszła!

Clara: (Wailing) Co my mamy czynić?

Tomek: (C) Czekajcie minutę (Closes door) Niech pomyślę (Goes up to Stas and looks at Zosia then turns to others) Gdy Zosia przyjdzie do siebie, wcale nie mowy o tem--to jest---co tam--(Points to other room) Rozumiecie? (All nod)

Stas: To prawda--Ani słowa aby jej przypomnieć o tem--Ona już przeszła przez tyle. Żeby byle kto mógł zwarjować od tego. Tomek, co ty myślisz że powinniśmy teraz robić.

Tomek: (Speaking in a low tone) Słuchajcie wszyscy---Wiemy teraz dobrze że jest ktoś w tem domu oprócz nas--Śmierć Syski dosuradcza temu--A Zosia dosyć strachu przeżyła. Ale jakoń--lub to co jest-- mogło się tu dostać (Looking at Kunnegonda)

Stas: Bóg wie. Syska i ja pozamykaliśmy wszystkie drzwi i okna. A gdy ty poszłeś spać. Ja przejżałem cały dom i nie widziałem ani słyszałem ni kogo.

Paweł: (L. of sofa) Naturalnie że nie--ten warjat--lub to co zabiło Syskę--się chowało za tą ścianą.

Tomek: Chciałem to samo mowić--ta ściana--może powinniśmy teraz zobaczyć co tam jest----a może powinniśmy czekać za policję (Opens door)

Clara: Nie idź tam i zostać nas tu samych.

Tomek: Do tego czasu może tam już nie ma nikogo--teraz--a może--- tam jest co o czem się nam nie śniło--(opens door and looks across hall)

Broncia: (Wails) Zamknij te drzwi. (Tomek colses the door, stands R. of it, looking off L.)

Stas: Więc co uczynię. Jak tylko Zosia przyjdzie, do siebie.

Clara: Oh, czy jej nic nie jest?

Stas: Teraz, oddecha regularnie--I przychodzi do siebie.

Paweł: Co ty teraz zrobisz?

Stas: Pojdę przez tą ścianę--i nie będę czekał nanikogo--nawet na policję.

Tomek: (Slams door and comes down C.) Poczekaj minutę--Pamiętaj że prawa--nikt nie ma wolne do pokoju gdzie morderstwo było

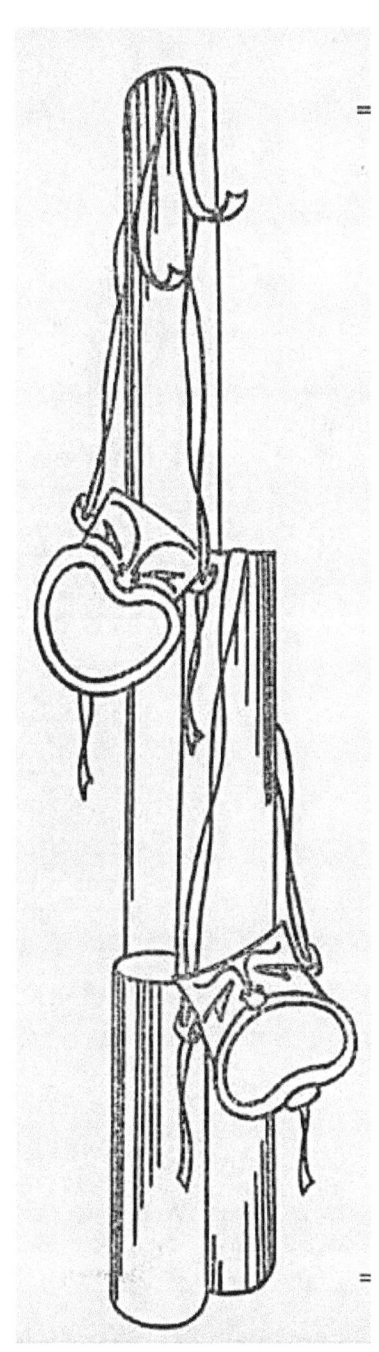

THE END

About the Author

PHYLLIS RITA ZYCH BUDKA was born in Schenectady, New York, and lives in nearby Niskayuna. All her grandparents came to Schenectady in the early 20th century. She attended St. Adalbert's Parochial School, McKinley Junior High and Mont Pleasant High School. After graduating from the University of Rochester with a Bachelor of Arts in Russian Language, she married Alfred J. Budka. They are the parents of Kenneth, Thomas and Christine and grandparents of seven. With Al's encouragement, Phyllis returned to school and received a Master's Degree in Mechanical Engineering from Union College. During her years at Union, she developed an interest in nickel iron and stony iron meteorites, and has published many articles on the results of her research.

Phyllis worked as a metallurgical engineer, retiring in 2007. As retirement neared, her interest in genealogy and local family history grew. Many trips to Poland and Lithuania have helped to discover ancestral history and build connections and friendships with living cousins, which continue with the help of the internet.

Family of Phyllis Zych Budka

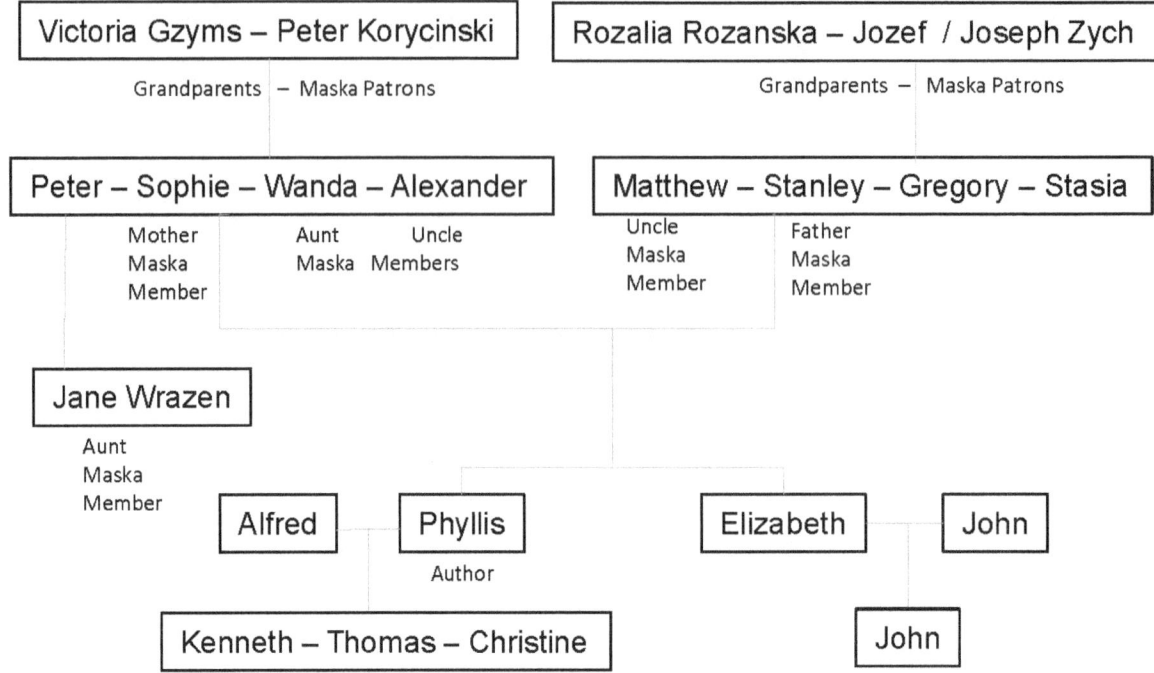

www.ingramcontent.com/pod-product-compliance
Lightning Source LLC
Chambersburg PA
CBHW080547230426
43663CB00015B/2737